Praise for *The Passionate Mind Re_____*

"Whether *The Passionate Mind Revisited* is for you depends on your interest in philosophy, human behavior, epistemology, and personal development. This ambitious, broad-ranging book is by necessity abstract, but for philosophers, Diana Alstad and Joel Kramer are miraculously clear and lead the reader by meticulous steps to some surprising conclusions." —**Diane Johnson, author** of *Lulu in Marrakech*

"Nobody does a more masterful job of folding back the fabric of our individual, cultural, and human attachments and revealing hidden denials, hypocrisies, and paradoxes than Diana Alstad and Joel Kramer. They are among the very few who can open hidden doors to rooms in your house you never knew were there. This book will change the way you look at things—perhaps everything. Are you courageous enough to risk that? Reading this book is a glimpse into what the human mind is capable of perceiving and the mindset of the evolved human mind in the next millennia." —**Kevin W. Kelley, author of** *The Home Planet*

"In 1974 *The Passionate Mind* took me on a journey into my deepest self; it made me dance in the dark. Now, in *The Passionate Mind Revisited,* the entire world is explored—the cosmos in which that self resides—is explored. The investment many children of the '60s and '70s made in freeing ourselves is now turned toward a globe in need of freedom from hunger, poverty, and violence. *The Passionate Mind Revisited* is a critical tool for social, political, and ethical transformation." —**Frances Kissling, former president of Catholics for Choice**

"A welcome infusion of clarity, brilliance, and inspiration that will very likely blow your mind. This profound book is a philosophical, intellectual, and spiritual Rosetta Stone—not a glib compilation of simplistic answers but a critical frame of reference that challenges the way we think about the nature of thinking itself. *The Passionate Mind Revisited* is essential reading for anyone trying to get their bearings amid confusing and contradictory claims and ideas that have long been promoted about the meaning of self-awareness and social consciousness. If you intend to delve into any other discussion of the powerful social, religious, psychological, ecological, and ethical changes confronting current and future generations, *read this book first* or you may miss the crucial context that will help you make sense of it all." **—Keith Harary, PhD, executive director of the Institute for Advanced Psychology and author of *Who Do You Think You Are?***

"The phrase 'looking inward' has become anathema to many social reformers who put their emphasis upon external action. In turn, this 'knee-jerk' activism has been criticized by those who advocate inner development. Diana Alstad and Joel Kramer believe that both approaches can occur concurrently and provide a framework for this process in this brilliant book. If the twenty-first century is not be the last gasp of humanity's time on Earth, the ideas and practices articulated by these two innovators will deserve credit." **—Stanley Krippner, PhD, professor of psychology, Saybrook Graduate School and coauthor of *Haunted by Combat: Understanding PTSD in War Veterans***

"A breakthrough in spiritual realism, pioneering in its confrontation of life's perennial tough judgment calls, and courageous in its intolerance of the crypto-scientific pseudo-spiritual gloss, this book will meet you where you really live." **—Jeremy Sherman, PhD, MPP, executive director of the Berkeley Consortium on Emergent Dynamics**

"*The Passionate Mind Revisited* has afforded me deeper, clearer, more pragmatic approaches to my work and to the future of humanity and life on Earth. My worldview and experience of the spiritual dimensions of life are both more grounded *and* more expansive from the exposure to their thinking and exploration of their ideas. Much awaits you in exploring your own passionate mind! And the Earth needs our passion and clarity more than ever."**—Rio de la Vista, former editor of *Windstar* and conservationist**

"In times of transition and not knowing, visionary artists dance with the possibilities that they sense emerging for us. Diana Alstad and Joel Kramer have seen a magnificent potential for humanity and have written down their insights in an inspiring and practical way. I recommend their book as medicine for all who are curious about what might lie beyond the present confusion and challenges." **—Marion Weber, founder of the Arts and Healing Network**

"Nothing today is more critical than making sense of our times and what they ask of us. Diana Alstad and Joel Kramer bring important insight and integrity to this difficult task. Spiritual and scientific sacred cows get equally unsparing treatment. *The Passionate Mind Revisited* makes a valuable contribution at both a personal and a societal level." —**Charles M. Johnston, MD, author of** ***The Creative Imperative*** **and director of the Institute for Creative Development**

"Diana Alstad and Joel Kramer are exciting critical thinkers for our times, who, as passionate individuals, offer us provocative insights to investigate and navigate our own terrain in transitional times. *The Passionate Mind Revisited* is a classic reinvented for this dynamic historic moment." —**Ganga White, author of** ***Yoga Beyond Belief***

"Kramer and Alstad argue with clarity and passion that the simplistic "be here now" mindset sweeping contemporary pop psychology tragically fails to account for how the past and the future are always part of how we construct any "now" and any "here." I found myself cheering at their insistence that negating the future in the name of spiritual enlightenment amounts to an amputation of our intrinsic capacity to take future consequences into account—a task of vital importance at this crucial stage in our evolutionary adventure." —**Keith Thompson, author of** ***Leaving the Left***

"It is clear that *The Passionate Mind Revisited* is a seminal book for our time. One of the core beliefs held by nation-states and most individuals is that 'more is better.' What a wonderful gift we have been given to challenge our unexplored assumptions to help us shift to a world that can fulfill us all." —**Wilford Welch, author of** ***The Tactics of Hope***

"*The Passionate Mind Revisited* is a promising re-visioning of age-old philosophical dilemmas in a contemporary setting with important social and political implications. The authors are poignantly aware of the effects that Eastern thought and practice have had on spiritually inclined individuals in America over the past half-century, and they challenge head-on many assumptions flowing from their own and others' earlier teachings. Their systematic demonstration leads to the stirring conclusion that a spiritually aware, caring life has to be lived future-oriented and in time—not in some timeless realm. By illuminating the roles of thought and diversity in a life of spiritual awareness, the authors' book would re-orient and rejuvenate spiritual work, bringing it back into the world of time to become more effective and socially relevant." —James Millikan, PhD, former professor of philosophy at Yale and University of Florida

"In this book, Diana Alstad and Joel Kramer have combined more than thirty years of writing, experience, and thinking to construct for the reader a unique lens with which we might examine our worldviews, ideologies, beliefs, fears, and hang-ups. We see more clearly the consequences of our collective failure to free ourselves from the spiritual and intellectual compulsions that have led us to the brink of planetary doom. The coauthors urge all of us, if we are truly serious about planetary survival, to continue the struggle to engage collectively in the evolution of our consciousness. I commend them for this book, a superb achievement." —Charles H. Jones, professor emeritus of law, Rutgers University School of Law

"*The Passionate Mind Revisited* is an excellent resource for expanding personal and social awareness. Diana Alstad and Joel Kramer integrate many cross-cultural and interdisciplinary ideas to illustrate how we can continue to grow, create, and expand during times of uncertainty and open to possibilities not considered before." —Angeles Arrien, PhD, author of *Signs of Life*

THE
PASSIONATE
MIND REVISITED

Expanding Personal and
Social Awareness

Other books by the authors

The Passionate Mind:
A Manual for Living Creatively with One's Self
Joel Kramer

The Guru Papers: Masks of Authoritarian Power
Joel Kramer and Diana Alstad

THE
PASSIONATE
MIND REVISITED

Expanding Personal and Social Awareness

JOEL KRAMER and DIANA ALSTAD

North Atlantic Books
Berkeley, California

Copyright © 2009 by Joel Kramer and Diana Alstad. Copyright © 2009 cover image "Passionate Minds" by Joel Kramer and Diana Alstad. All rights reserved. No portion of this book, except for brief review, may be reproduced, stored in a retrieval system, or transmitted in any form or by any means—electronic, mechanical, photocopying, recording, or otherwise—without the written permission of the publisher. For information contact North Atlantic Books.

Published by
North Atlantic Books
P.O. Box 12327
Berkeley, California 94712

Cover image "Passionate Minds" by Justin Young
Cover and book design by Suzanne Albertson

Printed in the United States of America

The Passionate Mind Revisited: Expanding Personal and Social Awareness is sponsored by the Society for the Study of Native Arts and Sciences, a nonprofit educational corporation whose goals are to develop an educational and cross-cultural perspective linking various scientific, social, and artistic fields; to nurture a holistic view of arts, sciences, humanities, and healing; and to publish and distribute literature on the relationship of mind, body, and nature.

North Atlantic Books' publications are available through most bookstores. For further information, visit our Web site at www.northatlanticbooks.com or call 800-733-3000.

Library of Congress Cataloging-in-Publication Data TK

Kramer, Joel, 1937-
  The passionate mind revisited : expanding personal and social awareness / Joel Kramer and Diana Alstad.
    p. cm.
  ISBN 978-1-55643-807-3
  1. Self-perception. 2. Awareness. 3. Thought and thinking.
4. Meditation. 5. Emotions. I. Alstad, Diana, 1944- II. Title.
  BF697.K683 2009
  128—dc22

                    2009020382

    1   2   3   4   5   6   7   8   9   SHERIDAN   14   13   12   11   10   09

*To humanity continuing its
evolutionary journey.*

ACKNOWLEDGMENTS

This book would not exist without our editor's unwavering support, wisdom, and encouragement. Kathy Glass believed in our work and has cheered, steered, uplifted, and guided us through the ups and downs of the creative process. Her sensitive, insightful, unerring advice on content and style was invaluable.

We are indebted to Elizabeth Kennedy, our project editor, the vital central spoke who kept the book on track and moving forward. Her expertise and belief in our work were crucial in bringing this unusual and unpredictable "co-revisited" project home.

A very special thanks to Lesa Kramer for her wisdom and loving, extraordinary, multi-faceted support.

And a special thanks to Dr. Jeffrey Rubin, whose wisdom, support, depth of insight, and willingness to make time in his busy schedule to help us cannot be overstated.

We're very thankful for Jeremy Sherman's expert advice and feedback regarding genetic conditioning and the current quandaries in evolutionary psychology.

Much gratitude to Justin Young, an exceptionally creative multimedia artist, who surprised us at the last minute with his beautifully fitting cover image gift "Passionate Minds." (www.Justin-Young.com)

Thanks to Suzanne Albertson, the book designer, for her stunning cover and interior design.

Thanks also to:

Professor Jack Semura for his astute perceptions;

Merlin Sheldrake, Dan Fried, and Kevin Kelley for their insights on cross-generational dialogue;

Margot Boland, Kevin Kelley, Jean Altshuler, and Sandra Carden for their advice on cover art;

Thanks to the supportive North Atlantic Book staff and to Richard Grossinger and Lindy Hough, our publishers, for their patience and belief in our work over the years.

TABLE OF CONTENTS

INTRODUCTION

to *The Passionate Mind Revisited*

*T*he *Passionate Mind* was first published in 1974, and to this day many people have told us that it is a touchstone for them in their lives. It presents a method of self-reflexively observing one's own thoughts and its internal structures simply and directly. Interestingly, many of the seeds of concern in *The Passionate Mind* have come to bear an assortment of fruit, from bitter to hopeful. *The Passionate Mind Revisited* enlarges upon this method to go more deeply into personal awareness of who one is. The personal is important in and of itself—all the more so now because it is people who make up the institutions and societies that have made the world what it is. The book's other major focus is moving from the personal to the social and the global.

The emphasis of *The Passionate Mind Revisited* has moved outward, into the realm of social evolution, in order to meet current challenges, both global and inner. We (Joel and Diana) believe that to better use the faculty of thought, it's essential to understand the nature and effects of one's worldview—specifically, how morality and spirituality are embedded in it. To do this, spirituality needs to be "brought down to Earth" by collapsing the separation between the spiritual and the mundane created by predominant traditional spiritual worldviews. We believe that this age-old false and destructive split that separates spirit from the world, and makes the world of lesser importance, is one reason why we are a species at risk. Since a worldview is a lens through which to view the world, if the lens negates or trivializes the world, this clouds one's awareness of and action within the world. This can cause havoc in people's lives as well as within the world at large.

We are social animals who have been socially retarded—in terms of treating each other "humanely"—ever since entering the power hierarchy stage that came with agriculture. This phase was conjoined with religious worldviews that reflected the imagination, magic and superstitions, beliefs, concerns, fears, power structures with their privileges and self-interests, and "knowledge" of those times. Because these old structures, many still in place, are a significant cause of our global problems and current social systems, we believe that our viability depends upon evolving socially. This for us does not mean becoming essentially different from what we are, but becoming better at being who we are—at being the caring, connecting social animals that our mammalian genetic heritage allows us to be. This means, above all, better at relationships—all our problems are relational at their core. This includes becoming better at caring and care-taking, at seeing the long-term implications of our actions, at constructing worldviews in touch with a fast-moving globalism, and supporting institutions that nurture human connectivity rather than an all-consuming and isolating consumerism. This is an enormous challenge. It requires a shift in awareness that we are capable of, but that has been conditioned and frightened out of us.

This book examines who we are, how we got here, and what we can possibly do to continue our evolutionary journey. We pay particular attention to worldviews because each is a lens that takes in and integrates experience that affects one's attitudes toward life and the future, bringing hope or hopelessness. They also lead to life stances that can become fixed, such as optimism, pessimism, skepticism, indifference, cynicism, and even nihilism. Throughout this book we weave in a worldview that we think is more viable and in touch with what is going on, and so offers the possibility of realistic hope for humanity's well-being and future. Should you find it worthwhile to take the journey of these writings, our hope is that you will get enough of a feel of the lens we are looking through to see if it's pertinent to you or if it can shed light on what concerns you. If not, we hope that it will, at the very least, leave you with vital questions to ponder.

Worldviews have either emphasized "being" or "becoming." The West, until the recent influx of Eastern thought, has been more involved in "becoming," where the flow of subjective as well as chronological time is real; progress is real; separation and boundaries are real; egos are what people come with, and individuation is not only acknowledged but valued. The eighteenth-century "Age of Reason" (the West's "Age of Enlightenment") used reason to overcome religious authority, dogma, and superstition. Western "enlightenment" has come to mean using intelligence, thought, intuition, and emotions to understand human nature and the world more deeply. This process does not primarily occur through the isolation of inner contemplation, but through the accumulated and shared experiences of humankind, where "truth" either withstands the tests of time or is modified with new information. Since Freud, there has also been a focus on inner life and psychodynamics that were structured and interpreted through very different worldviews and views of the mind than in Eastern frameworks.

In the East "being," which is identified with "timeless" states that are "outside of psychological time," has been traditionally more valued. Since thought generates the subjective sense of time and creates the past and future, it is looked upon as a hindrance to being in what is called the "eternal now." This worldview envisions the unity of existence as primary, with diversity being secondary at best, and the boundaries that create individual entities constituting a lesser order or even considered unreal. A flow of values has come from the unity worldview that look upon ego and self-centeredness, competition, and attachments to anything as not only blocking spiritual connection but as being the source of our earthly problems. Enlightenment for the East is a timeless unchanging state that is beyond thought, beyond attachments, and beyond the needs of a person or person's ego for personal enhancements. Here fundamental truth is static, eternal, and unchanging.

We have found both the "being" and "becoming" worldview foundations to be in their own ways deeply enmeshed in either/or thinking. Either diversity is the basic reality or unity is; either you are attached or non-attached; either you're competitive and feeding your illusory ego, or you are cooperative in the realization that you are connected to everything; either you are in thought, generating no-longer-existent pasts and non-existent futures, or your mind is quiet and experiencing the timeless ecstasy of "now."

Worldviews are constructions of the human mind as people attempt to glean some understanding of the situation and circumstances they find themselves in. Many worldviews are generally not put together out of conscious intention, but rather are pieced together through personal experience and such cultural accretions as tradition, science, social climate, intuition, and desires about the way the world should be. In a less globalized village, people have tended to incorporate worldviews as a whole; local religions, and more recently the scientific mindset, are popular examples. But more and more people are eclectically combining their beliefs from the global marketplace of ideas. We contend that any construction of human thought (including of course our current one in this book and the one from thirty-five years ago) is potentially fallible and needs to be subject to revision through the feedback and changes that life brings. Worldviews that are fundamentally unchangeable, no matter what, are authoritarian and increasingly outmoded because they cannot cope with a rapidly changing and diversifying local and greater world.

Over the course of years of examining ourselves as individuals and in relationships, we have not found either point of view—being (unity) or becoming (individuation)—able to fully capture our experience, nor have we found dividing everything into this or that to be an accurate picture of how the world actually works. We have found that the East's prioritizing of unity and the West's favoring of duality or multiplicity both contain valuable perspectives, but each offers only part of the whole picture. So for more than three decades, the two of us have been developing and fleshing out a way of looking at ourselves and at this particular moment of history from a perspective that views these seeming polarities not as distinct and exclusionary opposites, but as an embedded tension that is an integral part of the process of creation and destruction—build up and break down—and certainly the human condition. This tension creates an evolutionary momentum that ensures novelty and makes what people do, or do not do, matter.

We call this way of thinking and perceiving *dialectical,* not in the traditional sense of moving toward a predetermined end, but in observing how seeming opposites are actually intrinsically linked and embedded in each other, each being necessary for the other to exist, as opposed to the two opposites competing as exclusive realities. For example, spiritual realization is said to come when all vestiges of egotism have left. Instead of a simplistic either/or proposition, egotism and altruism in our view are not opposite ends of a continuum such that the more altruistic you are, the less egotistical. Rather we see egotism and altruism as part of an embedded relationship. If doing good for others did not make you feel good about yourself, there would be far less of it. The same is true for competition and cooperation. Teams and corporations cooperate in order to compete better, and that's often why people cooperate too. Cooperation and competition are interwoven in the evolutionary process because humanity's cooperative abilities have given us the competitive edge to reach and stay at the top of the food chain—that is until now, where our lack of concern for the future implications of our actions has put us and the world as we know it at great risk.

The Passionate Mind Revisited does not prioritize Oneness or unity, thereby making separateness and diversity secondary or a creation of unity. Rather it sees separation and unity as interwoven poles that create ongoing tension and relaxation in the universe, like breathing. This means that individuation, separateness, boundaries, and uniqueness of human expression are equally real and an expression of how spirit manifests. This book puts forth a worldview that emphasizes the embeddedness and dialectic within such seeming oppositions as the One and the Many, merging and individuation, the spiritual and material, separation and unity, control and surrender, cooperation and competition. Bringing the concept of worldview into the inquiry as one of the core organizing and filtering structures of thought enlarges the lens through which we may observe conditioning patterns.

At the core of Oneness "renunciate" practices is a negation of the reality of the world, matter, and self, along with a villainization of thought, separation, ego, desire, attachments, boundaries, etc. This has led to cultural confusion in the post-sixties West and in much of New Age thought. A more useful, and we think truer, worldview would synthesize the valid parts of both Eastern and Western worldviews and include valuing and protecting democracy, evolution, social justice, and so on. Spiritual activism and engaged Buddhism are steps in this direction—attempts to effect positive change in the world. It is vital that these acts not be limited by authoritarian worldviews, values, and processes.

Thought over the centuries has built the structures of society, morality, power, and privilege that have brought humanity to where it is now—to the brink of self-destruction. This is largely because we are seemingly unable or unwilling to utilize foresight to envision the consequences of producing more people and things indiscriminately. This has been coupled with an overall lack of concern, or very short-term concern at best, of how others and the resources of the planet are used and abused. So how thought has been used got us into this predicament, and we believe that it will take a different, higher level of far-seeing thought to get us out. If we're going to learn to live with each other in a viable (more sustainable) way, we must use our intelligence and emotions to do things better. This involves thinking about the future and potential future consequences with more clarity and knowledge of how things work. It includes an understanding of how the past is a vital part of what the present is now; and how, in a real sense, the past lives in the present as do the future's possibilities (especially as consequences of present acts). Our future will be largely determined by the ways our collective minds attempt to construct a viable future.

There is much talk in spiritual circles about the necessity of some kind of shift or revolution in human consciousness for humanity to become viable. For many this shift involves moving from selfish concerns to seeing oneself as totally interconnected to the whole planet and all the life forms of it. So humans would evolve from considering individual concerns primary and acting out of narrow personal perspectives to caring more about the good of the whole—in short, becoming very different from who we are, which has never worked.

We too believe a shift is essential, but we think it involves seeing with more awareness who we are, which can lead us to be better at it—without negating aspects of being human that are connected to being individuals in relationship. We agree that an expansion of social awareness is essential, but this can only occur through deeper understanding and insights into how we actually work, and what brought us to where we are, facing our own potential demise through a lack of awareness in dealing with each other and the Earth.

Past ideologies have attempted to convince or force people to set aside their own pleasures and prerogatives for the good of the group. This has not worked for many reasons, including the fact that a small elite authoritarian autocracy always defined the "greater good." There is an interwoven tension between individual freedoms and group cohesion that cannot be ignored in any solution that addresses the problems we face.

Although we have all had "timeless" moments that produced significant insights or brought great beauty, we are creatures that live in time and think a lot, not only about our personal future, but about the future of what we care about. We are also social animals whose fate and perspectives are totally tied into each other through what connects us, which are largely, though not exclusively, thoughts, emotions, ideas, and insights that are mainly communicated through words. The capacity to on occasion understand or misunderstand the sound vibrations that pass between people has caused great mischief, pain, and unintelligent misuse of our planet's resources. Communication when successful has also brought about the possibility of great communion between people, joy, and empathy in realizing that we are not alone, and deeper understandings of the nature of our nature and nature in general. Thought has allowed questions and ideas around such issues as meaning, spirituality, and whether or not there is or can be any purpose in evolution or meaning in an individual human life. It has allowed people to explore such issues as the relation between time and timelessness.

The commentary on Time (Chapter 8) has become one of the seminal sections of this book, not only because it best reveals the difference between worldviews and the relation between time and values, but because how time is dealt with (our conceptualizations of it and resulting actions) is crucial to our future and survival. The commentary on Evolution (Chapter 10) addresses the controversy between "intelligent design" and materialist scientific perspectives from within the worldview presented by this book, which gives a new and very different explanation for how evolution works.

In this revisiting and re-visioning, we have attempted to keep the conversational mode of the original book, which was composed of transcribed lectures. Joel Kramer was the speaker in *The Passionate Mind,* and for the sake of simplicity and continuity we have both (Joel and Diana) decided to maintain the first-person voice within the chapters themselves. However, *The Passionate Mind Revisited* is the result of years of conversation between us, and the actual writing of the book has been a shared enterprise. Following the basic text of most chapters is a commentary that aims to bring in current perspectives and concerns. Here we enlarge the social and evolutionary connections that we see as vital for a deeper view of what we can do to be more active participants in our own evolutionary process. The "we" in the chapter introductions and commentaries refers to our combined voices.

This is not a book that resigns itself to a diminution of human life and possibility in the face of the reality that the mechanisms and modes of human interaction that brought us to the top of the chain are now bringing us down. This is the way evolution works, by putting up a wall that seems insurmountable—and actually is, unless the species involved, us, can cut the Gordian knot by doing something really different, by springing out of millennia of conditioning and becoming a conscious ingredient in the evolutionary process.

This does not involve the slow process of genetic mutation and natural selection, which has been the fuel of the age-old, relatively nonconscious biological evolution. It involves an evolution in the evolutionary process itself, from the biological to the social, which does involve a shift of mind that comes from a broader awareness. Humanity has through concerted effort gone to the moon, to an extent harnessed atomic energy, mapped our genetic structure. In art, science, sports, and technologies we have had extraordinary achievements. What we have never done is turn our collective intelligence toward moving the world to where we can make the lives of people not only livable, but valuable and valued, which is essential for creativity to flower. If saving and elevating our species were to become the main focus of humanity, who knows what we could accomplish? In order to do this, we are being pushed by time and necessity to evolve socially. Sustainability cannot mean going back to a lesser life, but must offer an equal or better existence with more hope. And that can only mean connecting with each other more deeply and effectively as we engage in the human drama.

It is our hope that *The Passionate Mind Revisited* can bring more clarity and awareness both personally and socially. This includes the clarity to see that we are facing the necessity of consciously evolving to more social maturity. Are we up to it? We'd better be.

1. Authority

In the thirty-five years since *The Passionate Mind* was published the world has changed to the extent that not only is civilization as we know it in question, so is humanity's viability. Many people in observing the state of the world realize that we cannot continue doing what we have been doing and must together do something basically different, but what?

The Passionate Mind Revisited reexamines who we are, how we got here, and where our possibilities lie. To do this we are putting all authority and "accepted wisdom" on the table for reconsideration. All authority comes from the past, collectively from our history and individually from our experiences. Both have a powerful hold on how we envision present and future possibilities. We are not at all saying that authority itself is unnecessary and should be done away with, but rather questioning what is its basis, how it is to be used, and by whom.

The real problem is not authority—it's authority that is authoritarian. Authoritarianism has two basic traits: a person or ideology that claims to know what's best for others; and second, the authority is unchallengeable—not open to feedback and change when shown to be wrong. Authoritarian ideologies and their values have been a major element in our history and are still prevalent today. Our authoritarian heritage has greatly contributed to our current dilemmas and is blocking needed solutions. This is such a key issue that we wrote an entire book on it, *The Guru Papers: Masks of Authoritarian Power* (North Atlantic Books, 1993).

W hat we are going to be doing in these talks, which are ideally not monologues but discussions, dialogues between you and me, is to examine the fundamental nature of what it is to be a human being. In order to do this, it is necessary to actually look at ourselves as we are. That's not such an easy thing to do because we have deep-rooted self-images of who we are, all kinds of ideas about what we should be, and all kinds of desires as to what we want to be. This clouds our vision so that it becomes very difficult to see ourselves as we are. But it's not possible to see anything clearly until we come into direct contact with ourselves.

Much of what goes under the name of meditation, and also many spiritual pursuits, have one thing in common. They all have as a focus and core value a quieting of thought, a quieting of the whole verbal-mental process. One might wonder why do this? Thought plays an important role in life. We have been socialized and conditioned with thought. Our educational system trains us to have very active, very busy, comparing and competitive minds. And the sharper, the more clever, the better our intellect, the more society rewards us. We lead very active, very busy lives, always doing, always accomplishing. We reap the goods and rewards the world gives us for our achievements. As the world's problems and prices mount, our lives and minds get busier yet, with more challenges, fears, and responsibilities.

The essence of traditional meditation directs itself to temporarily stilling this whole process of busy thinking and living, to there being an occasional silence in oneself. The question is "Why do this? Why do this at all?" In order to see why it might be interesting and at times valuable for there to be a quietness of thought, it is necessary to look at what thought is all about. To see why bringing a meditative awareness into one's life can be a key to living creatively, it is necessary to see the nature and workings of your own thought. As we are thinking social animals, thought has a vital place in the scheme of things. From its inception, thought has been double-edged, as it has both furthered our well-being and been used destructively against others and ourselves. The ability to think has been a large part of our evolutionary success, yet how and what we think is at the root of our deepest personal and social problems. Thought both connects people and separates us. Because thought has a large hand in constructing our world, using it better with more clarity and foresight is necessary for meeting life's challenges.

In the time we spend together we are going to be examining the many facets of thought, how it works, its limitations, and why trying to quiet it has been getting more popular recently. A mind that's trying to quiet itself is at some level a very active mind—which is one of the paradoxes and quandaries of meditation. This gets into what's involved in quieting thought and whether or not thought *can* totally quiet itself.

Thought tells itself it is limitless, that it can handle all problems. All that is needed is the proper analysis, formulas, or systems. But there are some things the very nature of which thought alone is not equipped to handle. It is possible, if we are very attentive and interested, to see the limitations of the symbolic-verbal approach. To see this is to get in touch with the nature and limitations of thought, since thought operates with symbols. Many issues that we will be going into can only be approached by an aware intelligence that is not bound by thought.

In order to examine together how we work, we must first look at the nature of authority. If I am just another authority for you, then you aren't going to look at yourself. There are many authorities in the world. You go to one person and he says, "Do this," and you go to another and she says, "Do that," and a third says, "Don't do anything they told you; only I know what's right, so do what I say," and this is endless. I go from one authority to another and they all tell me to listen to them. What am I to do? I go here and I'm told to do this; I go there and I'm told to do that. So I shop around until I find someone who tells me what I want to hear and I believe that person. This is what is ordinarily passes for learning or growth, which of course is not learning at all.

Real communication rarely occurs when there's either dominance or submission—either being an authority or blindly following one. The very nature of such a dynamic destroys the energy of communion. If you examine the nature of dominance and submission carefully, you will find that they are not the opposites they seem, as both are used for control in different guises. Why do I dominate you or try to? I do it to get you to do what I want, to control you, or to make myself feel good, or to feel superior. Why do I submit to you? I submit voluntarily only if you have something I want. Perhaps I submit out of fear, which means there are experiences or other things I either want or don't want from you; so I submit in order to gain some control over you for my own wants. I do this by making you need me, for those who wish to dominate need submission and become dependent on those who submit. Submission to reputed authorities, which is especially rife in the spiritual arena, cuts off learning along with communication.

For communication to occur, there must be a sense of communion, a sense of connection, of exploring together. Real communication, which is not merely the superficial or surface understanding of words, occurs only when there's a sense of equality and an openness to each other. Only then can we explore with our total being the deeper questions that display themselves in living.

Most of us are largely secondhand human beings. Much of what we are, what we believe, the ways we move through the world, is secondhand, gathered or handed to us from books and other authorities, from our culture's conditioning, and from the experiences of others. So that actually we are just recreating the past over and over again. Being secondhand, taking on others' thoughts and beliefs in an unexamined way, occurs naturally to a degree, as we are all part of some cultural foundation that we take for granted—like fish, it's the water we usually swim in unconsciously. Unless something truly new can also find a way in, living becomes dull and habit-bound instead of interesting, vibrant, and responsive to the moment. Of course, as social animals we do learn from others, from their discoveries and experiences, and from our collective history. Humanity's evolutionary advantage is the ability to learn from the past as discoveries and presumed knowledge are passed on from generation to generation. The danger, especially in times of upheaval and change, is that the hold of the past can stifle necessary changes and growth. To prevent this, we must become more conscious. This means, among other things, freeing oneself from the authority of the past.

It doesn't matter what anyone else says, or what the great or wise say. We don't know that they're great or wise; we imagine they are, someone has told us, or we read a book and the book says they are. Becoming a more firsthand person, which is to become your own authority, is not so easily done. One obstacle is perhaps the greatest authority of all, the authority of the past, of tradition, especially spiritual tradition— whatever is held sacred or considered age-old wisdom. Tradition and history are important—not as a vise to squeeze the present into, but rather as stepping stones to grow from. Following what someone supposedly said hundreds or thousands of years ago is a hindrance to looking within. Even to be concerned with such matters is not to be looking at oneself. Many traditional authorities or books reputed to be wise or even sacred may not have been wise at all—or may not still be for these times. Often one cannot know what was actually said. The presumed original words may have been said or not. If they contained wisdom then, they may or may not be relevant now. The authority of spiritual tradition, which is among the oldest and thus potentially the most outmoded, is also among the most powerful in the world. It is imperative to now reexamine everything afresh, including what is considered sacred, to see what is fitting for ourselves and our times.

It's difficult to do away with all authority because it puts one in a rather frightening place, with little to hold on to. Yet real learning, which is not merely the accumulation of knowledge or the rote repetition of facts, never occurs unless we do away with authority. This also means a willingness to question assumptions and beliefs.

In these discussions we will be doing away with authority, so that we need no one, and then you can be your own authority—a light unto yourself. You can see within yourself whether what is being said is true for you or not. In order to become an authority for yourself you must come to terms with yourself. You must see yourself as you actually are, and to do this, you must look with a truly open mind. That is ideally what we are going to do together—look at ourselves, both individually and how we interweave with the world. But first we should be aware of some of the difficulties of communication.

My words are at best a mirror—a mirror for you to see yourself in. The words themselves are not what they purport to represent. Insofar as they are words they are always inadequate, always an abstraction. The nature of language is such that it makes real communication very difficult indeed. Take any word. Take a common noun like "cat." You know that the word itself is an abstraction and by that I mean something quite simple. Philosophically, to abstract means to fail to take account of. So if I say, "Here is a cat," I have failed to take account of whether it is a black or white cat, male or female, young or old, brown- or blue-eyed, with short or long hair, or an infinite number of attributes: its temperament, its relation to the room, to me, etc. If I were trying with symbols to describe totally the livingness of this cat, to capture it in words, I would have to string words out indefinitely. The same is true for a tree or even a rock. And even if I were able to use an infinite number of adjectives, I still would just have words, not a living cat. The living thing is not the word. A living thing is always moving, always changing.

Yet we are dealing with words here, and through words we are trying to discuss many things that are far more elusive than usual, things that fundamentally cannot be communicated by words alone. But however inadequate words may be in this arena, we have little choice but to use them in relating with each other. So with this in mind we should be aware that the word is not the thing. I will not be using words or thought in the usual ways or putting forth concepts or a belief system that can be grasped and mastered. Instead I'll be engaging you in self-inquiry, a mode of inquiry involving a different way of looking that comes in part from my own inquiry.

Another problem in these discussions is that it is difficult to truly listen, whether to me or to anyone. Ordinarily what we do when we think we are listening is to take in the words, translate them into something that we know or are familiar with, and then agree or disagree. If the words fit our beliefs, the things we are comfortable with, that we think we know, then the speaker is wise and we agree. If the words do not please us, do not fit our structures and beliefs or are uncomfortable, then the speaker is not wise and we disagree. That's what most of us do and call it listening. But agreeing is meaningless and beside the point in the arena of inner inquiry, while disagreeing is a distraction and a hindrance. If we are either agreeing or disagreeing, then we're not listening, for to listen there must be an openness, an innocence, a temporary suspending of judgment and the familiar, so that the fresh can possibly come in. This is not to say that judging is wrong or never appropriate. Judging, comparing, and evaluating are inherent in how thought works. Evaluating whether something makes sense for you or not is part of being your own authority. But if you are busily involved in either agreeing or disagreeing in the moment of hearing (and you can watch yourself do this as you listen), the new, which is the fount of growth and learning, does not readily come in.

I think that for many of us what we are going to talk about, and the way we will do this, will be new. Instead of you agreeing with me, I am interested in you using my words as a mirror to look at yourself. But you can only do this if you are listening with a curious and passionate mind. Only in passion is there a quality of attention fundamental to learning. Passion occurs when there is interest and care, an engagement of one's total being and a willingness to move into the new. You really have to care about seeing (in this case it is seeing yourself), for as soon as you say, "I know myself," learning stops.

Meditation involves techniques; it's something you do that temporarily removes you from external input—the world. What I refer to as a meditative frame of mind is an awareness that can pierce through the layers of our conditioning and allow living in the world in a very direct, intimate way. A strange irony in the practice of most meditation is that one is doing something to achieve an end—a quiet mind—whether focusing on one's breath, body, or an object, repeating a *mantra* (words), visualizing, or some other technique.

If thought is silenced, a meditative state may occur, moving you from "doing" to "being," where the sense of time leaves and it feels timeless. This state can bring a different way of observing that is direct, unmediated by the mind's usual filters. The shift from doing to being can bring an awareness that breaks through the limitations of thought and conditioning. This state of awareness can occur in any facet of life, including observing thought itself to see how it works. It involves letting go of preconceived ideas and agendas of what you want or expect so that you are in direct contact with what is, with no psychological distance between you (the observer) and what you're perceiving. Although some meditative practices can still thought, there is no guarantee they will also bring this state of unfiltered awareness. Thought can be still, but one's awareness can be in a pre-programmed and familiar place, like breath, *mantra,* visions.

I view these discussions as an active meditation that can possibly bring a shift of awareness that broadens your field of consciousness and allows you to experience a meditative state. It is my hope that through the process of examining together what it is to be a human being in the world today, by looking at many of the basic concerns of living, an awareness and a clarity will shine through the words.

One might ask, "Why bother with this kind of inquiry?" The tremendous push that most of us are feeling because of the pressures of the times is very demanding. Is not this whole involvement with awareness a very self-absorbing activity? Why be so caught up in oneself when the world needs our attention? The old order isn't working; the old ways, societies, and the world as we've known it are breaking down, and time is running out for finding global solutions. Our technologies have accelerated and exacerbated many of the problems inherent in the nature of being human. This includes our capacity for violence and insufficient concern for the far-reaching consequences of our actions. These problems have been mounting for centuries and are now quickly coming to a head. We are making the planet we live on uninhabitable, so our very survival is now in question. I am sure that most of the crises and extraordinary uncertainties of today are obvious to each and every one of you. Is there anything meaningful in all this inquiry to help respond to our overwhelming challenges?

In order to deal with what the world has become, it's essential first to see clearly how it is related to who we are, for who we are has brought us to where we are. The world we find ourselves in was created by humans and is an expression of us, so it will not change until we do. It is a product of our beliefs, fears, desires, perceptions, and power structures. Our social, economic, political, and other power structures are all created and perpetuated by the human mind. Our problems involve the nature and problems of being human, and unless there is a real change in people's minds and hearts, there is no real change at all. The external is a manifestation of the internal. The greed in the world is an expression of human greed, as is the violence. Social separation, war, and ethnic strife stem from conflicting beliefs and narrow identities. Later in looking at evolution, I think we will find that the basic question of survival gets down to whether or not we will evolve socially to be able to live in this world with one another.

It is essential for us to become conscious participants in social evolution. A shift of consciousness can expand personal and group identities to include the global, which also expands care. People care about what they identify with. Only if there is a shift in people's awareness will there ever be viable solutions. More awareness brings better thinking that can anticipate the interconnected, global repercussions of our actions. Awareness is growing in many places, and movements are afoot to create the popular and political will to overcome difficult challenges.

The world doesn't change unless I do, unless we do. The question is: Is it possible for an ordinary person, a person like you and me, to come to terms with oneself so that one can individually, personally (because it is all very personal) meet the challenges of living in these extraordinarily turbulent, dangerous, yet potentially creative times?

2. Belief

Our brains are built to wonder, probe, and attempt to explain life's occurrences and mysteries by creating beliefs about them. Our great gift of cognition is our capacity, with the help of language and emotions, to create thoughts, ideas, abstractions, and beliefs from our own perceptions and from the words and experiences of others. We then make assumptions, come to conclusions, form opinions and beliefs. Since the brain is a belief-making entity, it's not possible to not have beliefs. As with language, we have an inbuilt capacity to believe, but the content of the actual beliefs can be most anything.

We humans have a propensity to believe since at least some beliefs are needed to live. Beliefs about the nature of reality, the accuracy of memory, and the oncoming moment, day, or year are necessary to function and survive. Beliefs help us navigate daily life, make some sense of the world, sort out what we consider true and false, connect with other "like-minded" people, attribute meaning to life, and carry out countless other large and small functions. Believing that I must at times take the future into account fosters survival.

There are so many differing beliefs, each putting out tendrils to infiltrate and capture minds through conditioning, advertising, peers, social consensus, and the like. Beliefs can be counter to survival, narrowly self-serving, and as history has verified, deadly. So how to wend one's way through the minefield of beliefs confronting us? This issue is especially critical for these times because it has been the historical accumulation and passing on of beliefs that brought us here, to where our viability as a species is in question.

Beliefs cover a spectrum from malleable, thus changeable, to very rigid and fixed. Our minds are constructed to make our beliefs seem real, but like any construction of the human mind, beliefs are potentially fallible. So a major issue for these times is how tightly or loosely we hold our beliefs—are they closed or open to feedback and change? Closed beliefs are unchangeable and authoritarian, meaning not open to being shown where they're wrong. Since beliefs are a most significant part of what has brought humanity to where we are, unless we can better understand how they work within us and learn to approach them more critically, we will never get beyond warring with each other, and in the process tearing up the planet that supports us.

W hat we believe determines much of what we think and do: the way we move, the way we respond to people, how we think of ourselves, how we see the world in general. All of us have beliefs, innumerable beliefs, big and little about this and that. Some are unconscious and taken for granted because of the cultural context, and some beliefs come from thoughtful reflection. Often they are functions of habit, preference, and internalizing the conditionings and information (possibly unreliable) from our experience, parents, peers, society, advertising, media, books, authorities and seeming experts, the Internet, blogs, hearsay, and the like. Hopes, fears, desires, emotions, and wishful thinking also greatly influence beliefs.

What does it mean to believe in anything—a person, a leader, science, God, a worldview, a religion, an economic system, any system of ideas? Examining the structure of beliefs in general and how they work is a doorway into the nature of thought. For this it's important to see the structure of belief, not specific beliefs but beliefs in general. A state of intimate, direct understanding brings a confidence that, though certain at a given time, is not beyond revision. The nature of firsthand beliefs is that they can change if your experience does, while secondhand beliefs are taken on for many reasons, including preference, and they easily become attachments that are locked in.

Since closed beliefs are counter to survival in a rapidly changing, dangerous world, let's not initially ask if a belief is right or wrong, good or bad, life-furthering or -destroying, constructive or destructive, but rather just what it means to have closed beliefs that do not change with changing times or changing evidence.

Unshakable beliefs come in different forms. Some are closed for a period of time; others are closed–period. Some are closed because of personal and everyday experience (the sun will appear again tomorrow), while others bolster a worldview or religion, or placate one's fears. I think we will be able to look–inwardly look–and see the difference so that you can tell for yourself whether you are actually in a state of immovable secondhand belief or not. For this discussion, the content of a belief is more incidental.

I have a fixed belief about anything. How does this affect the whole internal nature of my awareness? Let's look at it personally, each of us. To be in a state of fixed belief usually means there is limited firsthand experience or knowledge of it. Beliefs that are fixed and unchangeable not only often result in violence, but they can trigger a potential state of internal violence–violence that can easily lead to external violence. Let us see the way this works.

As one moves through the world one encounters many beliefs, all jockeying with one another, vying for our minds. If you have a belief about anything and that belief is attacked by another belief–another system of thought, worldview, religion, another "ism"–what do you do? You automatically defend it, don't you? The thing to do is watch the way you work. Whether you defend your belief verbally to the other person or go away and defend it silently to yourself is not the point–you're still defending it. It's in the psychological structure of closed beliefs to automatically defend themselves when attacked.

Is defense that different from attack? To be defending a belief is often to be attacking someone else's. Such defense contains aggression or, at the very least, fear. In this whole process of belief there is the potential of defense and attack. You don't need to believe me–see it for yourself. You can observe how you operate with people in day-to-day living and see the structure of belief. As you move through the world, inevitably someone will attack or threaten (purposely or not) something that you believe or hold dear for belief-related "reasons." You can watch how you respond, because only then will you find out. Watch to see if you immediately defend it. You can watch this in others too. It is from this that violence results, internal and external. You can feel the tension in your body: in the physical constrictions, the tightening of the viscera, the tone of your voice, the flow of adrenaline, the aggression in the defense.

So that to be in a state of unquestioning belief is to be in a state of potential aggression, capable of leading to overt violence. In this sense, internal and external violence are not essentially different. We make the world in our image, and if there is internal violence it will usually express itself in the world. All one has to do is to look around in the world today. Violence and the threat and fear of it are pervasive. It's important to keep in mind that the beliefs we're discussing are not of the ordinary everyday variety that we all have, but rather those that do not change no matter what the counter-evidence is. Such beliefs can be so hooked into one's identity that people are willing to die and kill for them.

The line separating secondhand beliefs from internal knowledge is often murky, but how automatically you defend is a good clue. To find out if you have fixed beliefs and to identify them, you must watch yourself closely because defense is automatic. As soon as you're attacked you defend, either overtly by verbally attacking or punching someone (or wanting to), or by verbally attacking or quietly negating the person to yourself. You can observe this in the ways you operate with your family, at work, or in any relationship.

However, if I personally know anything at all firsthand, then a whole different process is involved that is not merely my conditioning, or adopting the current intellectual fashion, or conforming to whatever groups I identify with. Although the line between conditioned beliefs and firsthand knowledge is sometimes blurred, this surety of experience is different from internalizing a belief or ideology coming from some supposedly impeccable source or culturally accepted "reality"—all these are secondhand. Attributing someone's misfortune to the law of karma or God's will are examples of such beliefs.

If a man were to tell me that the sun comes up in the north, I might initially respond by saying that it really appears in the east. If he should continue to insist on it, I'd begin to wonder if he is putting me on or if he's a little quirky or insane, or whatever. Here you can observe in yourself that there is no internal psychological push to defend; this is something that you just know. When you have internal understanding that is not essentially based on what someone else says, then you don't need to prove it or convince anyone of it. Some beliefs are so highly conditioned, so ingrained, that it may appear as if no defense is taking place. Someone who feels it is hopeless to try to persuade an atheist that there is a God might not engage—but could still wish all atheists would somehow vanish. You could also refrain from defending in order to prove to yourself that you are not aggressive. But one's physiology is not easily fooled. Tensions, constrictions, glandular changes, the effort itself—all are clues.

The world's organized violence is all carried out in the name of belief. Beliefs of superiority, from religious and ethnic to age, gender, and the idiosyncratic, underpin or justify most prejudice, group hatred, and oppression. Even if the underlying motive is to gain power or territory, very high-sounding beliefs are needed and used to justify the violence. Seeing how this works in oneself (usually in less obvious ways) is essential for awareness. Of course, to see it is not necessarily to make it go away. Seeing the nature of your beliefs and how they contain the seeds of violence may motivate you to try to do away with or change them in order to become nonviolent. But the ideal of nonviolence is another secondhand belief. Trying to make your beliefs go away because you don't like them is avoiding yourself on the basis of other beliefs about what you should be. This creates inner conflict and stress, which is a form of internal violence.

At this point you might wonder, "OK, if fixed secondhand beliefs contain violence, and if I believe this and try to avoid it through effort, I'm just getting involved in belief in a different way, so what am I to do?" That is one of the important questions we will look at here.

Look, I see that I have many beliefs. I see that the hardened ones that have become interwoven with my identity create potential violence. I also have strong moral convictions that may be at odds with others' values—or even with some of my own. I see that trying to force a change in this comes out of another belief that I shouldn't defend my beliefs. This is an example of the many "binds of mind" that we will be looking at. The violence within beliefs can even happen with seemingly benign ones. The content of a belief does matter (in the world, if not so much for this exploration), especially if it engenders harm. But how a belief is held and whether or not it is subject to change is often more important than its content.

Let's take the well-intended, seemingly beneficial belief "Do no harm to sentient creatures." I may think this is obviously a life-furthering belief. Yet it's possible for even such a belief as this, if held unbendingly, to perpetuate the very thing I'm trying to do away with—violence. This is especially true given that aggression has its place in life's dramas. Physical aggression is part of our genetic nature (far more pronounced in males, but not absent in females), as one might suspect of predators, which we are. Aggression cannot be entirely eliminated, but it can be curbed, though not by ideological force. Through awareness of our aggression and insight into its nature and the implications of its casual usage, we can change its expression by channeling it into, say, creative competition.

In some places people don't kill rats or mosquitoes because belief in the ideal of total nonviolence is so deeply ingrained. In the guise of revering the sanctity of all life, rats are allowed to roam the streets, biting and infecting children—which actually happens. So in the name of nonviolence, greater violence is committed, which is the way of many beliefs. This is an example of being more concerned with upholding the purity of beliefs than with their effects in the world—a tragic example of how beliefs can blind you and block natural care.

We are looking at how beliefs work and how they can filter perception. Though they can bring comfort, they can easily become deadening structures that keep you from changing, and that includes making essential evolutionary changes. They remove one from seeing the world clearly and living in it creatively. If I have a closed belief about anything, it means I have cut off inquiry. Instead of looking, I believe, and that's a dulling, habit-bound way to meet life. It stiffens me and makes me tired. To see this—really to see it—brings forth movement. Later, we'll look at the nature of this movement.

The world is full of mind predators trying to infiltrate minds with images, ideas, and beliefs (what some call memes) to manipulate hopes, desires, and fears for power and profit. We tend to move toward good feelings and away from unpleasant ones, so there's a great tendency to incorporate beliefs that make you feel good or tell you what you want to hear, while rejecting or ignoring what doesn't. Since this is mechanical it's another way that beliefs filter awareness. If I see the way beliefs work, I see that the brain makes beliefs seem real—that's part of being a belief. Otherwise they're merely held as opinions, on a spectrum from strong to tentative and uncertain. Questioning basic beliefs can initially bring confusion, anxiety, or conflict, which is why it's usually avoided. Yet if you recognize that any beliefs can be fallible, you may at least hold them more loosely. You may believe as I do that there are life-furthering beliefs and life-denying beliefs, but what is life-furthering or threatening must be open to feedback and reexamination. For me, this is not a merely a belief issue but a survival issue. This is why I've been focusing on how beliefs work, particularly rigid beliefs.

What we're discussing here is a way of looking at what is—not what I want to be, not what others tell me I should or should not be, or what authorities say, but a way of looking at what is. Looking at yourself is not analysis, not introspection, not analyzing and tearing apart something that has happened in the past. It's not that at all. Looking is something quite different. I'm discussing a way of looking at yourself and the world around you that's just available and can open up living in new ways. It's about a way of looking with awareness at anything—not just internally, also at the world and at others, and at yourself as embedded in the world. This way of looking with awareness is not mine; it's not a possession or an invention. It's just there. All one has to do is look. Nobody can do it for you.

If I look only at what I want to see, then I don't look at all. If I want to understand anything—a flower, a child, anything—then I must observe it. I must watch it carefully. If I'm involved in trying to make it something other than what it is, trying to change it, improve it, I'm no longer watching it as it is. Of course things do change and are influenced—I can watch how that occurs too. An added element is that if something affects me, I usually try to influence it if I can. But even though I may have a vested interest in its direction, my influence may not be unwelcome and may be beneficial for all concerned. I can observe all of that, which helps me to see more clearly.

This is especially true of oneself. If you really want to understand what you are and how you work, you must observe yourself. Ordinarily when I look, I don't look in order to see. I look with an eye toward changing into something else—to please others, to be more in line with my values, or simply to feel better. Trying to become better or different makes observing myself more difficult, yet the reality is that I often do want to become better. I am interested in changing, being happier, healthier, more fulfilled, realized, spiritual. So one of the things that I am is someone who does try to change myself. I can watch that too and see just what it means to be involved in beliefs of what I should be or desires of what I want to be, without trying to change the fact that I'm trying to change myself.

I can observe that the effort involved in attempting to change comes from ideas that I should be different; and that many of these ideas are unexamined beliefs and values conditioned into me from an early age and reinforced by society or the groups I identify with. Changes that involve effort mostly come from beliefs. If I watch myself wanting to be something other than what I am, I can begin to see the movement of that which is me. All of this lives in thought. What thought does is judge me according to my beliefs, and I say to myself that "I'm not good enough." What is trying to change me? Is it not thought (based on beliefs, judgments, memory, and desire) that is always trying to make me into something other than what I am? To judge yourself lacking is a sign that your beliefs are causing you pain and conflict—forms of internal violence. This does not mean that you should be entirely content with yourself and not explore what might bring you growth. But causing yourself pain tends to inhibit growth, by shutting your energy down.

Thoughts do elucidate what ought to be, which can be appropriate in a given context, but most ought-to-bes are beliefs, beliefs that can interfere with seeing clearly. To say that you don't like what you see means that you are judging it. Judgments can be so strong that they cloud real seeing, which in the moment springs one out of the filters of subjective reactions and judgments. However, if judging is what you're doing (and we do judge), you can observe that too. So how does change occur that is not trying to mold me into pre-conditioned values, second-hand beliefs, or ideas from the past, that is not being forced, that is in touch with the unique moment? Where does it come from? Ultimately, it comes from one place—the clarity with which you see yourself. It is here that one's will, which is sometimes necessary to counter ingrained habits, focuses and brings change without effort or force.

Please understand, I'm not saying that judging in itself is wrong. Our uniquely human capacities to discriminate, compare, and evaluate help us to make sense of what's going on. But most of us have unexamined, often unlivable core values that we judge and beat ourselves with. Instead of being curious about who we are, we often judge ourselves as not loving or giving enough, as being too selfish. The types of changes we ordinarily seek are pre-programmed by these values. In making an effort to live up to them life becomes struggle and conflict instead of an exploration into who you are. In trying to change yourself it's interesting to ask, "Who is trying to change whom?" If you're trying to match your ideals, remember that many of these ideals are conditioned at an early age and remain unexamined, so it's likely that you're repeating secondhand programs, the old. Real change, which involves growth, moves into the new, the unknown. People say they want to grow, but by growth they usually mean keeping everything about themselves and their life that they like, getting rid of what they don't like, and getting more of what they like. This is not how real growth occurs. Growth is like shedding an old skin, which is ultimately freeing but could include letting go of some of what you like. Belief in unlivable ideals brings conflict and resistance to change, as such ideals usually come from outmoded worldviews that are locked in.

How do you know if your beliefs are appropriate for you, or even at all livable? In order to approach this you have to see who you are with some clarity. I can observe my beliefs and self-judgments. I can observe that they make me dislike aspects of myself and that as a result I live in conflict. I can observe the fact that I don't like some of these beliefs and want the judgments to go away and stop bothering me—and yet they don't. (Unexamined conditioning is not under one's control and needs to be made conscious through seeing it clearly.) All this is conflict, and I bring my conflict into the world. In observing this I see myself with more clarity, which brings change of a different order.

Why do I want to change? We have an idea that there is a way to be that is different from and better than the way we are. This "other way" is often nebulous and itself changing as we hunger after something else. If you look you'll see how conflict is involved with some beliefs. And the more I try to force conflicts away, the more conflict I create. If I'm in conflict, that's what is, and if I can see that clearly, with awareness not judgment, that clarity can bring a movement of a different order, to an unexpected place.

The fact is that we are manipulative social animals. We attempt to manipulate ourselves, our surroundings, and each other. This is part of being human; so I'm not saying that one shouldn't want to change oneself or the world. It's natural to want more control over our lives, to chase after security. The danger is that with too much control you keep repeating the past—past habits and pleasures—blocking change. Following your interest is different, as you don't know where it will lead. It can bring another kind of change that's effortless, coming from passion and awareness. Life is change, and one changes with or without effort. Nor I am saying that using will or intention to move yourself is never appropriate. And moving out of deeply rooted conditioning patterns that are not serving you does at times feel like an effort. But will and intention are just one way to bring change into life. When you see clearly, that seeing itself moves you into an unforeseen place. The movement may be immediate or it might point to the necessity of using your will to move through ingrained habits. You may see something very clearly, like the need to exercise, and then marshal your will or find a more creative and enjoyable way to do this. This, however, is not coming from belief but from clarity. If it is true clarity, the will can be strong enough to break through the resistances of habit without conflict. Action from lack of clarity often generates the kind of effort that stifles creative movement.

Seeing that change is inevitable, the question is do we have some say in which direction it goes? If we do, then becoming part of the momentum of creative change is participating in the thrust of evolution. Whether we do or not can be endlessly argued, but having a worldview where our actions make a difference brings energy for positive change. Many of us see a great necessity for change, but it's important to be aware of the binds in trying to change. The difficulties of meeting the new creatively would lessen through a more open-ended relation to belief. To see how beliefs work is to get in touch with a different way of looking at "what is." Since awareness is the direct relationship with what is, a living awareness that sees what is freshly can bring a momentum for change. Unless we become capable of believing with more awareness and changing through more clarity, it's doubtful that we will meet the challenge of these times.

There is much talk about the need for greater consciousness involving some kind of shift. It's crucial to get more comfortable with uncertainty in a world of vast, complex, and rapid change. Becoming curious and questioning how fitting one's beliefs are for these rapidly changing and dangerous times is a change in consciousness.

Question: We live in an age of science that affects what many people believe. Scientists can be pretty dogmatic too, and scientific beliefs are secondhand for most people. So would you please discuss scientific beliefs?

Answer: The difference between religion and science is that religion is about justifying beliefs; science is ideally about discovering what's true and verifiable within the scientific paradigm and changing if shown wrong. Take evolution, for instance. There's plenty of scientific evidence for it and none for the Genesis creation story, but fundamentalists try to find tiny loopholes to justify what they believe. For literalists, belief in the Bible and dogma takes precedence over evidence or even harmful consequences. They start with belief in the Bible and then look for evidence to fit their beliefs instead of searching for whatever truth can be found independently. Scientific "beliefs" are in actuality hypotheses or theories that are open to modification by new evidence, facts, or anomalies. Even though many scientists resist new evidence out of attachment to the reigning paradigm (and their investment in it), if human bones that predated all other mammals were found, the theory of human evolution would have to be revised, because approximating the truth is ultimately more important in science and eventually wins out over those theories that are self-interested and resistant to change.

Question: You talk about seeing as if it's objective and in a mental vacuum. But isn't one always seeing out of some point of view, some worldview or other, or a mixture? Can one see anything without a worldview?

Answer: Just being in a human body is being in a particular structure that influences and to an extent determines how a person perceives, takes in, puts out, and integrates information. So too do we bring the totality of who we are to every living situation. This includes our conditioning, worldviews, and the like. The awareness or seeing that I'm speaking of has the capacity to pierce through our filters and the accumulations of the past so that in that moment one can see newly or freshly. This can change a worldview or unhook you from automatic, conditioned responses. But this is an ongoing process, since today's insights can change a worldview or become tomorrow's memories that can reinforce your worldview. Worldviews have a way of congealing insight into a reiteration of the old. However, in times of extreme turbulence, there is a push to reorganize one's viewpoints that is part of the evolutionary process.

Question: Doesn't our past experience affect our seeing too, making what we see subjective? You seem to think it's possible to see or perceive objectively, freshly, untainted by the past. Where can objectivity come from since we are all subjects with our own unique layerings of experiences?

Answer: This question has some similarity to the one above, although it's posed more abstractly. The controversies between what is subjective or objective have raged throughout history. Some argue that objectivity is impossible. But few of us would flatten the world into either the absolutely objective or subjective—especially if we realized the implications of doing so. Thinking of either of them as "pure" makes it difficult to acknowledge a middle ground where some viewpoint could be more or less objective than another. How you evaluate objectivity depends on the worldview you are operating from. Although any construction by the human mind is potentially fallible and will probably be refined or surpassed in the future, this doesn't mean that some perspectives are not more objective or truer than others right now. The question then becomes "What criteria can enable people to maintain that there is at least some objectivity in their point of view?" For me, an awareness that breaks through old perspectives to see something new is one of the indicators of seeing beyond the limitations of one's subjective boundaries. Although this does not make the "seeing" an absolute truth, as it is potentially correctable by a future awareness in a later situation, it's the best we have available. In this historical moment where our viability is in question, it is vital to observe the world and ourselves as objectively as we can.

Question: Much of what you say doesn't seem to follow necessarily. There seems to be a sense in it, but it seems to me that the way you look at things is just one possible way out of many. In listening to you I get a feeling of surety that might be called rigid or dogmatic. I agree that when the mind is trying to see into the nature of its own workings, how it sees is limited by its own perspective. So what you are saying could easily be just one way of looking at things. How do you know that what you are saying isn't just that?

Answer: You talk as if there is an almost infinite possible number of ways of looking at things with one's mind and then ask, "How does one know that the way one is looking at things is more correct than any other?" Is that not the question?

Questioner: Basically.

Answer: Looking at things as if there were an infinite number of ways to look at things is actually just one way of looking at things. There is another way—and that is to just look at them. If you will do this in yourself then perhaps the endless questions of intellectual justification will cease. To need intellectual justifications for all aspects of living is in itself just one way of looking at things. It's not possible to look without a worldview, so one has to be open to feedback and see if it's valid over time in many situations. One may not even know that one is looking through a worldview since part of having one is often thinking it is an unfiltered view instead of a mental construct. We all build some kind of worldview out of experience, intuition, preference, the accumulation of what we consider knowledge, and very often rigid conditioning. So the information and other inputs we take in are filtered through our overall worldview. This is so whether we are observing internally or externally.

The question then is: Is it possible for a mind to pierce through the structures the mind builds for integrating information and look not only out of the cages of its conditioning, but to really look without filtering? Is it possible for a mind in a given moment to be free? I am fairly sure that most of you at some instant of your life have had a flash of insight and in that instant everything looked different. Though the intensity of that moment faded, some change in you remained. Although moments of searing clarity are not in one's control, if you become aware of how the mind conditions itself and know the nature of the worldview you view from, moments of piercing through the structures of your mind to an unfiltered clarity become more likely. This is how new insights occur that can change or modify a worldview.

Question: Since beliefs seem to be relative to their culture and society, how can anyone determine if one belief is more life-furthering than another?

Answer: The realization that perception and experience may not reflect external reality has come and gone throughout history. Many modern relativists hold that because all beliefs are subjective, tied to experiences and embedded in unprovable and competing worldviews, it's impossible to know what's true. This is a position that can be defended but not lived by, as reality however defined has a way of intruding into beliefs. This is not my position. Our perceptions and the brain itself are slippery and unreliable in some areas, but not all. The question is whether our nervous system evolved to connect with certain aspects of the reality of the external world that we can experience—or is it all just a fabrication of our internal structure? A bird and a human may experience a tree differently, from a different viewpoint, but that does not mean they are experiencing something different. You can't land on a branch that's not there. People have words and concepts to give feedback and check others' experience. The capacity to align mentally is built in the brains of humans through language, symbols, beliefs, values, emotions, and goals. One reason there is consensus at all is that there's a reality to agree about. Another is you can pierce through filters and images and get in touch with something real. So although objectivity may never be absolute or perfect, neither is everything totally subjective. There is a scale from subjective to objective. Almost everyone would want to be able to say that some points of view are more objective, more true, than others.

To give a crucial example: there's compelling evidence for the belief that our species is at risk—projections based on personal experience, science, and actually seeing (via the media if not firsthand) the breakdown of physical systems. Just like some views are more objective than others, some values are more functional and life-furthering than others. Whether beliefs and values are constructive or destructive is crucial to know, but hard to prove. Everyone believes that their beliefs are the most true and their values the best. So what is life-furthering or threatening must be open to feedback and reexamination. Here the process of establishing what really matters is vital. Defending something on the basis of what's good for humanity to become viable is different from most defense because you can make a telling case for it. Defending values and resolving conflicts can be evolutionary instead of violent if it's done in a way that brings more empathy and understanding to all sides. There's a difference between making a case for your values and being aggressive and degrading toward those who differ. Trying to persuade others by justifying and defending life-supporting values fits into what humanity now needs to survive because now more than ever our beliefs need to be as accurate and in touch with what's going on in the external world as possible to make the right changes. This includes recognizing our collective needs for each other and the interwoven web of life that makes our life possible. It's crucial to acknowledge that human fallibility will need ongoing revision. We also need to see more clearly what's going on and our part in it, both historically and now.

Democracy is best for feedback-based belief and values. The challenge is to make it work better through an educated and open-minded citizenry. The nature of our beliefs and the governments we create, and how well we can deal with an uncertain and perilous future, will greatly determine who we become and if we can create a viable world that will support us. Becoming better believers with more objective beliefs is a prerequisite for better democracies as well as needed social evolution.

Question: What's the relation between beliefs and values?

Answer: That's an important question. Values are a special type of belief, a more complex issue that could be a separate topic. People have two basic kinds of beliefs: about what's considered true and what's good or bad—that is, what they consider facts and what they value. So far I've mainly talked about the beliefs that people consider true. Beliefs claiming a factual basis have an external referent in the world, oneself, God, whatever, while all moral or ethical values are about "what ought to be" instead of "what is"—what one should or shouldn't do. These ideals are abstract concepts that do not depend on referring to anything tangible in the world. Simply put, if you have a value, it's because you believe it has value. So belief in values needs to be approached somewhat differently. Moral values (morality) are actually rules, ideals, or guidelines for relationships. Since they're at the core of daily life and group identity, moral values are generally accompanied by strong emotions. Valuing can also be conditional upon mere functionality. (I value my computer or my car until it wears out or needs to be replaced, or until something outgrows its usefulness.) These are not the kind of values we are looking at.

Differing values around important life issues, like beliefs about whether facts are true or not, need to be debated in the democratic marketplace of ideas. With values that are controversial, ambiguous, or inconsistent as isolated statements, only probing discussion can reveal all that's involved. For instance, two people can each believe they value life, one being against abortion, the other for it. What's really involved here is whose life should be valued more, the mother's or the fetus's, and why; and more importantly, who decides, and on what basis? But values do not live in isolation; they're usually embedded in a worldview that justifies them. The nature of the worldview is a determining factor in what values are believed in, and whether they are held as closed or open. Since authoritarian, thus closed, values can often be made to sound benignly innocent and pure to mask underlying control agendas, it's much easier to see if a worldview is authoritarian than to see if an isolated value is fixed or malleable.

Question: So values are either closed or open like other beliefs?

Answer: Yes, moral values can be like secondhand beliefs—rule-bound, inflexible absolutes that are not modifiable with changing circumstances. An example is "Always tell the truth no matter what." When values are unchallengeable absolutes (rules, commandments, and often unlivable ideals), this means they're subordinate to a rigidly held ideology, worldview, or cause that's more important than the values. Likewise, if the worldview is authoritarian, the closed and immovable beliefs and values that are part of it are dogmatic too. A hidden power agenda is typically masked by lofty ideals to protect the worldview or authority behind it. Protecting the belief system takes precedence over everything else. Here values are secondary to a more basic belief in the pronouncements of an absolute authority. (God says life is sacred.) So authoritarian values are a smokescreen for protecting an authoritarian ideology or power structure.

Closed beliefs usually come out of authoritarian hierarchies of power where people care more about their place on the hierarchy of privilege than the harmful consequences that the ideology justifying the hierarchy has on people. For example: changing its stance on birth control would undermine papal infallibility, so the Catholic church perpetuates vast suffering and ecological destruction caused by overpopulation—all in the name of God and the sanctity of life. I call this "ideological uncaringness" when authorities and their followers care more about their beliefs than people. So here too there is a strong connection among beliefs, violence, and global harm.

Question: Is defending values different from defending closed beliefs?

Answer: Values that are open to dialogue, feedback, and change are of a different order than rule-bound ones. Valuing and defending justice and believing that harmful actions toward people are wrong is about defending people, not beliefs. When "honor killings" of women or sexual slavery are condemned, people are claiming that certain actions are harmful, not just beliefs. Truly caring moral values that aim at something outside themselves, like the betterment of humanity or saving the world for future generations, are not locked in like fixed beliefs are because they are conditional on whether or not they help or hinder their overriding (external) concerns. Deeply held moral convictions and values that benefit others, like human rights, democracy, and women's equality, are of this type. They're about protecting people instead of a worldview or power hierarchy.

Some values need to be defended to make the world better. So defending what you care about and want to protect—life, human dignity and potential, the Earth, through valuing free speech, fairness, human rights, protecting children, minorities—is different from defending closed belief systems. When people are the priority, not closed core beliefs, the values are a means of furthering a life-enhancing agenda that is open to discussion and change if some other way looks better. Defending such values need not be aggressive, although aggression can occur if emotionally triggered. Justifying values on the basis of what will make humanity viable is different from attack when it's based on facts and objectivity as to what's actually needed. Arguments for viability have an inbuilt flexibility when the result is more important than any specific value. You justify them as best you can, but as long as such convictions are shown to be better for humanity, they're not the kind of fixed beliefs we're discussing. You're really saying, "I hold these convictions because I think they can improve the human condition." But if you hold onto them no matter what, they too are closed beliefs.

Question: You talk as if saving humanity should be our top priority. Not everyone agrees with that value. I know people who think if humanity became extinct we would be getting what we deserve.

Answer: Yes, some do contend that saving humanity is a value that humanity has not shown itself to be worthy of, and that the world would be better without us. That's a value judgment—a negative one coming from humanity's past and present behavior. (All values are based on something.) That judgment usually reflects either cynicism or hopelessness about human nature (cynics are usually disappointed idealists), or repulsion over the horrors and scope of human cruelty, greed, and stupidity. This is an example of historical thinking that can be countered by focusing on human potential and the nature of evolution.

My view and beliefs concerning humanity are not value-free either, as I value the general well-being and continuation of human existence. Nor is my view of values and beliefs value-free. It seems obvious that not only is a shift in values needed in this time of turmoil but also a change in what they are based on and the way they are held. Since my worldview is evolutionary with values geared toward fostering survival, I start with a basic, overriding value that all or most people would agree with. People want themselves, their children, and future generations to survive. So here is a fairly universally shared value. Whether or not we can evolve socially quickly enough to do so depends largely on having functional, evolving values as opposed to immobile, outmoded, dysfunctional ones, which are usually authoritarian.

Values don't live in a vacuum but are a particular order of beliefs that derive from whatever worldview or views and experiences one has. Like other beliefs, they occupy a spectrum from rigid and closed to open and malleable. When living things and the Earth take precedence over concepts, values are changeable through feedback that looks at what supports the human community. Fixed values that unquestioningly support tradition and the *status quo* have led us here but can lead us no further. Our survival depends on having values that are able to keep up with the needs of the times and thus further life instead of leading to a dead end.

Question: You haven't talked about tolerance, but it seems like that's what we need more of. Would you agree?

Answer: Not exactly; it's not quite that simple. For instance, the concept of religious tolerance has come to include not being critical of others' beliefs. But tolerance only works well if all the players play by the same rules. Respecting people's rights to have differing beliefs does not mean that one must respect the beliefs themselves. How tolerant should one be of intolerant viewpoints whose aim is to do away with tolerance or democracy altogether? Tolerance needs to be redefined to encourage discourse that can question the validity of any belief based on its impact on people and the world.

Religious tolerance is essential for religious freedom, which is a prerequisite for democracy. However, the religiously intolerant have no qualms about attempting to eliminate and even outlaw any religious disagreement. They often utilize voting to try to eliminate democracy. Therefore, the concept of religious tolerance also needs reexamining because if the tolerant tolerate the intolerant, there quickly will not be any tolerance left. So I propose the following: People have the right to believe what they will, but anyone also has the right to criticize any belief, especially if it can be shown to be harmful. Instead of complying with the taboo against questioning religious beliefs, if a belief can be shown even to be potentially harmful, it should be challenged and questioned within a democratic arena of discourse. Historically, beliefs that could not stand on their own were made sacred to prevent challenge. No belief should any longer be too sacred to question. In fact, even more than other beliefs, those deemed "sacred" should be suspect, since such beliefs and values have been blindly passed on for hundreds and thousands of years.

COMMENTARY:
Being Better Believers

We all have beliefs that we believe to be true or more likely true than what we don't believe. Over the course of our lives most of us have discovered that many beliefs we've had and many that our historical predecessors have had did not stand up to whatever criteria for truth the beliefs rode on. Yesteryear's knowledge often becomes today's superstitions and uninformed or ridiculed beliefs. But not all beliefs change with conceptions of what truth or knowledge is or isn't. This is especially true of beliefs derived from worldviews that have been a long-term foundation for values and morality. The relation between belief and what is considered knowledge is difficult to pin and changeable. Even if you believe that science, logic, and rationality are the only source of true knowledge, you also believe in other things that science does not deal with, including values, what meaning if any existence contains, and countless other aspects of life. Given the potential fallibility of beliefs and what is considered knowledge, how are we to wend our way in this uncertain terrain?

Many beliefs have an emotional content that makes them seem real and certain. When a belief is experienced with strong emotions, a mechanism in the brain enhances them and makes them seem true. That's why such beliefs are so powerful and why we focus on them here, especially those that do not change with changing evidence. Beliefs with their certainties are one of the greatest propellants of action that come out of the conditionings of the past. Beliefs in a large way have made the world what it is today. We cannot with certainty know that our knowledge is true; but we can with more certainty know what we, and at times others, believe.

Although beliefs can be merely wish fulfillments, reflecting people's preferences and desires and quelling fears, they also are connected to a human need to understand the world we live in and our place in it. Earlier worldviews were formed through revelation—by shamans, prophets, presumed enlightened beings, avatars, or whatever gods the people believed in. They all had creation myths about where we came from, along with a morality code—how we are to act and worship once we're here, and where we're going over the long haul, including after death.

Beliefs construct worldviews; worldviews in turn have embedded in them beliefs, values, and justifications for their presumed truth.

A worldview attempts to provide a somewhat coherent picture to believe or have faith in, or that you think most likely, regarding what existence is about. Faith is a subset of belief that values ignoring all evidence that contradicts the worldview. Tertwillian, a medieval Christian apologist, coined the statement *"Credo ad absurdum"* ("I believe because it is absurd")—the gold standard of faith. We call traditional worldviews authoritarian, as they purport to come from a higher wisdom that ordinary people cannot challenge. Belief that any group or person has sole access to the truth that all should obey has and still can foster violence toward non-believers. The pressure to conform has historically been reinforced with ostracism, physical fear, torture, maiming, and death.

While other social animals relate much more instinctively, the capacities to understand and believe are essential to making us the evolving social animal we are. Beliefs both unite and separate us. They allow us to communicate, connect, and bond with others, to form, align, and unite in groups. But throughout history the beliefs that united us have also separated us from others by creating identities that breed feelings of superiority that in turn justify intolerance toward "outsiders." Most human horrors have been and are brought about by childish worldviews still implanted in many minds both to explain our existence and control us by keeping us in our place in the power hierarchies. These varying worldviews construct identities that create groups of people who give their primary allegiance to the group, with their primary (or only) concern being for those who share the same beliefs and identity. Within these groups there is great pressure for unexamined conformity, which is the necessary key to maintaining whatever security identifying with the group brings.

Outsiders tend to become the "other" and are treated with a different set of rules and moral constraints—often with less care or inhumanely. In some cultures even today, outsiders of the dominant group are viewed as being in some way less than human and made *de facto* slaves. This includes societies that consider women to be secondary or men's possessions. Slavery as an institution could not have taken hold without defining slaves as an inferior race or ethnic group. Such beliefs often become lethal when intertwined with the more overtly male genetic predatory tendencies toward violence and killing. (Women's aggression manifests in less physically violent, lethal ways.) It's worth repeating that in today's world much if not most organized violence involves the clash of different beliefs—religious, ethnic, racial, nationalistic, and other worldview differences. Mass rapes and civilian killings are more likely in wars with ethnic differences, the extreme form being genocide.

Holding on to narrow cultural identities that emphasize differences instead of similarities is the source of ongoing hatreds and strife that are ripping countries and the world apart. Violence, killing, and various crusades against outsiders are too often promoted and even justified as sacred. No matter what their anger or political justifications, few would be suicide bombers without believing in a religion that assures them of an afterlife with great rewards.

The greatest changes in history occur when worldviews and moral orders break down because they can no longer adequately deal with the changing times. When this occurs the traditional vector reasserts an even more conservative posture, while those in the modernism vector struggle to find new solutions, values, and meaning in life. The deepest, most intense, and we think the most dangerous polarity of belief involves the worldwide battle between the forces of the old and the new for people's minds that we call "the morality wars." People living according to older traditions try to hold on to their worldviews and values by attempting to block the wave of changes unleashed by science, technology, and the shifts in worldview and values that greater understandings of the cosmos brought. These old traditions come from religions that see science as destroying the mythos that the religions are based on. They also rightly see that although science can compromise these old worldviews, it cannot offer either personal or social values to replace the loss and bring about a workable social order.

But since proponents of these authoritarian worldviews and moralities try to return to the past or preserve the *status quo* by sacralizing tradition, they cannot cope with or adequately compete in the modern reality. A world of spiraling change demands feedback-oriented instead of tradition-dictated solutions. Given humanity's sometimes contradictory predilection for both power and continuity, those in tradition-bound patriarchal religions want to use the fruits of science and technology that empower and enable them to compete—computers, airplanes, motor vehicles, electricity, arms, and their almost endless spin-offs—without changing worldviews or gender and familial roles that originated hundreds, sometimes thousands of years ago.

Science as it now stands has its own answers or beliefs about where the universe and life came from, what we are to do while here, and where the universe is ultimately going. The Big Bang theory (that some call science's creation myth) has everything coming out of nothing, and since the universe is infinitely expanding, with galaxies ever more rapidly accelerating away from each other, eventually gravity will lose hold and the universe will cease to be capable of supporting life as we know it. While we are here, our genetically programmed job is to reproduce, keeping our gene pool in play as long as we can. So if your worldview is totally circumscribed by science, it does not present an uplifting view of our place in the scheme of things. It is in this arena that those who proclaim the necessity of intelligent design have an emotional advantage in their beliefs over "cold science," as they anthropomorphically presume that "design" implies a designer, which feeds traditional ideas of a God who puts people at the head of the rest of creation. (When examining evolution we will propose a way that meaning can be found in existence without a separate entity that's the meaning-maker.)

In these dangerous life- and species-threatening times, it is necessary for all beliefs, especially those coming from old traditional authoritarian sources but also modern ones coming from science, to be subject to honest reexamination. Many of us today witnessing the obvious crises we face realize that our survival must involve some kind of shift in consciousness. We see such a shift as coming from the evolutionary process that constructed us, now moving us to the necessity of evolving socially. What this involves in part is the need to become better believers. Beliefs about the world and ourselves are where our excursions into truth and meaning end up, and to a great extent they shape the future through us. As long as rapid change remains part of the human landscape, better, more open-minded believing is needed that strives toward objectivity. Also crucial are feedback and survival-oriented beliefs offering hope, as well as a deep concern about humanity's future that can transcend historic beliefs known to divide people and groups. That we are all in this together is a popular and true refrain. Social evolution involves the internalization of our shared plight. To meet it we need more accurate, life-furthering, constructive beliefs that do not deny the importance of the external world, which humanity has had a large hand in fashioning and is now destroying.

Most people's beliefs about values, right and wrong, and how people should treat each other and the world usually come from upbringing, culture, and personal experience. Our thoughts and beliefs brought on our current problems, and a social awareness that includes new ways of thinking and believing must get us out of them. People need to become better believers through loosening the way beliefs are held—being curious, open to change when warranted, trying to understand other views. Whether or not understanding other views influences our own, it can bring more empathy and respect.

The relativism more prevalent in modern societies has to an extent undermined absolutism, but not sufficiently to eliminate the assumed causes of superiority and strife. This is because an absolute relativism flattens values and places them within cultural contexts that are not to be judged from without, which removes the ground for critiquing dysfunctional beliefs. Many relativists hold that it's impossible to know "the truth." Some go so far as to say that truth is nothing more than the consensus reality of a particular time. Yet the observation that all knowledge and beliefs are potentially fallible does not mean that beliefs about the world, oneself, and values all have equal weight. Some beliefs are closer to being objective than others. Even though absolute truth may be beyond our grasp, we need to be wise enough to foresee the consequences of what could occur if we ignore the signs of danger surrounding us.

We acutely need pan-cultural values we can believe in to bind us as a global community with the common concern of viability. Not all values need be relative to a given culture or merely based on preference. Because values are embedded in worldviews, if your worldview values life, intelligence, and people treating each other with care and dignity, then from that point of view some values are more valuable than others. If different worldviews share common values it's easier to reach accord. This does not make the values viable—we have seen that the fundamentalists of different religions have more in common with each other than with the modern people of their own culture. Pan-cultural agreement is not enough if the values are archaic. There's an urgent need for values with pan-cultural agreement based on improving and protecting the world in ways that would bring hope to most everyone. This can lead to the overall benefit in basic ways and is a bottom-line priority of social evolution. This will involve a shift in consciousness, including a shift toward more fact-based and process-oriented worldviews that allow for uncertainty, change, and potential fallibility. Social awareness is the next step in the evolution of evolution.

Humanity is facing the difficult necessity of people expanding their beliefs and identities such that the primary identity is our common human and global identity as citizens and caretakers of planet Earth, with the others being secondary. Identities that make people feel special may be a necessary and can be a positive factor in life, but "special" need no longer mean superior if such identities are not based on authoritarian "sacred" (unchallengeable) traditions and worldviews or wealth or power. This shift can come from a change in consciousness that realizes we're all in the same boat together, a boat that will sink unless we as a species enlarge our identities and build shared values capable of addressing global problems. Cultures that cannot change values with changing times rigidify, wither, and eventually self-destruct. It is under such circumstances that violence in many forms becomes an inevitable outcome, with hatred, anger, desperation, and hopelessness being rampant. This causes more and more angry and disenfranchised people to become willing to take others down with them. Those who don't care if they live don't care if you do either.

If societies fostered curiosity, open-mindedness, and tolerance instead of prejudice and fear in order to control and manipulate people, humanity would have a far better chance of overcoming its self-induced crises. Human intelligence coupled with technological know-how exists to possibly turn ecological disaster around, but still lacking are the values that can bring the will or trust among groups to make human viability the ultimate global priority that it must become for us to survive. The nature of our beliefs, and how well they can deal with a fast-changing, uncertain future, will greatly determine who we become and if we create a viable world that can support us. We need to become more aware of beliefs and their potential fallibility, which will make us better believers.

3. Pleasure and Desire

Many evolutionary biologists and psychologists see us as essentially controlled by our genes, whose agenda is their propagation through sexual reproduction. Genes hook pleasure into reproduction, and in males, pleasure is also tied into aggression, so the strongest male wins out in reproducing the next generation. Pleasure is related to other biological needs as well to ensure satisfying them.

Genes have little concern for the vehicle that conveys them through generations, so our bodies are merely convenient carriers. In humans a brain evolved concerned with the well-being of the individual carrier—our bodies, ourselves. Our brains produced minds that can circumvent the simple genetic program through both understanding and creating values related to an interest in ourselves and what we care about. Seeing clearly how pleasure works in us is a great help in unhooking from the mechanical aspects of pleasure that are not aimed at our well-being.

W hat are we searching for? We are all looking for something, aren't we? What is it that one seeks? There are many names for it: happiness, fulfillment, meaning, self-realization, inner peace, joy, enjoyment, love, well-being, harmony, peak experiences, "being in the zone." Many of these things we wish for are hard to describe and even harder to seek. A question that can be more easily approached is "What is the nature of seeking?" This includes the arena of so-called "spiritual seeking" for mystical states, enlightenment, bliss, ego-loss, nirvana, and the like. Becoming "more spiritual" usually means better or "more selfless"—more loving, caring, empathetic, compassionate, giving, altruistic, detached, mindful. If we look beyond the words, beyond all of these names, I think we will find that what they all have in common is wanting to feel good, and even to feel better and better. Although what we seek goes under many names, good feelings are pleasures.

Looking at both pleasure and the search for it in order to see how they work is an inroad into the nature of desire, seeking, thought, and the human condition itself. Wanting to feel good or better is one of the powerful mechanisms that drives us. I'm not saying it should or shouldn't be this way, nor am I negating pleasure or criticizing desiring it. Rather, the hope is that becoming aware of how these elements work can help create a shift in consciousness that will make our relationship to pleasure more realistic in the sense of being aware of potential consequences for yourself, the environment, and the world, and more enjoyable because you can feel good when pleasures are in line with what's appropriate for these times.

Many different experiences can give pleasure, and they are not the same for everyone. However, all pleasures have certain aspects in common. Pleasures exist in the body as feelings that we enjoy. This could involve satisfying biological needs, having sensual or aesthetic experiences, and a whole spectrum of more cerebral satisfactions like winning a chess game or a bet. A shift in bodily sensations or emotions always occurs, however large or slight. The feelings can be increased or diminished by thought, but they fade fairly quickly to memory. The pleasure in bringing back the memory pales before the original experience to varying degrees. This is one reason we tend to seek more and greater pleasures.

This seeking is actually the product of desire. Desire puts you in time, because within desire is an expectation, a belief or hope that getting the objects of desire will bring good, even better feelings. Desire is endless, from desiring a tasty dish, love, a trip to Bali, to winning a Nobel Prize, conquering the world, or immortality. There is no certainty that a desire will be realized, especially if it's an unrealistic fantasy or a programmed goal, or even a once-known pleasure. Even if realized, the desire may not bring the expected enjoyment, for wanting and liking are not the same. Researchers have found that humans are generally pretty bad at predicting what will make them feel good over time.

Wanting pleasure beyond satisfying physical drives seems to stem from a uniquely human, inbuilt, restless discontent instilled by evolution to prevent stasis and foster competition. The continual desire for more prevents getting stuck in any ongoing pleasures. In other words, this dissatisfaction fuels pleasure-seeking. Desire, like fear, is a gateway to being controlled through manipulation of our dissatisfactions, drives, and genetic programming. We are conditioned by society to want success, however defined. Predatory advertising panders to and exacerbates this by preying on our fears and desires. When we do find a way to make ourselves feel better, we soon take it for granted. It becomes the new baseline of expectancy and then we want more. Other desires capture our attention that we imagine will make us feel better yet. We quickly adapt to whatever pleasures we have, which brings more desire, because desire and its mirror image, fear, are the fuel that we run on.

Have you ever noticed that bad or unpleasant feelings seem to hang on longer and be stronger than good ones? There is a sensible evolutionary reason for this too. Good feelings dissipate sooner to leave space for protective fear and anger warnings of threat that are more crucial to survival. This is another reason why we continually seek a state of feeling better through the accumulation of whatever we are conditioned to think will do so, whether wealth, power, status, material possessions, or spiritual credits. We seek ways to improve ourselves and become a better person, believing that will also make us feel better.

Desire aims at something you don't have, which usually involves the hope of feeling better through one form of pleasure or another (including all acquisition). So desire, like pleasure, is double-edged. Like pleasant memories or daydreams that can keep you from experiencing the uniqueness of the ongoing moment, desires can bring sorrow through dissatisfaction, feelings of lack, disappointment, envy, and resentment. On the positive side, desire can bring interest and the motivation to change, as well as the pleasures of anticipation. Many "spiritual" worldviews maintain that pleasure, desire, and the attachments they inevitably bring feed the ego and prevent spirituality. This is not my view. I am not judging, villainizing, or trying to eliminate wanting pleasure or having desires or attachments. Quite to the contrary, desire for pleasure, growth, and goals like saving the world are powerful and important core motivators that move us. Goals contain desires. What would your life be without desires and goals to inspire and motivate you? Desire, like love, makes the world go 'round. It's a fuel that evolution runs on. The problem is not desire itself; it's what we desire and the ways desire can be manipulated—whether by gurus, leaders, corporations, or a social system that equates human worth with accumulation. Attachment to what you have or want is inherent in being a social animal because you're attached to what you care about. This is part of bonding.

Desires and attachments can be beneficial or detrimental, depending on the situation. My interest is in seeing how these motivators of our lives work in us and how we can use them to live better. The more awareness we have of their workings, the more we can free ourselves from social manipulation and obsolete conditioning patterns, even genetic ones. Some people maintain that wanting to be happy is the bottom-line desire, not pleasure itself. It is true that pleasures come and go, while happiness is an amorphous, many-faceted state that in any given moment may or may not contain pleasure and may even have pain. Happiness that is not fleeting usually involves meaning, quality of life and relationships, work and general satisfaction, goals, and an overall outlook containing some wisdom and emotional awareness. Although happiness can be desired, it cannot be sought. It is a result of how a life is led, with no guarantee of happiness either coming or remaining. One reason we are focusing on pleasure is that seeking pleasure to be happy rarely brings lasting happiness, as many pleasures are short-lived. So pleasure-seeking as a way of life or as the meaning of life is ultimately not fulfilling, although in times of spiritual/moral breakdown, pleasure and feeling good understandably do take on more importance and meaning.

After its initial immediacy, pleasure lives in memories and anticipations. To be seeking pleasures, whether trying to satisfy physical desires (eat, sleep, sex) or more complex ones (power, adulation, respect, altruism), is to be in that moment of thought in the past or future. When thought remembers past pleasures, the pleasure itself is in the combination of thought and the body's cells that contain the residue that "remembers" the pleasurable experience. However, it is thought that remembers and desires.

It's natural and healthy to prefer pleasure over pain. Yet if offered the option of a painless life, I would not choose it. It's as important to see the place of pain in life's dramas as pleasure. Growth for many is a value, and rightly so. As life is change, one either changes by growing or by becoming more rigid. Real growth often involves periods of confusion, discomfort, pain, and even suffering before a new direction evolves. In most every life there are moments when one looks back and says to oneself, "I've really grown." Upon looking carefully at the process that brought about the growth, one realizes that it was rarely free from pain and suffering. They were the feedback that something in one's life was not working. Without them there would have been no motivation to change. Pain, like necessity, is the mother of invention. I certainly am not advocating the cultivation of suffering as a means of growth, unlike some traditional worldviews that do present it as a means toward spiritual realization. Pain and suffering do not have to be sought because they are potentially around the next corner. But fearing them and leading a life geared at avoiding them as much as possible cuts you off from the adventures of the unknown and inhibits growth.

Growth also comes from revising goals to meet changing times. Desire that's aware of the necessity of change brings motivation to grow through intention and will.

In seeking, you mostly seek the known—how would one seek the unknown? Suppose I were to tell you to go ahead and look for something totally out of your ken, something completely out of your experience.

Where would you look? How would you know when you found it? You would only know if you recognize it. You only recognize something if you already know it. However, upon seeing the necessity of change, you could try different things to see what's fitting.

Actually, what we usually seek are things and experiences we hold in memory or that we have heard of and imagine to be pleasurable or at least good for us. Five minutes ago, or last year, twenty years ago, I had an extraordinary experience that now lives in memory. That experience—whether it be the initial blush of young love, the joy of having a baby, an idyllic time or exciting trip, succeeding at something, an experience in nature, or an altered state—whatever it was, I have cherished it over the years. When I'm feeling bad I think of it; it warms me, and I say to myself, "Wouldn't it be nice if I could feel or be that way all the time, or at least more than I do now?" When we seek, is it not usually this that we seek—a repetition or intensification of the known? You can only seek something that has happened or that you imagine. You cannot seek the new because it's unknown; you can only seek the old. So most seeking perpetuates the known.

People talk of wonderful experiences or states of being. Books entice you with promises of continual joy and bliss or delights beyond the mundane. You say to yourself, "That's for me." Then you search for the key to unlock the door to all these goodies. What are these "goodies"? Do you not simply translate all these ideas into other words or images that come from your experience or hearsay? Please look in yourself and see if this is so.

Searching for the "unknown" is simply seeking ideas that are the creation of thought. Thoughts can rearrange themselves to appear new, yet these products of imagination are mostly not really new. Although thoughts that come out of awareness and insight can be creative, our thoughts are usually the old in disguise. It is also very easy to get wrapped up in the pleasures of the search itself, in the excitement of anticipation, relishing the good feelings it will bring. Searching for the meaning of life, the fountain of youth, questing, even spiritual seeking are like the hunt in that the quest itself is often more exciting than reaching the goal. It gives life meaning and a worthwhile challenge that once achieved may bring some satisfaction, but soon afterward dissatisfaction or desire sets in again.

On occasion something captures our interest—nature, a symphony, a book, a conversation, a novel idea. The compelling thing about being truly interested is that you forget about yourself while following where the interest may lead. Interest commands attention and generates energy in you to follow the interest. These feelings of aliveness are pleasures that during those moments of total attention feel timeless. (You're unaware of time passing and of yourself.) At some point you become aware that the unique energy of being so engaged is enjoyable—you remember it. The memory puts you back in time with perhaps a desire to return to that quality of interest, which you may or may not be able to recapture. The memories of the experience, which often include evaluation ("I really liked that total focus"), place you in the past and create a desire for more of it (the future). I'm not presenting this as right or wrong, but rather as how we work. We want to enjoy life and also to know that we are enjoying it. Liking or disliking an experience involves evaluation, which we are programmed to do for survival and to give us a sense of direction.

This is the interface of control and surrender. We want to be taken over by interest and passion, which we hope will ignite our creativity and bring us to unforeseen ways of connecting with the world and ourselves. We also want to take control of this momentum to ensure that we won't go out too far and perhaps be hurt or significantly damaged. If there were a formula that ensured the right balance between control and surrender (letting go), choices would be easier to make and life would be far more mechanical. There is no formula. The ways that people attempt to deal with control and surrender have repercussions on their well-being, satisfaction, and even happiness. Although happiness itself cannot be sought, some of its elements can be developed, while others involve surrendering. Simplistically, happiness is a life context where one feels connected to others and the particular times one finds oneself in, loves and is loved, and is engaged in something one considers meaningful that is greater than mere self-enhancement.

There are ways of being that can enhance or diminish happiness. But in these times that demand deep changes in the way we do things, there is little assurance as to the results. Consequently, a pervading undercurrent of fear tends to lead people toward more self-absorbed activities. "Follow your interest" as a touchstone can be a way of breaking through conditioned habits and reaching a place that is more beneficial for oneself and humanity, but that depends on what your interests are. No one can really know or tell you what your interests should be, but if they involve the accumulation of personal wealth, power, or status through traditional routes, these are neither new nor a recipe for happiness, nor do they meet the historic moment. So although following your interests can engage you and on occasion put you into a timeless mode, it is not a panacea for a meaningful life. It can bring pleasure, but as we've seen pleasure is double-edged and not always focused on the greater good.

The pursuit of pleasure has inbuilt limits that can diminish growth and creativity because living "fully" is not always pleasant. The nature of pleasure is that you want more. If overeating didn't have stop mechanisms like indigestion, we could eventually eat ourselves to death; some manage to do this anyway. Not all pleasures have stop mechanisms, and many can be highly addictive—power, money, nicotine, sweets, alcohol, shopping, even adulation. The pleasures of power over people have led some to attempt world domination. The pleasures our species has enjoyed of being on top of the food chain, enabling us to use the resources of our world casually and with little forethought, are leading us toward self-destruction. In times of crisis there is a great pull to rely on old known pleasures, however temporary, in the attempt to feel good.

So I'll return to examining how pleasure works, but with a view toward becoming more aware of its two sides.

You have a pleasurable experience. What do you first become aware of at such times? Does not the evaluative process come in? You say, "This is wonderful; I love this"—or whatever it is that you say. Then perhaps you wonder how you can experience it again. How can you do it a lot, or tomorrow, or next year? Isn't this the kind of thing that happens? It is here that one begins to discover the nature of pleasure. The experience of that moment that gave you pleasure had a timeless quality. It could make you feel different, perhaps a bodily warmth, transported by beauty, or a sense of connection or insight or success. You may be able to shift back and forth between the feelings and knowing that you're enjoying the feelings, until you lose interest and do something else. You may later try to repeat that moment or look for it again.

Actually, the pleasure of the good feelings is of a different order than the realization that you're experiencing pleasure. Evaluation of the pleasure itself can be a pleasure of living in the body, but it also has a cerebral component where you are enjoying the enjoying. The feelings and emotions are still in the body but are now colored by thought. Although pleasure lives in the moment itself, that pleasure shifts, fading into memory as you evaluate it. We not only want to feel thrilled, we want to know that we are feeling thrilled. The original experience may have had an extraordinary quality, an energy. But that is changed, different, as soon as evaluation comes in. Then the timeless moment is no longer timeless because there is an evaluator, an experiencer who is having an experience that contains evaluation, which means there is separation between the experience and experiencer. As soon as you're aware of having an experience, it's different, isn't it? When the evaluation occurs, that's what's going on, not the original experience itself, which is now in memory. You may still be involved in the original experience (let's say being captured by someone's uniqueness and feeling good that she likes you). I'm not saying one shouldn't do this. Evaluation comes in and we may draw pleasure from it—it's just what we do.

Can you see how this works for you, not the words, but the actuality of what it means to be evaluating? Not whether I should or should not be evaluating, judging, or comparing it to another moment (which is of course just evaluation), but how evaluation works in living. Strong experiences leave a residue in thought and in the tissue—in the cells themselves. If the memories are pleasurable I can bask in the warm memory of them. The joy or pleasure of the timeless moment eventually leaves; I cannot keep or own it. I can keep the memory of it; it's part of me. I can't repeat it exactly or reenact the joy I felt in the moment. Watch it. See how it works for yourself. You may tell your friends what a fine time you had or how good you felt. You plan to repeat the moment, perhaps hoping next time to intensify it. All of this contains a component of thought. There is never a next time, because it's not quite the same. As you are walking away from the original moment, you work it over in your mind, holding it to you, trying to extend the pleasure through memory.

Seeking pleasure is a very human thing to do; we all in our own ways do it. I'm not judging it or saying it shouldn't be pursued. Pleasurable memories and anticipations can be good for your physical and mental well-being because they can trigger similar, though less intense, beneficial physical effects. I'm observing how pleasure works and pointing out that one cannot seek the unknown, the truly creative, which is where many of the precious qualities that people want actually flourish. It's important to see how pleasure and seeking pleasure work in oneself, which is mostly on automatic. Awareness of the nature of pleasure and its mechanical aspects allows more freedom in action. This awareness is an example of a meditative process in living. This topic is especially important for these times, as it has been humanity's unaware pursuit of pleasures (particularly short-term ones) that has greatly contributed to where we now find ourselves.

Although seeking pleasure can bring known pleasures (companionship, favorite walks or scenes, music, foods, travel, sex, and the like), there is the potential of sorrow within repeating familiar pleasures, or in basking in memory and desires. For in seeking the known I can miss the thrust of life. As I'm telling myself how fine I'm feeling (or felt), I'm removing myself from the potential that the living moment holds for me. I may fail to connect with a friend more deeply or to smell the perfume of the woods, for I've removed attention from the moment to thoughts about past and future pleasures. Here's where the potential of sorrow lives. How does this work? While reliving an experience I remove myself from life's newness, its challenge. Life is a movement, and when there is this space between me and it, I remove myself from this living energy, and in this separation there can be sorrow.

Although often shifting, attention is always on something–the question is what's more rich, interesting, or important for you in a given moment. Sometimes this separation is just a shift of attention to something more interesting. But when it dulls living, it contributes to the feeling of not ever being or having enough: that I am not good enough, not smart enough, kind enough, rich enough–spiritually or experientially. The truth about pleasure is that ultimately you never get enough. No matter how much you get, it's not enough. So pleasure-seeking, which is thought creating desire, is double-edged. The dynamics of pleasure can keep you from totally engaging with life in the moment, which is where joy, communion, love, and creativity lie.

Pleasure and pain are two sides of a coin: they both promote desire. We desire ever more pleasure and ever less pain. And at times they intermix. There can be pleasure in pain: in sad yearnings, in nostalgia, in longing, and in the bittersweet quality of self-pity. There is also pain in pleasure as I try to hold on to it and see it seep away. To see clearly how pleasure and pain work brings degrees of freedom and possibility that can move one out of the tyranny of the past, whether it be old pleasures or pains.

Pleasure and beliefs can also be interrelated. I often pick my beliefs insofar as they will give me pleasure or allay fear and doubt. There is much pleasure especially in conditioned beliefs. The beliefs that I am most attached to are the ones that bring security and certainty, that are comforting and reassuring and allow a more pleasurable state of mind. You can see this for yourself. The more uncertain and frightening the world is, the better conditioned beliefs make me feel and the more I cling to them. If I believe spirituality is about feeling good, the better that my beliefs and practices make me feel, the more they reinforce my spiritual beliefs and worldview and seem true.

One can observe the pleasure of dominance in terms of beliefs. Beliefs that become part of my identity can separate me from you by making me feel a little better, superior to you, which is pleasure. I believe in capitalism or socialism or atheism or science or quantum realities or Buddhism, and these beliefs make me better than you who do not believe as I do. If I'm a Buddhist and you are a Christian, I think it's better to be a Buddhist. If I felt it were better to be a Christian, I'd be one. Of course, I can get extraordinary pleasure out of being better than you, or I can feel sorry for you, or pity you in your wrongness or your naïveté.

Beliefs also prop up group and personal identities, which will be discussed later. See how much energy, how much time you spend each day building structures that make you feel better than you would without them. A problem is that many beliefs that make people feel better are not necessarily conducive to a well-functioning, caring society. The more alienating, divisive, and uncaring a social order is, the more people will cling to beliefs like racism, nationalism, and religious and cultural intolerance that make them feel superior. But the energy that is put into feeling superior negates life. Each time I convince myself that I'm better than you, which is one of the few pleasures available to many people, I dull myself with self-congratulation that cuts me off from any real connection we might have, which is another root of sorrow.

Ours is a sorrow-filled world of separate beliefs and identities competing with each other for supremacy. The pleasure I get from feeling superior separates me from you and groups from each other, creating extraordinary sorrow, violence, and needless tragedy in the world. To see this, not to try to make it go away, not to negate it, just to see the way it works, is a vital inroad into the nature of oneself, including identity.

We tend to think in terms of high and low desires. I may create hierarchies of desires and evaluate them according to my beliefs—"low" desires for material gain, power, or sensuality; "high" desires for God, spirituality, peace, and a better world. But whether a desire is high or low, better or worse, they all partake in the structure of desire. I'm not saying that all desires are on an equal footing or that one shouldn't have preferences—we all do. Certainly desiring health is healthier than desiring to be worshipped. What we usually consider "high" and "low" desires very often come from our social conditioning. An example of a healthy or "higher" desire is a desire for my beliefs to approximate truth as best I can. This changes the way I hold beliefs and is better for me as well as the world.

As we become discontent with known pleasures, it's not unusual to become bored or jaded and look for new, greater, supposedly higher ones. I may turn to spirituality, searching for bliss, higher states of consciousness, and mystical experiences. Mystics, spiritual authorities, and books promise ecstasy or bliss of one type or another and describe spirituality as feeling wonderfully special most or all of the time, or even throughout eternity. Believing them arouses desire, and I search for those who can tell me how to get there. The promises of spiritual authorities carry the weight of tradition—especially when they fit my yearning for something more. I come to view spiritual experiences as providing the greatest possible feelings, which are pleasures. I may have had mystical experiences and long to repeat them. Special practices may make me feel better and give me predicted experiences that reinforce my hopes and beliefs.

The mind is so clever; thought is so sly. It says, "Well, all right. I see that pleasure and desire can contain sorrow and that to seek anything usually means seeking pleasure. So I'll stop seeking pleasure. I'll train myself not to have desires through one practice or another." Why do this? Don't I think that if I can stop seeking pleasure, which is sometimes called letting go of desires, detaching from wants, then I'll feel better? So that wanting to let go of desire has the same core desire within it, the agenda of feeling better. Detaching from desire has the not-so-hidden promise that new and wonderful, more sublime, more spiritual pleasures will come one's way. Of course this is just another elaborately disguised seeking of pleasure. The desire to be desireless is but another desire. The thought that because it purports to be spiritual it's superior to more mundane desires shows how the mind justifies any desire it is attached to.

Letting go of desires, especially unrealizable ones, *can* make you feel better. Detaching from desires is a control mechanism of mind that can be very useful in freeing oneself from old programming, since many of our desires have been conditioned into us. But since desire is part of the motor of change, attempting to let go of desire totally (as some worldviews recommend) removes you from the creative momentum of life. There's real danger in dampening one's emotions, intuitions, and creativity—the danger of being "detached" from inner wellsprings. Creativity does not spring from being detached. I seek, and I see that it's in my nature to seek pleasure. Sometimes I find ways of feeling good that are satisfying, but many times I don't. If I'm happy and satisfied, well and good; then for the moment there's no problem. But if not, I see that seeking pleasure can remove me from life, creating sorrow, which brings more desire—a self-perpetuating loop of pleasure and pain. Then I want to stop, to escape the loop, but the very wanting to stop is another way of seeking pleasure, so there's great conflict.

Looking at pleasure, there seems to be no way out of its conflict. If I try to get out of it, the trying itself puts me back in. So what can I do?

Is it possible to be free of all this—to move freely and on occasion break out of the confines of my nature, to move with a freedom that is a freedom in action that pierces through the limits of the conditioned mind? The question we've been contemplating is not whether there are better or worse desires, or more or less pleasurable pleasures, but rather how desire and pleasure work in us and how they can hook onto anything. An answer to the question of "What to do?" leads to the basic question of whether or not it's possible for an ordinary human being, not a saint or a guru or an expert, to see how this whole process works, and in the seeing itself to move in that moment out of the conditioned habits that pleasures and desires generate, so that they are no longer problematic in living. Is it possible?

Of course, if I were to tell you it's possible and you were to believe me, we'd just be involved again in belief. It's important to find out for yourself if it's actually possible to come into direct contact with the nature of pleasure and desire—to see it. To see when they're appropriate and healthy and when they might not be. It is awareness that sees how this is a part of how you mechanically work, without judging it in yourself, and this awareness opens the door to its own movement. To further address the question of what is one to do, we'll examine the nature of fear, freedom, and choice. There are another doorways to understanding from the inside the nature of the mind one lives with.

Question: You opened by saying what happiness, fulfillment, etc., have in common is pleasure—but not all the time—maybe kind of like a lowest common denominator. What are the other qualities of happiness, and how is it different from pleasure?

Answer: I said that happiness, contentment, and a sense of fulfillment are not what I mean by pleasure. They are more of an overall quality of life, a context that you operate from. This does not mean that once you're happy you always will be as circumstances of life change, both internally and externally. Pleasure is designed in us to be short-lasting, and so it comes and goes. When you are happy, the likelihood is that you will have more pleasure than when not. However, pain and suffering can move through happiness too. I did say that happiness itself cannot be directly sought because it is the outcome of many factors in a life, such as the quality of connections with people, whether love is in your life, and whether you feel you have used your life well.

Question: Can you further distinguish between liking and wanting?

Answer: This is essentially differentiating between pleasure and desire. When experiencing what you like, it gives you pleasure. You assume that if you experienced the same thing again (or something similar), you would again like it. We tend to identify ourselves by our likes and dislikes—I like chocolate or sex and dislike pushy people or pressure. Your anticipation of what will continue to give you pleasure may be true or not, since repeated pleasures have a way of losing capacity to ignite good feelings. Desiring, whether to repeat the intensity of a pleasure or for some more profound or growth-producing experience, does not ensure that if you get what you're aiming at, you'll like it. The old adage "Be careful what you ask for; you might get it" points to the history of desire. Desiring is part of the human condition. It's what we do to ameliorate the built-in discontent we have with habit and the repetitive. Desire is necessary for change and can move us to evolve socially, which is necessary for our survival. The problem with desire is not that you have it, but what it aims at. The question is whether your desires, both personal and social, are life-furthering or -diminishing.

Particularly in these potentially transformative times, I view an overriding desire to get as close to the truth as we can, whether pleasant or not, as essential to the furthering of life and our future well-being. Desires are in our minds, coming out of beliefs and creating goals. Having beliefs that are in touch with the truth of the reality we are facing makes possible the realization of life-affirming goals. Hope brings energy that can contribute to making the needed changes. Hope, like belief, needs to be grounded in realistic possibilities to be effective. It is here that your awareness of how you work is the key.

Question: Many people are worried about widespread drug use, which is related to pleasure—especially addictions. What do you think about drugs and about how this issue is being handled?

Answer: The use and abuse of drugs offer many examples of the connection between pleasure and pain. Drugs can give immediate pleasure or relief of some sort, but if abused they either create problems or lead to painful lives that cause pain to others too. This also brings social problems—although often not the ones that the government designates and focuses on. For instance, it's a well-known fact that alcohol and nicotine are harmful drugs that cause many more deaths than all other drugs combined.

Most drugs—socially acceptable or not, legal or illegal, prescription or over-the-counter—are destructive if overused, with some being more addictive and harmful than others. (Here I'm not using the term "destructive" evaluatively, but rather physiologically and psychologically, and in terms of whether the way a drug is being used causes problems.) Drug use of all types is prevalent in most walks of life. This poses special dangers for the young—especially because accurate public information about each drug and their actual effects is censored and replaced by propaganda that the young mistrust and ignore, leaving them victims of adult misinformation and policies. A highly sexualized society that unabashedly uses sexuality to sell products, while withholding information about sex, birth control, and preventing sexual diseases, likewise treats the young worse than shamefully by putting their lives at risk in an era of AIDS. The young are unfortunately the hapless victims of adult prejudices and subsequent mishandling of crucial issues. These are examples of real social problems.

In the vain hope of trying to solve what is designated as "the drug problem"—or at least trying to get elected by pandering to and exacerbating the public's fears and ignorance—politicians outlaw drugs and proclaim a "war" on drugs. The health industry builds profitable rehabilitation centers; society does this and that; but what society doesn't do (given that people will continue to take drugs) is focus on harm reduction and making protective scientific information available—both about prescription drugs and drugs considered anti-social. Overall, society is not even looking at the real problem. Instead of reducing harm, the government actually causes more harm with the billions it throws at eradicating illegal drugs and flooding the judicial system with non-violent offenders.

The problem of drugs is not drugs alone. The problem is that they offer many people either relief or a more interesting alternative than their lives without them. As long as that's the case there will be a continuing problem with drugs. For example, heroin is extraordinarily dulling, but it does relieve pain for a time. Unfortunately, people who feel hopeless or stuck in a seemingly endless grind are very susceptible to an easy way out of a shabby, degrading, or even just flat and boring life. Drugs become the focal point, offering respite, a community, and a meaning of sorts or at least a goal (pursuit of the drug). The underlying problem is the fragmented and disconnected reality of many people's lives. So you cannot merely treat symptoms and expect a deep cure. {See the chapter on addiction in *The Guru Papers*.}

The use of drugs will not decrease unless there's a change in people's lives. It should be clear by now (once again, decades after learning this lesson) that outlawing drugs—prohibition—does not solve anything and is usually counter-productive, causing even more harm. Much of the old order is breaking down, partly because the way it deals with difficulties is unaware, dysfunctional, and destructive—that is the real problem.

COMMENTARY:
Pleasure and Power

Going under the assumption that to us seems self-evident, that humans are a species at risk, we see our only possibilities coming from evolving socially. What this must include is becoming aware of the parts of our nature that have contributed to our present plight. The ways we have tolerated, accepted, and even participated in the casual use and abuse of our planet and each other have been conditioned into us and our prevailing social systems for millennia.

But that's not the whole story: The ways in which pleasure and desire are tied in with our predatory nature, and the extent to which this is institutionalized, have shaped our history and social and personal habits and behavior. In our early ancestors, survival was more immediately and overtly linked to predation and cooperating in bands to hunt, which our genes linked to pleasure. This shows up in modern garb in the varied pleasures of cooperation, competition, and aggression.

Desire for pleasure and fear of pain or death are emotions that activate approach/avoidance mechanisms. Desire and pleasure attract; fear and pain repel. They both have a biological survival basis. The evolutionary underpinning of pleasure is genes and other biological mechanisms that reward and reinforce behavior that increases fitness for survival (eating, sex, child-rearing, relationships, success, learning) and is thus worthy of time and attention. Feeling good was originally a reasonable sign that things were safe, while feeling bad was a warning.

Although pleasure and pain are interwoven and we are wired to respond to the immediacy of both, they do not operate in the same way. With pleasure, the quicker the gratification, the more seductive and reinforcing it is. But most biological pleasures (like food and sex) have inbuilt stop mechanisms that make them more fleeting than the so-called negative ones (fear, anger, sadness), because the biological pleasures were originally less important for self-protection and imme-diate survival. Pleasures are usually short-lived because they quickly habituate and are taken for granted as the new baseline—in modern parlance, luxuries rapidly become necessities. Novel or more intense pleasures then capture our interest and desire. Without biological satiety to bring one back to a functional homeostasis, pleasures can easily become what in cybernetics is called a positive feedback loop—the more you get, the more you want. This self-perpetuating, end-lessly demanding loop of going for more eventually leads to self-destruction. This is why humans are so susceptible to the next hit of pleasure and all the manufactured desires of consumerism. There is often more pleasure in anticipation and desire than in real-izing them, as pleasure whets the appetite for more desire, especially if it is not as satisfying as hoped or imagined. Longing often con-tains more emotion than having.

Rather than stemming from our genes themselves, global problems result more from how our genetic programming has been institution-alized and greatly amplified by technology, which has now been mag-nified to dangerous, out-of-control extremes. Political, religious, and corporate exploitation of our genetic mechanisms triggering pleasure, desire, and fear is commonly done solely for power and profit, without limits or qualms, and with indifference to the destructive consequences. Aside from the potentially huge (but relatively untapped) powers of con-sumer awareness and boycotts, this exploitation is only offset by what-ever regulation governments with heavy corporate influence can manage to impose, fund, and oversee.

Technology has devised a seemingly endless number of enticing things to consume that give short-term gratification with no stop mech-anisms—aside from lack of money. Corporate advertisers have come up with countless scientifically based, devious ways to manipulate our genetic programming around pleasures, desires, and fears to get us to buy their products and increase their profits. So people work hard at often unsatisfying jobs partly to keep buying an endless array of things to reward themselves for doing what they don't want to do.

All we have is our time, which makes it priceless. Essentially most people are caught in an elaborate system where they sacrifice their lives by selling their time to enhance someone else's profit. The more dissatisfied and overworked, and the less free time available, the more people turn to products and entertainments for consolation. This is an example of how the inherent intertwining of pleasure and pain is pertinent not only personally but socially. The better we understand how we work, the better we can protect ourselves from our own appetites and the exploitation and manipulation of our programmed conditioning and addictive, contrived pleasures. Once again, the seeing can be the movement—in this case, away from mechanistic, unthinking behavior.

A consumer society makes acquisition and pleasure-seeking the meaning of life, whether consuming things or collecting experiences. Since short-term reinforcements of pleasure are powerful, similar to hunting for sport, the act of shopping itself (hunting for products and deals) can be more engaging than acquiring. Although the technologies that magnify and multiply the pleasures of consumerism are relatively new, it has become clear that whatever they have brought us has overall not been the fount of expected lasting happiness and fulfillment. Linking pleasure so powerfully and virtually exclusively with consumption has increased our collective stress, health problems, and worries. As the reward for sacrificing to uninspired work aimed at creating the goods that feed short-term pleasures, consumption is a closed circle resulting in a society of greed, moral vacuum, and shallow hedonism that falls short of true happiness. This thwarts the healthier, happier, evolving society that could develop from fostering satisfying pursuits, fulfilling relationships, and the leisure needed for the joys of learning and growth throughout life.

Consumerism gone awry has led to an unsustainable, perilous world.

The relentless accumulation and seeking of pleasures and profits without caring what this leaves in its wake is at the root of many global problems, including ecological ones. To evolve socially in a viable direction requires a shift away from values based on quantity (accumulation) toward prioritizing the value of quality. This means offering people a freer, better-quality life with time for themselves, their relationships, and their interests—and time to care about and act upon the larger concerns affecting our well-being as a group.

We are not only "wired" to seek pleasure through desire, we naturally try to avoid pain. Yet as we saw in looking at how pleasure and pain work and are interconnected, growth rarely comes without some pain. Self-protecting to try to avoid pain as a main agenda can inhibit relationships and growth experiences that could later bring deeper or more profound growth. Knowing this can allow one to enjoy the pleasures that come and when possible use the inevitable pains to grow.

Pleasures without controls bring pain; pain can be feedback that habits need to change, or at least be examined. This applies to society as well. The globalization of desires for consumer pleasures has exacerbated worldwide pain, anger, jealousy, hatred, and violence. Humanity's need for deep transition results from its old ways not working, which increases pain on every level—from within families to the famines and violence occurring on a grand scale. Because we are bound by habits, with unwieldy social structures and institutions that resist change, only being up against the wall of necessity (as we now are) can ignite the global and political will to push and support needed change. Though this transition is painful to many, it is also an opportunity, for it can open the gateway to survival through transforming socially. This can involve the initial pain of letting go of certain old, highly conditioned pleasures as a necessary prelude to a different value system. Shifting collectively from valuing quantity to quality will bring a safer, better world for more people.

As social animals, we have used our remarkable ability to communicate to both cooperate and compete in ways that enhanced our predatory capacities. Like our other pro-survival instincts, predation is programmed to be pleasurable (the better not to be eaten). The willingness to kill is a power that manifests in the pleasures of the hunt. Our inbuilt aggression is more physical, violent, and overtly recognizable in males, while female aggression is subtler. The human predilection to construct power hierarchies that assign different values and status to people is linked with competition. Discovering hierarchy as a way to manage and control a large population increased the spread of human power. This gave rise to the spoils of conquest, war, and the unholy alliance between rulers and religion. Hierarchies have been founded, maintained, and kept in place by violence and threat. Some leaders ruled through sheer brutality, but commonly kings considered to be gods justified their rule through religion and the promise of "keeping chaos at bay." Killing and the threat of violence is and always has been the bottom line of power and power hierarchies. Since men are better at "protecting" and killing, this biologically based dimorphism led to a "sexual order" (a social order sometimes called patriarchy) where power is sliced by gender and gives men the public, institutional power. (The Freedom commentary in Chapter 5 describes the sexual order and how it is a core part of global problems.)

Power is one of the greatest, most insatiable, addictive, and potentially corrupting of pleasures. It has been and is a foundation of social hierarchies, dominance, and violence. Its pleasures are naturally greater and more compelling for those toward the top of a hierarchy, the "bosses" of commerce, religion, or state who benefit from the world as it is—divided into ethnicities, classes, religions, genders, rulers and ruled, haves and have-nots. This produces identities and groups that feed on the pleasures of power, privilege, and superiority, profiting as best they can from the separations that create a sorrow-full world.

The problem is not power itself or that people want power—it is how it's obtained, maintained, and institutionalized to benefit the few, and carelessly used and abused. Far too often the motive for abuse is simply greed. Those with power are mostly conservative, as their main wish is to conserve the structures that maintain their position.

We see power as value-neutral—like energy and electricity, which are also powers—so we are not against wanting, having, or using power *per se.* Everything depends on the situation and how power is used—the human element. In the human arena we look at power as the capacity of an individual or group to influence the direction of others or of one's surroundings. This could include influencing how others think and act, and what they do with their lives for good or ill.

Power over others understandably has a strong stigma attached to it. But in certain appropriate situations requiring leadership to accomplish a goal or task, "power over" definitely has its place, as does hierarchy itself. Many tasks in life require using power over someone (hierarchy)—including on occasion raising a child. No one would want to fly in a jet where the captain did not have the power to tell those on board what to do. We call this type of power (and hierarchy) that ends when the task does "task-driven." It stands in stark contrast to power-driven people and hierarchies where the real priority inevitably becomes perpetuating their power—usually under the guise of lofty ideals.

Many people and hierarchies that act as if they are task-driven are actually power-driven, including religions who claim their task is saving (or enlightening) souls while they avidly and unfairly protect their privilege and tax exemptions—funds that, instead of promoting their beliefs, could go toward saving bodies from hunger or homelessness. Unlike religions, corporations do not mask their venality, their official *raison d'être,* as their by-laws make profit for stockholders the bottom line, formally preventing it from being the welfare of people or the planet. (Corporations have started making feeble public relations efforts to temper their ruthless public image, but "stockholder value" remains the bottom line, not the production of a product that helps people or protects the environment.) This has to change, especially with corporations that affect life systems.

Most if not all people want power. We all want some control over how we feel and the direction of our lives—or at least we want to not be routinely bothered by others. Having and using power to do what one wants brings pleasure, whether from winning a contest, planting a garden, or opening a child to the wonders of the universe. The attraction and attachment to power, either to our own or to others with power, is part of the human condition. We as a species have always been attracted to power because it has survival value and brings many types of rewards and pleasures. Our innate curiosity about how things work has vastly increased our powers through tool-making, which led to technology. We've always been eager to expand our capacities and skills (forms of power) through knowledge, inventions, and discoveries that enlarge our horizons and possibilities to fashion the life we want. This has exponentially increased our power as a species, allowing us to reap both great pleasure and pain. Now we need to learn to use this curiosity and our skills socially to fashion a better world—one that works better for everyone.

The ways we humans have approached and used power and institutionalized it is a core cause of our predicaments. So once again, the problem is not having or wanting power, but power being used without care, intelligence, integrity, and foresight. If the accumulation of power and money (which is stored energy, a form of power) continues to be the ultimate pleasure—so great that it overrides consequences and concern for others—this does not bode well for societies, the world, and humanity.

We cannot escape our desires for power nor its pleasures. The fact that power has become extraordinarily value-laden makes it very difficult to observe its workings in oneself and others with some objectivity. Its gargantuan benefits and abuses have placed the concept of power on a continuum from the ultimate reward to the ultimate evil. Instead of villainizing power or seeing it as an evil to overcome, people and institutions must shift to using power more for species viability than for self-enhancement. To do this, greater awareness is needed of the nature of power, its attractions, corruptions, and implications—including the nature of self-interest. Then it can be controlled and regulated more intelligently and effectively.

More objectivity is necessary about how we utilize and institutionalize our power as a species, because the far-reaching consequences of its usage will determine the quanta of our pain and very viability. To make power the villain skews the analysis from the start, along with the strategies for changing how it is used. One must know the real problem to solve it. Just as the problem is not in pleasure and desire *per se* but in their lack of stop mechanisms, in the power arena especially the problem is the lack of social stop mechanisms—particularly on those whose main concern is protecting and enlarging their own power.

Democracy is an essential part of social evolution that, when functioning well, is feedback-oriented. The more people want the truth, the more politicians can tell it. So a more aware citizenry is essential. Democracy's bottom line is that it enables power to change hands bloodlessly from the bottom up, through the vote. Modern democracy is historically young, with many flaws that can be attributed to people still operating under old authoritarian worldviews with unlivable ideals that politicians think they have to pay lip service to, although they often do the opposite to enhance their power.

One of the great challenges facing us in evolving socially is how to use power without being a slave to its pleasures. The social dimension brings great complexity and new challenges to the issue of power: How can those with less power regulate those with more? How can power change hands without violence, and with honesty, fairness, and integrity? How can it be structured and distributed more equitably and sanely? How can it be placed in the appropriate hands for a given task? And how to get those with more power (including corporations, governments, and other institutions) to make human viability and the necessary well-being of people and the planet their top priority? The technology to move in this direction is here, but so far the human and political will, mutual trust, and required collectively held values are not.

The warning signals are all around us that the evolutionary mechanisms that got us here are not going to keep us here. Evolution has also given us possibility, through using our minds, awareness, and care, to break through deeply rooted habits and to evolve socially by being conscious participants in our own evolution. The challenge is great, but what other choice do we have?

4. Fear

In some historical moments, fear is pervasive throughout the world. We are living in one of those times, here in the opening decades of the new millennium. Fear is the focus of this chapter—what the mind does with fear, its dynamics and mechanisms. In other animals fear comes in the moment of perceived danger and leaves when the danger subsides. In humans the fear can linger and get stuck in thought as well as in the musculature. Though the mind cannot eliminate the raw animal nature of fear (nor should it), it can see the workings of fear and how this transfers into thought. This awareness can break through the mental habits that fear brings so that a creative response is possible.

If we care about our children, being concerned and even fearful about their future is not only understandable in these times, it is potentially valuable foresight that can be put to good effect—whether directing it outward (into action) or making one's children more aware. Through our own cleverness, misuse, errors, and lack of foresight, humanity has put itself at an evolutionary cusp point that will determine its survival. Fear is a survival response signaling danger. With the world becoming more objectively frightening, fear has a more important role than ever. So burying realistic fears through denial is not the best overall strategy. It is a conundrum that the more one cares about what's going on in the world, the more fears this can arouse. An evolutionary question for these times is: how does one live with fear intelligently, effectively, and awarely?

The issue is not whether fear at times has value, but what to do with it. Instead of considering fear as an enemy to be conquered or done away with, it's more productive to investigate fear's double-edged nature. As a protective instinct, fear is a potential ally in life's dramas and a prod to creativity, but it can close people down, making them more mechanical and less responsive (and possibly physically unhealthy). By seeing in yourself how fear is linked in thought with belief, desire, pleasure, and conflict, you can experience the mechanical nature of most mental fear. This is very helpful in limiting fear's negative impacts. Noting how fear and desire are inextricably intertwined is not a condemnation of either (unlike what one finds in many spiritual frameworks). Rather, it offers the possibility of transmuting fear into action that can complement the desire that most of us have for the well-being of ourselves and those we care about.

Fear is mostly the mind projecting into the future. It is often a subjective filter that can limit awareness and distort the appropriate response. *The Passionate Mind* discussed ways that individuals can free their own minds through seeing the mechanical aspects of thought, including a focus on what the mind does with fear. In the present book, this discussion is extended into the societal arena. In these particularly fearful times we are faced with the challenge of learning to live with fear such that it moves us forward toward viability instead of toward inappropriate, destructive, and authoritarian behavior.

As the world becomes more dangerous, fears naturally increase. History has tragically shown that when fear becomes rife it rises from the personal to the social like a cloud that permeates everything. People become susceptible to charismatic belief systems and authoritarian figures that allay fear at the cost of the people's power and rights. These times need the creative input and response-ability of as many people as possible. The manipulation of fear is a dangerous threat to democracy that needs to be countered by greater awareness.

Fear is a core part of our evolutionary and genetic heritage, part of our animal nature, and essential for survival. Anger, fear, and sadness signaling trespass, danger, and loss are self-protective emotions, each indicating a specific response for a given situation—fight, flight, or freeze and conserve energy. Fear is an intrusive warning that over-rides other things, triggering alertness and energy to deal with threats. So fear has its place in the human drama as part of the challenge and response of living.

Approach/avoidance mechanisms like pleasure/pain and desire/fear are basic human motivators. People move toward pleasure and try to hold onto it; they move away from pain and try to protect against it. Desire and fear are the fuel that accompanies pleasure and pain. We literally could not survive without them. At the simplest level, wanting to live (desiring it and its necessities) and not wanting to die (fearing, thus avoiding that which can destroy us) is part of what does in fact keep us alive.

A strategy for dealing with fear coming from Eastern religion (and now adopted by many Westerners) is to be present in the "eternal now," which cuts off future projections like fear and desire. Although the East's insights capture much of what thought does with fear and desire, the solution offered of detaching from them has serious limitations. The ongoing present contains causality from the past and is pregnant with real consequences and possibilities for the future. So while temporarily cutting off fear may at times be conducive to inner peace, it is no more adequate for countering real threats than the "ostrich approach" to danger (i.e., head in the sand).

To promote "transcending" or detaching from fear and desire through quieting (or at least taming) thought and its projections assumes that these feelings and even thought itself can be sufficiently controlled through techniques. This assumption points people in a wrong direction, since anyone who has tried to conquer desire and fear eventually learns that this cannot really be done. Attempting to eliminate them is just the mind projecting into the future its fear of and desire for these states. The idea that people can and should be free of them is not only misleading, it is potentially harmful. The Eastern renunciation approach denies essential parts of being human, including the vital effects of fear and desire in our lives. The question is not how to be free of fear forever, but whether it is possible to have a liberating relation to it in a living situation.

Like belief, pleasure, and desire, fear has two faces. It can bring creative responses or inhibit them. It can propel much-needed change or bring dangerous, destructive reactions. Even with immediate visceral fears of being attacked or falling, if fear takes hold it interferes with responding fully to that moment and so adds to the danger. Unlike most animals, humans live with an awareness of time, which gives us the double-edged gift of foresight. We need to predict consequences, and yet this ability can create fears that rigidify the mind and body, limiting full responsiveness. What we will be looking at together is where fear as a mental projection can hinder creative movement and therefore our lives. To do this we'll examine how the fear that lives in thought is rooted in our conditioning, in order that a new relation to it—and to our conditioning—may develop.

I am afraid of many things: of being hurt, of not living fully, of loneliness, of not succeeding, of losing the securities I have. I'm afraid of not realizing my fullest potential, of my laziness, of not measuring up, of not being spiritual enough. I'm afraid that the pleasures I had yesterday will no longer be tomorrow, or that my loved ones won't still love me. There is great fear in living. Ordinarily what we do with whatever fears plague our mind is invent systems and beliefs to try to make fears go away or control them as best we can. But the specter of fear is potentially ever-recurring. There are the background fears that shadow life and are easily triggered—the world's mounting problems, economic and political crises, fear for my children's future, fear of illness, of aging, of my own and others' deaths. Fear can eat into our minds, becoming the fuel that most of us run on. I'm even afraid of not having fear—that if there were no fear in my life I'd be more self-destructive. I'm also afraid that without ambition to drive me I'd vegetate, and life would pass me by. Without fear, what will move me? I can try to forget about it; I can pretend it doesn't exist; but fear lurks in the shadows ready to surface when triggered and influences so much of my movement.

The immediacy of physical danger aside, fear and desire are often intertwined and can generate each other. When there is fear, desire is always in the background. Psychologically, if there were no desire, no ambition, there would be no fear. If you didn't want anything at all, would there be anything to lose or be afraid of? As soon as you want or like something, a part of that desire is the potential fear that you won't get it or keep it. I'm in love today; I want to make sure this love stays in my life, so out of fear I begin doing things to secure it. I want to live forever, so I'm afraid of death. I want you to like me, so I operate with you in certain ways out of fear. I'm not saying you should or shouldn't do this. Desiring and fearing are natural. We're just looking at the nature of the fear that lives in thought. An awareness of how fear and desire work in tandem can be freeing.

Fear and desire, like many oppositions, are not that different. Fear is actually the desire for something not to occur, while desire contains the potential fear that it will not be fulfilled. Although desire does not contain fear experientially as long as you're very confident about its realization, that confidence can be shattered in an instant. Insecurity triggers the fear underlying desire. Please understand, I'm not suggesting that we try to throw out desire and ambition in order to do away with fear, or that it should or should not be this way. Not wanting to be hurt or to lose something you love is natural.

Fear and desire also wrap around pleasure. Moving from one pleasure to another, one can observe the fear of missing out, of loss, of not getting more, of it not being enough, coupled with the desire for greater, more lasting pleasures in the future. So I continue out of fear, trying to recapture the old pleasures and securities. All this lives in thought.

Fear tends to be egocentric, which is not to say that it's good or bad, just that fear involves itself partly with my pleasures, my experiences, my health, my security, or whatever I care about. Am I going to get enough? Will the pleasures that I have continue? This is not necessarily limiting since the spreading range of my care stretches beyond me to my family, my loved ones, the world, the Earth, the future—all of these have to do with what I care about, my wants and wishes.

To be living in time as we mostly do is to live with fear and desire. Fear is thought as it projects in time out of memories of what was to anticipations of what will be—likewise with desire. Fear always contains assumptions about the future—that something will or might occur and that I won't like it. It's important to see that it's practically impossible to be afraid of anything that is happening. If I point a gun at you, you're not afraid that I'm pointing a gun at you. You're afraid that I'm going to shoot you. If I've shot you, you're not afraid of being shot; you're already shot. You're afraid I'll shoot you again, or that you'll bleed to death or be scarred or whatever. So most fear is not a response to what is, but rather to what might happen.

When there is fear there is also conflict, conflict with what is actually happening. In a dangerous situation, "what is" is danger. I want to be safely out of it, but fear lessens my ability to respond fully. Thinking about possible outcomes is where fear can freeze action. I don't want to die or lose an arm or leg, so here is a want, a concern for what will be, which removes the energy from what is, and while it occurs I am immobile, in conflict. So fear can be a self-fulfilling prophecy. The more it puts me out of touch with the living situation, the more my fear may come to pass.

The same is true in regard to psychological problems. In inner conflict, am I not afraid that I will make a wrong choice, or that to go one way is to miss out on more profound experiences? I am so afraid of missing out. All of this binds me. When a response is not total, it is often fear that removes one from real responsibility, which is actually responseability—the ability to respond.

To see one's fears in daily life, and to see that where there's desire there is usually fear, is to delve into the nature of thought. Although survival needs and drives have a biological basis, it is thought that wants and has whatever ambitions it does for status, experiences, and pleasures, whether of the mind or body. From an early age I have been conditioned to be ambitious by society and by parents. Society wants us to produce; our parents want to be proud of us so they can take pleasure in identification. All of this is very comparative, for success in the eyes of others is only gauged in competitive terms. I only know if I'm good or successful if I'm better than you. Schools condition us this way with grades and rankings. Our criteria for what it takes to be a good person comes from mostly unexamined values, ideals, and beliefs that have been conditioned into us, so that ambitions often aim toward nothing more than secondhand ways of propping ourselves up. Ambition, fear, belief—these are aspects of living that most of us act out daily.

There are many types of fears—anxieties, nagging worries, insecurities, vulnerabilities. Fear comes in all sizes. Troubled times bring even bigger concerns: fear that everything we have lived for may fall apart, fear of crises and catastrophes, that our country and the world are coming unhinged—the environment, the economy, democracy, food, fuel. Such fears can loop around the mind endlessly.

Is it possible to live without being continually enmeshed in fear—to experience, on occasion, being free of fear? In order to answer that question for yourself, you must get to know fear, not with a removed observation but seeing the fear from within. Get to know it and see how it works. See where its roots reach into you. See how the mental seeds live in the past and are always projecting into the future. Fear is a great teacher. To watch fear, to attend to it, without trying to make it go away, to just watch it while being in it is to learn about yourself. It's a key to finding out the nature, depth, and degree of your attachment to various ideas, feelings, thought structures, and ways of being. Seeing how thought wraps around fear can give you a greater range of possibilities in dealing with the insidious tendrils of fear.

Fear can teach me about myself in relationships, where some of the most important and interesting learning occurs. Social fears of not being liked or accepted can be self-fulfilling prophecies as they generate inappropriate gestures and reactive responses. I may want something from you—your attention, affection, assistance, or some special privilege. So when we meet, instead of relating to you spontaneously and naturally, connecting with you in the present, I'm self-conscious and off center. My tension and often transparent, inept attempts to influence you turn you off. Wants and needs are agendas that aim at the future. If I need something from you, I can observe what needing does in our relationship. Being needy makes me feel one down so I'm nervous, ill at ease, and fearful I won't get it. The sound of my voice and my body language reflect my ambition, even if it is simply wanting you to like me. To see the way wanting works is to see how often fear is part of relationships.

When I see a cripple or the homeless begging, I'm uncomfortable. I turn my eyes away; I'd rather not see them. In turning away I close down to my environment. I'm afraid that if they want something from me, I might feel some obligation because of an idea or belief that I should in some way respond. Please keep in mind that I am not implying this is wrong. I'm simply observing how fear in living usually works.

I'm a woman walking down the street late at night. A man comes toward me and asks for a light. I'm afraid of him. I'm trying to make him go away. I can feel the adrenaline flowing, the tightening of my viscera. I watch the thought manifest: "This man may want to hurt or even kill me." The fear expresses itself in my voice, face, posture, and body movements. If fear makes me more alert and responsive it can help protect me, but when it gets entwined with thought it throws me off. If it makes me appear weak and nervous it invites victimization by predators.

There is fear in so much of living, in so much of relationship, not only with strangers but with my mate, my lover, my child. I'm afraid you won't like me or that you'll hurt me, or lie to me, or leave me. I'm afraid of not finding a mate, or of loving someone who's not right for me. There are fears around having and not having a child.

To be aware of a fear is the beginning of learning from it. What do I want? What are my concerns in an anxious situation? I don't want to be hurt, judged, rejected, or exploited. I don't want to lose what I have— a fulfilling or at least a comfortable and secure life, a cherished mate, my good standing in the community—all of which breed fear.

The habits of mind that accumulate over time continually reinforce themselves. Cellular memories from traumas and accidents when reignited by similar situations trigger fear, but here too thoughts and memories reinforce the fear and can even be obsessive. These are repetitive ways of thinking and of structuring the world in such mental patterns as beliefs, values, fears, hopes, ambitions, and images of oneself, others, and the universe. Since the ways you think about yourself and the world are the basic building blocks of personality, they can be rigid. Fear circumscribes the structure of personality or ego, so when these structures are challenged, fear arises. Fear often expresses itself through attack and defense to shore up and protect the challenged structure and alleviate the discomfort that fear brings. Fear can also be submerged, giving one the illusion of not being afraid.

Fear can be a sign of resistance to newness and change, to opening one's boundaries, and to movement into the unknown. Since we hold the world and ourselves together with thought, seeing past some of the conditioned filters of thought can challenge the fabric of our lives, initially bringing resistance. There's resistance to letting go of aspects of one's life or whatever one is attached to. Breaking through the filters of one's conditioning to a more objective perspective often involves the shattering of images and illusions. Seeing beyond subjective filters can bring newness and a sense of freedom that moves you into a more real and profound relation to life. But it can also be frightening because it releases an energy that can move you out of control. All of a sudden, you may not quite know who you are or what you're going to do. Paying attention to your fears can show you where your conditionings lie and expand your awareness. The awareness I'm talking about is a way of seeing the totality of what is—through living it.

If I see that dwelling in fear is counter-productive as well as unpleasant, stressful, and unhealthy, there's a natural tendency to let it go or want it to go away. Yet as we've noted, one cannot ultimately control fear, just as one cannot get rid of desire. It's there. Some claim it's possible to be permanently free of fear by detaching from every desire. Underneath this formula, of course, is the fear of becoming attached, but if you care about anything, becoming attached to it is both natural and inevitable. To want to be free of fear all the time is to be afraid of being afraid. Some people adopt a fearless, devil-may-care image or act recklessly to convince themselves and others that they are free of fear. This is only fear in disguise.

Many surface fears hide deeper ones that are emotionally more difficult to live with. Underlying the fears of daily life are the basic existential fears—fears of loneliness, of deep inadequacies, of aging, death, and dying. These deep fears either move us or shadow our lives. The more they remain unconscious and unacknowledged, the more habitual our responses to whatever newness the moment brings. These perennial fears are a hidden basis of what makes us mechanical. Fear and anxiety once activated can keep fueling themselves by hooking into different forebodings. As the deeper fears cannot be so easily controlled or conquered by techniques, trying to do so creates another bind of mind. Trying to repress them often just generates more superficial fears that are easier to tolerate. So what am I to do?

If I really see the nature of these binds, I shift from trying to quell fears to becoming curious about how they work in me. Here I may come up against a sly trick of mind. I say, "Yes, I'm going to try to see how fear operates in me." But as I'm looking, I'm looking with an eye to making it go away, hoping that if I see it properly, then perhaps it will disappear. That isn't simply looking. That's being involved again in an idea, in a hidden agenda of conquering fear. So once again, I see that anything I try to do can recreate the very thing I'm trying to escape.

Fear can be as great a psychological danger to living as a tree falling on you. It's relatively easy to see physical dangers, but the psychological dangers of living, the inner dangers (such as rigid beliefs and unlivable values), are not so easy to see because they become part of our personality. The very seeing of any of these dangers is a movement that by its nature cannot be pre-programmed. You never know which way you're going to move before movement occurs. It all depends upon the nature of the stimulus or danger facing you, which is always different. Seeing what's appropriate is a movement, as is seeing the direction to go. Seeing a danger that has built up over time, like ecological demise, initiates a movement that takes time to resolve—but here too awareness creates the momentum.

But out of our desire for security, out of our wanting to know, we want formulas; we want it programmed. Fear, however, is an ongoing challenge; there is no formula that can ultimately rid one of it. Formulas are followed by those who, out of fear, sidestep the continual newness of the challenge of dealing with fear when it arises. A fundamental fact is that we are also afraid of ourselves, of what we will do. So fear tends to compound itself.

Fear blocks creative thinking and fosters reactive and rash behavior. Real learning, real inquiry, real freedom only occur when fear is not in control. If I'm afraid that in seeing myself I'll not like what I see, I won't look. If I'm afraid that what I'll see will not be acceptable to me or fit into my beliefs, I remove myself from learning. If I'm afraid that inquiry will remove me from familiar pleasures or change me, growth stops.

Fear is the opener of doors. For to be the fear—which is not to be running away from it but to be living it, so that the fear at those moments *is* me—is a change in awareness, a turn of mind. I tend to treat fear as an external thing, as if there were something outside me that has come in and taken over. But the reality is that a part of me *is* fear when I'm afraid. The intimate, direct relationship of being one's fear so that one sees it while experiencing it, sees the way it works, its psychological danger and how it can shadow the moment by displacing the living immediacy one is confronting—that seeing can bring movement. The movement could be something I do, or a shift in how I hold the fear. To see the sorrow in fear as it removes me from direct living may enable a movement to come about. But if I look in order to move, I'm not really looking.

Seeing how what we've been discussing is all interconnected—how it all works, and how so much of it is related to the way we think about things—can change one's relationship to it. Although awareness does not itself occur in time, the lessons from it live in memory and can be cumulative over time, leading to greater self-understanding. Learning from experience involves not only interpreting the past, but also reinterpreting it in the light of new insights—whether as individuals, countries, or humanity as a whole. Human history is our collective memory as it is continually redefining itself by those alive in the ever-moving present. All that we have been looking at—belief, pleasure, desire, ambition, fear—are linked in fundamental ways. Because these aspects of life reside mostly in thought, this means we have also been looking at the nature of thought. To see the way these thoughts and emotions operate, how they are related, to observe them, is to see their mechanical aspects. To see fear totally is to see in it beliefs, desires, pleasures, inner conflicts. To see conflict totally is to see fear. To see any one of them clearly opens the door to seeing them all. It is seeing myself. All of this lives in me, and though I continue to fragment myself with thought, I am actually not fragments but a whole person, a living being.

We looked at belief and saw how closed beliefs and aggression are similar, because attachment to such beliefs is at the root of much violence. We looked at pleasure and saw how to be continually seeking pleasure (and to be seeking anything at all is usually to be seeking a form of pleasure) is to be seeking the known, past joys, something that we had or heard about. To be continually seeking more pleasure results in a sense of incompleteness, which brings sorrow by creating the gap between the "is" and the "ought"—what is and what we think we want.

We looked at fear and saw how desire and fear live with each other. If there is no wanting, there is no fear. We want this and that, the security, the knowledge that past experiences will be repeatable. We want all kinds of things. And if we see how fear and desire are linked, we see how wanting them to go away is playing the same game again, because the desire to be desireless is just another desire. The reality of it—as we've said—is that like fear, desire is a core part of being human, an essential motivator and source of passion.

Freedom from fear does not come from having any ideas about what that means. We saw how, in order to utilize fear as the great teacher it is, one must actually *be* the fear, live with it as a moment-to-moment thing, see how it crops up, how it can destroy real relationship in the moment. To see fear totally, to see it as the psychological danger that it can be (which isn't to try to change it) is a shift of awareness that has its own movement. By experiencing the nature of fear, a freedom can come that is different from anything that one seeks.

Care is a bridge to others and the world. I care about what I value and love; I care about what matters to me—which includes caring for others and what they care about. But the wider the spread of my care and empathy, the greater the potential for fear because it is linked with what I care about. In many situations that appear hopeless, with too much pain or anxiety to cope with, people detach from empathy and care by limiting what they identify with. It can be a form of self-protection. This is not unreasonable, as being paralyzed by fear or empathy serves no one. But the tactic is double-edged because this type of self-protection easily builds a bunker mentality geared at keeping the pain out. If I don't have children, if I don't care about the future, the world, or humanity, or if I withdraw into myself, I do have less to worry about. But emotional control gained at the price of relinquishing care and passion for others' well-being is not only empty, it is not what the world or people need at this time. The evolutionary question is how to live with fear intelligently, effectively, and consciously in these fearful times. It's essential to get to know fear in a way that does not depress or paralyze you emotionally or freeze responsible action.

The world's well-being requires developing improved foresight. Addressing the possible consequences of our collective actions requires taking the future into account like never before, so the problem is not that fear is thought projecting into the future. Fear as a warning is part of that crucial capacity of foresight. The evolutionary crux is how useful and realistic the projections are. Thought as future projection is only deemed a failing in worldviews that consider the past and future to be nothing but the illusory products of thought. From there it's an easy (but erroneous) step to making thought and ego the source of all problems. But for those who believe that the world is evolving over time, the ongoing "now" contains the accumulations of the past as the seeds of the future that will become the ever-present "now." Without a past and future, the present would not exist—and without intelligent forethought, neither will we. If taking the future into account is a prerequisite for survival, worldviews that deny the reality of time and the value of thought are obviously counter to survival. We'll go into this in more depth when we look at time {in Chapter 8}.

If you care about human survival and a viable future world, there is indeed much to fear today. But our unique talents and concerns have the potential for a multiplicity of positive actions that can transform the fear to creative response. Necessity truly is the mother of invention that propels evolution, which uses crisis to forge change. Crises that put survival at risk are an inherent part of evolution, and this realization can bring more peace as you face your own and the world's challenges.

Question: Doesn't fear keep people out of dangerous situations? The memory of having hurt myself and the desire not to do so again protects me.

Answer: Of course fear may keep you away from known dangers, but it can also keep you from exploring the unknown. The question is not whether fear can keep me out of danger, but rather how is fear a hindrance to living? Certainly I can to some extent keep danger out by enclosing myself and narrowing my life. Yet living has its dangers. The new always presents itself; if I have not continually built strength by responding to challenge—which is what learning and growth are about—then when danger comes (whether physical or psychological) fear can bind me. Some basic security—not worrying about rent and the next meal—may be necessary to be open to change. But if through fear I remove myself from challenge and attempt to make my life too secure, then I become dull and habit-bound, which is perhaps one of the greatest psychological dangers.

Question: Don't parents need to teach their children what to fear in order to protect them?

Answer: Instilling fear and guilt are two of the easiest ways to control others, especially your children, so one has to approach this issue with awareness. Much protective teaching is done in terms of fear. Being very young obviously makes some adult protection necessary, particularly when the adult knows that the child is not equipped to deal with something. Since a core part of living and learning involves response to challenges, knowing what is appropriate for a child is one of the major responsibilities of being a parent or a teacher. Again there is no formula. A toddler in the road may get run over, so this child must be taught to be afraid of the road. But if out of fear parents remove children from extending their capacities, or forbid them to do many things, they don't grow, flourish, or learn to be independent. Teaching a child to fear something that should be feared is one thing, but using fear inappropriately conditions a child to be fearful in the world, which is not a good survival mechanism.

I'm not only afraid for my child, I'm also very afraid for myself. Often fear is inculcated not mainly for the child's well-being, but to quell one's own fears. I'm afraid my child will get badly hurt or even die, and I'll blame myself and be devastated forever, so I implant my own fears about the world. Again what we're dealing with is linked with desire: I want my child to be safe, to succeed, be happy, or be a certain way, so I control and restrict my child to protect myself or get my way. Seeing when my self-protectiveness and fears are appropriate and when they can harm my child's development—making mistakes and living with uncertainty—are the ongoing challenges of parenthood.

Question: This discussion borders on how fear is used for social control, yet you haven't talked much about that.

Answer: Fear and desire, reward and punishment, the carrot and the stick, are powerful ways that societies obtain and maintain control. The specter of fear can be more powerful than pleasures and rewards, whether anticipated or realized. Fear makes people want to control what they fear, and if they can't they give their power to those who claim they can—under the illusion of creating safety for themselves. Fear can easily be manipulated to create self-protective bunker mentalities. History is rife with collusions between church and state, and all kinds of lesser protection rackets, that defend power hierarchies. Politically, a fearful populace gives up its rights in the name of self-protection and national security. In religion people turn to fundamentalism and unquestioned beliefs that on a surface level soothe their fears. Reactions are vicious circles that contain the seeds of the things being reacted against. Authoritarianism blocks challenging information and feedback, tethering creativity and intelligence. All these reactions make the world more backward, violent, corrupt, and perilous. So societies whose primary mode of control is fear create self-fulfilling prophecies.

Question: A lot of what goes on in my mind is fear. What you've said gives me a lot to reflect on—can you tell me anything else that can help?

Answer: The mental content of the fear that lives in thought contains assumptions and future projections from your experience, habits of mind, and conditioning. These may or may not be in touch with the real likelihood of future possibilities. Although you cannot eliminate all realistic fear, you can alter the way your mind holds it. Given that many fears originate in thought and are composed of it, thought can be an inroad to allaying fear by questioning its assumptions to see if they are ill-founded and whether a fear is realistic. One assumption that is always part of fear is that I will not like what I fear could happen. This too may be uncertain or wrong. My perspective or attitude may change; I may come to see crisis as an opportunity, or that it has an unforeseen silver lining or the possibility of one. With events that I cannot control (earthquakes, plane crashes, terrorism), realizing that worry is counterproductive and focusing instead on things I can do something about can alleviate fear in general.

Finding believable sources of hope and possibility can counteract fear. Hope contains desire for a better tomorrow for myself, children, the world. This is natural, but what is needed today is constructive hope and not just a sugar coating of simplistic beliefs that temporarily allay fears. Using our awareness to see clearly what is going on, including what is realistically fearful, and acting out of whatever capabilities we can muster to make a better situation is the only hope we have. Feeling hopeless brings despair and freezes action.

Potential catastrophes and global crises have so many variables that no one can know how it all will turn out. If one cannot muster credible optimism, at least one can adopt a "possibilistic" attitude—given so many unknowns in all directions, including the positive. The potential for human intelligence and creativity to meet the present urgent global survival challenge, when combined with the inbuilt desire to survive and an awareness of who we are and how we got here, at least offers possibility. In any case pessimism, fatalism, cynicism, and nihilism are not good strategies for success.

Positive action that addresses the fear is an effective antidote. It may connect you with like-minded people—another powerful antidote and source of hope. It puts you on the side of evolution because an evolutionary trajectory has an energy that we can participate in.

Both mental and physical techniques can remove the immediacy of feeling afraid—from breathing and relaxation to different types of drugs. Various methods of behavior or thought modification can help people cope with fear. If the fears come from old programs that have hung on and are not that pertinent to your current life, these methods can have more lasting effects and be healthier than mental loops of fear going 'round and 'round. Although fear may remain in the background, the energy that fear releases can be turned into positive action.

Question: It seems that those who believe in any of the religions are happier and less afraid. That's one avenue for dealing with fear. What about that?

Answer: Organized religions have all used fear, desire, guilt, and belief to capture, keep, and control followers. If you believe what they tell you and do what they say, they will allay your basic fears about death and give a ready-made meaning to life. Religions offer simplistic answers that tell you what you want to hear, death being the core fear they specialize in. All of this, whether it be the promise of heaven, of a better next life, or whatever religions promise, panders to fear. If I believe them it's because I want something they claim to offer—love, protection, security, and above all, a better afterlife or eternal life. Their "answers" play to people's existential hopes and fears, telling them that basically everything is all right because some higher intelligence is in charge, making sure that everything turns out according to a cosmic plan. So you can relax, because all you have to do is believe and obey.

Religions can bring *individuals* solace from existential issues, tragedy, and death through beliefs. Being part of a community of like-minded believers provides an identity and reassuring source of security. But many people don't realize that the difficulties in their lives and relationships often stem from the very beliefs that provide solace. The less people are in touch with what's really going on, the more individual lives and the world become dysfunctional. Because unquestioned religious beliefs can result in separation and often opposed and competing identities, individual and communal "security" is only gained at the price of a more divided, violent, frightening world. The good feelings that religion offers individuals come at society's expense—a vicious circle that breeds more fear, making people increasingly needy of and susceptible to religion.

Question: Will you talk about worrying? Knowing that it's all future projection does help, but I can't stop worrying.

Answer: Obviously, worrying is one way that fear displays itself. We're also afraid that should we not worry, danger could catch us off guard. Or that we would not get out of life what we want. Fear is the fuel many of us run on. Take away the fuel and what would move us? We can literally be afraid of not being afraid. We saw earlier how fear can be a motivator, a call to action, or it can distort and hinder the ability to respond in the ever-oncoming present. Since most worry doesn't help, why worry? Why do we spend so much time creating the tensions and binds (psychological and physiological) that worry brings, creating pain for ourselves? It's really important to see that much of it is me doing it to myself. Worrying a lot can be seen as feedback that clarity for action is lacking. Worry is fear without clarity of movement. If it just spins obsessively, not going anywhere useful, it stifles the energy necessary for action.

Worrying, which actually is a form of pain, is one of the easiest ways of feeding personality, of not abandoning oneself to life in the moment, which is to temporarily disappear in the psychological sense. Thought expressed as worry assumes that the "I" worrying now will be the same "me" in the future that I'm worrying about now. Worrying comes out of memory. The memory deposit lives in the cells, and its physiological aspect is expressed as tensions and tightness in the body. The feel of these tensions becomes familiar and we call that feeling tone "me." To continually feed these tensions is to keep the known "me" intact. Worrying does it quite nicely. Fear creates a sense of continuity through time. I may worry so much because it keeps the illusion of a static, unchanging me around. Worry is a way of attempting to keep the self secure, protecting it from the unknown and therefore change. Unless the focus within worrying eventually leads to insights, worrying shadows the present and can adversely influence an outcome or situation—becoming a self-fulfilling prophecy. With insight we lessen the strangling grip of fear.

5. Freedom

The original *Passionate Mind* discussed freedom as an inner inquiry about what it means to be free in oneself in the process of living. The focus was on self-inquiry to see one's nature and how one works. Freedom is many-faceted, and there are multiple ways of thinking about it—personal, social, political, philosophical, and spiritual. Usually involved are "freedom from" internal or external constraints or "freedom to" move your life through choice, in accordance with your desires.

For most of history, neither freedom from external factors (social structures, poverty, injustice, oppression) nor freedom to make many life choices was possible for most people. Freedom as such may not even have been a concept, let alone a value or goal. In rigid, highly structured societies with little room for individual initiative or privacy and no way to effect social change, it's not surprising that the worldviews promote acceptance of external conditions, surrender (to tradition, roles, and prescribed duties), and turning inward for fulfillment. This creates a static milieu of resignation and fatalism. The more turmoil in the world, the more insecurity, fear, suffering, and breakdown, the more people turn to spirituality in an effort to find inner peace and freedom.

Eastern spirituality purports to offer inner freedom from life's tribulations through renunciation (literally renouncing the self) and detachment. In other words, if there's no way to get what you want or escape what you dislike, you can deemphasize wanting and liking, desire and preference, because inhibiting desire and detaching from unwanted internal states is more under one's control than most externals. So like the Stoics of ancient Greece, the Eastern focus is on "freedom from" inner things—from desire, attachments, and ultimately from the ego or self, which is viewed as the source of all problems. The ego is said to disconnect from the spiritual source that unites and thus is seen as the basis of dissatisfaction and sorrow.

The mind's distractions and perpetual chatter are presented as a tyranny, endlessly creating desires and attachments that feed the ego. The dissatisfaction and sorrows that attachments can bring are to be overcome through practices and disciplines that quiet thought and supposedly diminish and eventually end desire. Detaching from the concerns of ego and surrendering to one's fate (karma or God's will) are made the highest spiritual values—to be rewarded in an after-life, if nowhere else.

Anyone who seeks inner freedom confronts a basic paradox inherent in any quest that defines freedom as a type of liberation from human wants, fears, and concerns. The desire to escape or free oneself from anything contains within it the seeds of the very bondage that one is trying to escape. For example, trying to still thought has the thought behind it that stilling thought will make you feel better, or get more of what you want, or make you a better person. The desire to be desireless is another desire. The desire for ego loss and perfection comes from the ego, as does all desire. The push to conquer one's ego in the belief that ego loss will be the ultimate experience bringing perfection and bliss is really self-centered activity in disguise, with the oft-hidden hope that selflessness will somehow be self-enhancing. Thought creates the concept of ego loss from secondhand sources or memory's projections and strives toward this accomplishment, which is more ego activity. This is another example of what I call "the spiritual paradox."

Likewise, asking "How do I become free?" similarly places you in a paradox, and even more important, it is not really an answerable question. For questing after freedom always involves ideas about what freedom consists of. The ideas I have come from the state of not being free and therefore involve projections of what it would be like not to have my current problems. Freedom here again is freedom *from* something—my problems, fear, desire, anger, competitiveness, whatever. My ideas of freedom are limited by my beliefs, worldview, and values, and as I try to force myself into the mold of the idea or ideal, I am limiting freedom right at the start.

But if freedom is looked at as a dimension of action rather than an escape from something, as a living process instead of a goal, the paradox dissolves. The most important thing about questing or questioning is the nature of the quest or question. The real question (as it can be answered and thus is potentially more freeing) is not "How do I become free?" but rather "What is it that binds me?" I can never find out how to be free by seeking freedom. I can, however, find out the nature of what it is that limits my awareness and responsiveness because that can be directly perceived. I can discern the nature of the binds that limit freedom. Freeing oneself comes with awareness of how one works, and with the ongoing intention to gain self-understanding. Binds limit exploration, just as releasing them permits learning.

Most people want to be free. At least they think they do. But what does it mean to be truly free in the actual moment of living? For me, the most important meaning of freedom is freedom in action. This means having the clarity to respond totally and appropriately to what the living moment is presenting. Clarity often eliminates choice and initiates action that does not leave a residue. Although options will most probably be part of the process initially, if clarity comes there is no choice but rather unfettered action, which is where real freedom lies. Let us examine this.

One of the ways the word *freedom* is commonly used is "freedom to" instead of "from." "Freedom to" typically means having choices and the freedom to choose. Seemingly the more choices I have, the freer I am; so I try to create a life with more choice in it, with more and more possibilities, and I consider that freedom. A life with options, opportunities, and alternatives is freer than one without them, and contemplating them in the present feels more liberating. But having potential future choices is very different from the moment where you are actually experiencing the necessity of choosing. Through exercising free will, making decisions, weighing alternatives, projecting the pluses and minuses, you choose. Isn't that one way we ordinarily think about freedom?

When I actually face a choice about anything—should I go to this movie or that, take this job or that, go to Hawaii or Mexico, work or relax, get married, have a baby, whatever the choice is—what is always there? What lives in choice in the moment of facing it? Conflict lives there, doesn't it? If I knew what to do there would be no choice, no conflict. I may have the opportunity to decide whether to do this or that, but in actual living situations, if there is conflict, in that moment is there freedom? Any situation of real choice contains indecision and with it, conflict. Should I do this or that?

Please look at it in yourselves and see what happens when there is choice. See how action is frozen, bound in conflict. The important thing is to see how it works in you. If there were no conflict, there would be no choice. Of course, with trivial choices like what cereal to eat or TV show to watch, there is no problem because the outcome has little or no significance. I'm talking about choices where one at least thinks the outcome of the choice has some importance for one's life. Since today's world creates extraordinary conflict, there also appear to be innumerable choices. We move from one choice, one decision to the other, trying to resolve our conflicts. But choosing from a lack of clarity can bring uncertainty, conflict, and the fear of making the wrong or not the best choice. Being in conflict is uncomfortable and tense, so the tendency is to want to escape it as quickly as possible. But decisions made out of conflict generally create more conflict—not necessarily immediately, but later on. Making a quick decision out of confusion or uncertainty can initially alleviate the feelings of conflict, which usually return when you start second-guessing yourself ("I should have done this or that") as wondering or regret emerge, or new conflicts are generated. If the choice is finally made out of uncertainty, this often creates a residue of doubt and even the potential of long-term regret.

Real freedom comes from clarity. The very need to make a decision, the very act of decision-making, is an indication of conflict. If you're trying to decide anything, you may as well wear a sign around your neck reading "I'm confused." If you knew what to do, if you saw clearly what's appropriate, there'd be no decision. You would know, and you would do it. In the moments when you're trying to make a decision it's possible to see clearly that you are confused and in conflict. To see clearly that you are unclear is seeing something clearly. This is seeing what is, which brings a movement or shift to a different way of holding the situation. You may see a more appropriate alternative, or drop the whole thing, or put it on hold until more clarity comes.

This clarity does not occur in time. While deciding occurs in time as thought weighs options in an effort to figure out the best choice, this seeing is an insight that breaks through the calculations of thought. However, the process of trying to choose may be a necessary or useful precursor for clarity to come. A problem is that in many instances of facing choice, this seeing what's appropriate does not come. The world's demands often do not allow enough time for a clarity that can eliminate the uncertainty of choices. Time pressure, social pressure, pressure at work can all propel you to decide before seeing what to do.

So if clarity is not there and the internal or external pressure to make a decision is insistent, what is one to do? You may resign yourself to exercising choice out of necessity, telling yourself, "I may not be making the right choice, but given what I know I'm doing the best I can and I'll just have to live with it." We have all faced situations like this. The reality is that circumstances force all of us to make decisions prematurely that are not based on clarity. It is simply my hope that seeing the nature of such choices can point the way to more clarity. Though not every situation of having to choose will move to clarity, if clarity becomes a value, there'll be more occurrences of it, because valuing clarity makes you more alert for it. Remember, the focus here is not for me or anyone to tell you what to do. What I'm doing throughout this inquiry is presenting how I see aspects within the human drama working as doorways for you to look at yourself and your life. Conflict and choice are examples, as are the other topics being explored.

Let's consider another example to show the difference between facing choice in the present and future options: I'm lucky. I've just inherited a large sum of money; many new possibilities (choices) appear to open up. Should I take a trip? If so, where? Should I leave my job? Buy this or that? So I feel that new freedoms have opened up out of all these new options. Choices have come my way. There doesn't appear to be any problem or conflict, yet there seem to be many choices.

If you look at it closely you'll find that this is not a situation containing real choice in the moment, so of course there is no conflict. For what I am calling choice here is just thought dwelling in pleasure and fantasy in the anticipation of fulfilling desires. I'm not really concerned with what I'm going to do. I'm just lost in the pleasures of the idea of being able to do many things. Should pressures bring about the urgency or need for a real choice, then conflict might come.

If one's alternatives are all unpleasant, such choices contain greater fear and even more desire for them to be resolved or go away. Must I really have an operation? Which doctor should operate on me? Should I tell my best friend that his wife is involved with someone else? Clarity is all the more vital in the face of painful and difficult choices. If you have the luxury of taking time, clarity may still not come, but urgency often brings it if one can resist the urge to hurry the process. Here I'm not looking at the ideas we have about freedom or what makes a life feel more free than others. I'm looking at the actuality of what I am when I'm confused—when I need to choose without knowing which way to go or what I want, and when I'm morally conflicted about what I ought or ought not to do. I am asking is there freedom when there is conflict? I may have the idea that, yes, I am free because I have the power to do this or that. But that's just an idea. I am talking about the living fact that when I am in conflict, all of what I conceive to be freedom is just thought as it plays in its ideas of freedom, which often creates more conflict. This is what I mean by saying that the only real freedom in the present is freedom in action. Freedom is responding totally to the living situation.

Look, I am a young man. I want to paint. My parents want me to be a doctor. Doctors make money; artists generally don't. My parents will support me in medical school but not in art school. I don't know what to do; I'm in conflict. The pressure is mounting because the school term starts soon. I must choose. The medical school accepts me and I go there. I struggled to decide while confused and now it's over. I feel relieved for a while after the initial release of tension that decisions can bring. I made a choice out of conflict, and for years I have been living with it. Fifteen years go by and I realize that I've never felt very fulfilled as a doctor, but my life, security, and identity are built around it. That's just one example of how much of life is lived in this fashion. Whenever an action is done out of conflict you can tell, for there is always a residue in thought. The residue is of course regretting, wondering, or replaying the choice in one's mind. Regret lives in the mind with residues in the body. When the mind plays in the "what ifs" of bypassed and bygone choices, it can be an indication that decisions were forced while in conflict.

If I am in direct relationship with what is, with myself as part of the total picture, then there is no conflict. When I see something clearly, directly, immediately, this awareness brings movement without residue.

I'm walking through the forest. Suddenly I hear an explosive crack and the huge tree above me is falling. I see this—I see it is falling. To see the tree falling is to move. There is no choice, no decision, no thinking, no conflict. I don't say to myself, "Should I move or not?" or wonder which way. If I did this, the tree might hit me. It's not that first I see and then through a decision, a rational process, I decide to move or determine where to move. To see is to move—immediately. This instinctive reflex in the face of physical danger is a metaphor for the simple yet often hard-to-grasp nature of the clarity within awareness—the seeing is the movement. In life's more complex situations that contain rationality and judgment, seeing usually doesn't come in that automatic way. But when seeing does come, it likewise moves you without choice, and it too is out of time.

I'm walking down a beach and a very young child is thrashing around in the water a couple of yards out. To see a child in trouble is to move. If I say to myself, "Is she actually drowning or is she only playing?" then the child could drown. You may wonder any number of things when you don't see the nature of what is. But to see that a child may drown is to move. Because someone else is in danger, not me, judgment is involved; but here too when you see clearly you move. The seeing is the movement. When there is seeing, there's a total involvement, a total relationship, as in those moments when the experiencer is not separate from the experience. This is not an ontological (reality) statement where the seer is literally the seen. It points to there being no mental or emotional interference with observing and acting.

Seeing an immediate physical danger clearly is relatively easy. The situation has a demand, an urgency about it; your whole being is alive, alert. What of psychological dangers and the subtle complexities of living? Some psychological dangers such as immovable beliefs, outmoded habits, internal conflict, and narrow identities that promote feeling superior prevent living fully and creatively and are as real a danger as a tree falling. I do not move from them because I don't see them as dangers. My vision is clouded by conditioning, by fear, by social reinforcements and the need to belong, so that I'm not aware of the ramifications and danger of such mental underpinnings. To see a psychological danger with a clarity and directness, to see its urgency, is to move from it. From this seeing comes movement that may not be what you want or expect, but movements come when there is a shift in awareness.

I, however, do not see clearly. There is enormous conflict in my life. I want to be free of it, but I see that trying to free myself of it comes from the conflict and simply creates more of it, and wanting it to go away removes me from what is; namely that I am in conflict. Within conflict is the desire to resolve or escape it, to be out of discomfort. What am I to do? When one sees all this, the effort to do away with conflict stops. Then even though the conflict itself may not leave, some of the pain of it does, because struggling to force a decision while confused just adds to the stress. Much of the pain of conflict resides in the effort to get out of it; that tension is relieved when the effort to escape ceases. Now my attention can turn instead to observing the nature of the conflict. If there is no urgency to decide, I can surrender to the conflict and allow it to be. If I wait to see clearly, there may be no need to decide. If I live with the conflict awarely, getting to know it intimately—what it's made of: the fears, desires, assumptions, projections, and external factors that compose it—this often brings unexpected alternatives and more creative solutions.

It sounds complex but really it's simple. It just involves seeing it totally: conflict feeds on itself. Decisions made through effort to resolve a conflict usually create more struggle. The only time more conflict is not created is when the action is effortless. So to see that I have conflict, neither to accept nor deny it, nor to try to make it go away, but to see how it affects me totally, to see its roots and its seeds in my conditioning—to see all this can bring a clarity of awareness as to what I am.

Freedom from conflict does not mean it will never again arise. Conflict is a normal part of living in the world. The question is how do you deal with it, as it can either freeze action or motivate necessary change that can fulfill the desire for something better.

To be alive is to be living with challenges that demand responses. Challenge by its very nature always contains something new, something different. If the response is to be adequate, then it must also contain something new and fresh. Because most of us usually respond out of habit, out of past conditioning, the response is often not adequate—it's not a response to the new moment. Inadequate responses create dross in memory in the form of regret or guilt: "I should have done this; I should have done that. If only I had said this. Maybe I should have gone there. I regret this or that." When we are laden with such thoughts, we are even less apt to respond to newness with newness.

I'm not saying that one should or could eliminate or "conquer" one's conditioning, which is absurd, for how can one eliminate the building blocks of oneself? By "conditioning" I mean habits of the mind and body that are programmed through genetics or experience. Overcoming the fact of conditioning is impossible. Conditioning is part of the organizational principle of universal energy that builds patterns and systems that are the stuff of life, for without it there would be no life. At the same time conditioning is often a hindrance to freedom since habits constrict by channeling the new into old patterns. This reinforces the tendency to go on automatic, which limits awareness and creates attachments to familiar pleasures and securities that can block real change. Experience by its nature conditions, so that moving out of it is an endless process. Freedom lies in springing in the living moment from patterns that limit the field of what is possible.

Please understand I am not saying that we should never respond from the past. Of course our past experience conditions us and is a factor in any movement, for this conditioning is part of me. Our past is part of who we are, what we have learned, and it not only lives in memory but in the way experience has reorganized us in our cellular structures. I've learned that an oncoming car could hurt me. It's not a belief; it has come from being in the world. Obviously an infant would not know this. Part of the total seeing of the car is the understanding that roads are dangerous. By understanding I mean something personal, firsthand. You being totally what you are, and cars and roads being what they are makes the living relationship.

Creative movement, which is a total response to challenge, to what's happening, is a movement into the unknown, out of and beyond one's conditioning, so something new occurs. You do not hold it in thought by remembering what you did; you are right there to meet the next moment. Of course, the movement itself conditions you, so that when another challenge occurs total movement springs from that, too. Living with awareness is a moment-to-moment thing, a continual thrust out of the old into the new. For this to occur there must be a direct connection with what is happening.

Many of us seek peace, and by "peace" we ordinarily mean either to be at peace with ourselves or to reach some state of equilibrium in which we are not overly affected by life's trials and tribulations. Some people try to achieve peace by cultivating an inner state of non-attachment where the vicissitudes of life do not affect one's equanimity. When we want peace what we are actually asking for is a removal from what's bothering us. We think peace is a life without problems, but that's unreal. Problems are challenges, and challenge is the motor of evolution. Life without them would be a dull thing, as it is through meeting problems that most growth occurs. And that of course is a moment-to-moment thing because what I am is a living being, a changing, flowing being. The problem is not that there are problems; it is that I do not respond to them completely. What real peace is—which has nothing to do with any ideas one has about peace, which is not a turning away from life— is action without conflict. To move in the world without the residues that conflict brings is to move freely, to be at peace. But how do I do it? How do I manage this in a world of incredible tension, extraordinary violence, and seemingly endless sorrows? In this world of demands and fantastic desires, how does peace come?

For this to occur I must not only be more aware of the world I inhabit, I must see myself with more clarity. How can I see the world through a dirty lens? I cannot actually see another human being in relationship unless I know the vehicle that is seeing—in short, unless I am more aware of myself and how I work. Although such seeings do not occur in time, they are cumulative over time and can result in a self-understanding that is freer from self-judgment, bringing more peace with myself and my nature. When the problems of living are met totally and creatively so that one is free to move on to the next challenge, there is peace. I am not presenting a constantly available state of freedom. Clearly in a world so full of conflict it is not possible to be free of it all the time. Freedom is not a possession one can own but a momentum that one can participate in.

Question: Should we stop wanting to change since wanting to change causes conflict?

Answer: I'm not saying that we should or shouldn't want to change. The desire to bring change ignites will and intention that can motivate without conflict. The fact is that we often do want to change. Isn't that true? To say to oneself, "I shouldn't want to change because if I don't want to change, then maybe something good will happen to me" is just to be in the whole thing again. If you want to change you can observe exactly what it means to want to change. "Here is what I am; here's what I want to be." There's a gap. I can observe this; observing whether the gap contains conflict is to watch oneself. One can observe the nature of the gap, its goals and desires, whether they are realistic or truly beneficial.

It's not changing the fact that one wants to change but watching what wanting to change does to living that brings movement, that brings real change. Look, to live is to change. You can change by becoming more rigid, more set in your ways, or by becoming more flexible, more responsive in meeting life. Seeing the need for change, in oneself or the world, can be seeing what is actually necessary, especially since the world isn't working. This can marshal one's will and intention for a better world. Here one can meet resistance that can also bring conflict—in others, institutions, or in oneself. But here, too, living with the conflict may bring a clarity that moves you, and that's where freedom lies.

Question: Are you free?

Answer: Suppose I were to tell you that I'm free. What could this mean—that I'm free all the time, or mostly, or sometimes? Would you believe me? You could speculate endlessly about whether I am or not, but it doesn't matter for you. I am not presenting myself as an example of anything. I'm attempting to look at how the world, other people, and myself actually work. What matters is if you see for yourself whether these words help bring you more clarity. You must answer that question. What I'm saying is the result of my life-long inquiry into the nature of myself and the world that I find myself in. But remember, I am not saying that I or anyone can be free all the time. I'm saying that to the degree your awareness is unclouded by outmoded conditionings, there is more potential to be free.

Question: Is regret always a feedback of lack of clarity?

Answer: Not always. Regret can come in many forms, especially over extended periods of time and change. Even actions coming from clarity may have expected or unexpected consequences that can in time shut out other options. Say I did in fact see clearly that I could not be satisfied without painting so I accepted the risks and consequences of following my passion. Later on I may not like the consequences, but disliking them is not necessarily regret. Moving into the unknown entails risk and choices at times having downsides (unexpected or not), so even with clarity regret can later stem from what develops—whether from internal or external changes. I might come to regret my choice as the world changes or I do. The economy may become more shaky, making it harder to survive in my work. Regret can also occur through learning or changing over time. I may see that I chose the wrong father for my child as life reveals more of who he is than I could have known at the time. When I'm sixty I can regret not having a child, but it was fine until then. However, the regrets that come from a lack of clarity in the moment of living feel different from those that come from learning or from future changes out of one's control.

Like life itself, moving into unknown territory always contains the possibility of unforeseen risks and rewards. Life does not offer a redo button. Going along one path usually rules out others. The woman who eventually comes to regret not having a child had many years of enjoying the other options that came from being child-free. She could become a surrogate aunt or grandmother or find any number of ways to have children in her life. Part of being an adult is living with where you find yourself and finding a creative solution to what's facing you.

Question: I don't understand what "not in time" means. It seems to me that movement that comes from seeing could involve choice and time. Why couldn't it be true that responding to a falling tree or anything still involves choice, but the choosing is quicker, perhaps in milliseconds? The choosing may not be conscious. You talk about the seeing and the movement being one, but physically, that's not how it works. It takes time—however short—for light waves to get to you, more time to reach the brain, then more time for the brain's messages to reach the muscles. Why in all of this is there not time for choice?

Answer: "Not being in time" is an experiential not a physiological state. I'm fairly sure we've all had such moments. I think you're partly asking, "Doesn't it take time, however rapid, to see, and is there not even more time between the seeing and the response? And, if this is indeed so, then choice could occur in all instances of response." Is that what you're asking?

Questioner: Yes.

Answer: Certainly the physiological models used to explain behavior all have time as an element. In fact, the nature of intellectual explanations necessarily contains time—going from here to there takes time; causes bring about effects only in time, and so forth. Yet even in physical science the nature of time is not such a clear-cut thing. From an internal point of view, does seeing ever occur in time? We have an idea that the process of perceiving and internalizing the external world takes time.

Let us look at the nature of the internal and the external. Most of us consider the skin to be the dividing line: everything inside is internal and "me," and everything outside is external and "not me." A bird is singing in a tree. Where is the sound of the bird? Is it in the vocal cords of the bird? In the air waves as they touch my ear? In the tympanic membrane? Along the auditory nerves or behind my ears in the brain itself? Where is the sound of the bird—out there or in me? Internal or external? Actually, the sound is neither in the bird nor in me, but rather in the total relationship. When there is total relationship, at that instant the division between the internal and external is not there. When there is sound it does not take time to hear the sound. There is just sound. When one sees anything, there is no time. Here by "seeing" I do not mean just sensory input, although it certainly includes that. I am talking about a total relationship.

Does the response that comes with direct relationship take time? Time only enters when thought looks back at it. The seeing and the response are not separate. Only thought in trying to understand, which includes trying to recognize, separates perception from action. Newness can never be recognized. Only the old, the known, is recognizable. The seeing of challenge, which by its nature is new, and the response to it are not divided. They are one. Thought, which after the fact wants to explain the response, creates time by putting the explanation in causal terms. That is, it makes the challenge the cause, and the response the effect. When thought is analyzing totally mechanical events, it can be creative in explaining the sequences, but only in mechanistic terms. Seeing totally, which never occurs in time, has its own movement, which is in that moment choiceless. Of course the movement that comes from clarity can span a period of time. What I'm saying is that the awareness initiates that momentum.

Question: This choiceless awareness that does not occur in what you call psychological time and cannot be pre-programmed to occur at will seems to me to be amorphous and not within our control. So how do I use it to be free of conflict?

Answer: I am fairly certain that we all have had moments of choiceless awareness, whether it results from an oncoming car, being "in the zone" athletically, or having a deep insight that clarified a problem. The more you are aware that such insights or timeless moments do not come from control itself (which is a mental activity) but from a letting go of pre-conceived notions, the more you see the value of those moments and the more likely they will occur. When those moments pass they live in memory, and the more you have the more they accumulate, making it easier for them to occur. Life is a balancing act between control and surrender. Being in control for most of us is more comfortable, while letting go involves uncertainty about where you will end up. Yet passion and creativity come from moments of letting go. Control can be used to create a context for letting go by consciously changing habits or merely taking a long walk in the woods. This is akin to opening a window. A window needs to be open for a breeze to blow in, but there is no guarantee that it will.

Question: Democracy is related to political freedom, which is crucial for the world now that authoritarianism is encroaching from so many directions. So can you say a few words about that?

Answer: We need a social context for freedom that protects and fosters it to help us respond creatively to the enormous social challenges. I define democracy as government where changes in power are without bloodshed, and the citizenry has the power to eject the leaders from below. Democracy is the best arrangement for a feedback-based value system. Although authoritarian systems can make more rapid changes, it's at the expense of keeping the populace childish and afraid to take initiative. Dictators and oligarchies, no matter how benevolent or intelligent at any given moment (which is never a sure thing), are not subject to the kinds of feedback that democracy brings.

The world needs democracies that have learned to move quickly and effectively, which is only possible if the citizenry is sufficiently educated and their beliefs and values are amenable to feedback in this fast-changing world. They need to understand the issues and their implications for the future, and not be inhibited in expressing their will. The challenge is to make democracy work. Many elements are necessary—for example, safety nets, government regulation of the economic, health, food and other sectors, free speech, the rule of law, and education that not only teaches the "facts" of the times but teaches people to think for themselves and rewards them for it. Basically a democracy can only be as democratic as the minds of its people.

Question: These talks sometimes make me feel helpless because while listening it all seems to make sense, but it doesn't stay with me, and that's frustrating.

Answer: I look at these talks as planting seeds that can grow on their own over time, without effort. One of the problems of listening to me may be that you want to understand in usual ways what is being said. What we usually mean by understanding is for thought to wrap around the words and turn them into a consistent, familiar, or comfortable structure. Then one can say, "I have it. I understand. Now it's my possession," and regurgitate the ideas on command. The difficulty is that I'm not presenting ideas in the ordinary sense. I'm looking at what is. Thought can never really possess what is, never totally wrap around it and own it. To truly understand these words one must understand oneself. To understand oneself is always a movement, a moment-to-moment thing. And although one can understand oneself better over time, as soon as you say "I know myself completely," you are talking about the past, what you were, which now lives only in memory. Trying to hold on to the words can distract from really listening. The words don't matter—how you see for yourself does. Opening up a different way of looking can result in a shift of awareness, and seeing the nature of one's filters can bring more self-trust and self-understanding.

COMMENTARY:
Whose Life Is Sacred?

For thousands of years the concept of freedom was almost entirely focused on inner freedom, given that the world's civilizations were not conducive to social freedom. Personal freedoms regarding how we move through the world, who we can marry, how to educate our children, what kind of status and possibilities we have, and countless other aspects of living affect how much real freedom of thought and action exists in a social order. Since people rub against each other, the freedom to do what one wants is always constrained by others' wants.

We have been emphasizing the imperative to evolve socially to meet our human-induced crises, but what would that look like? Evolution is about the future, so starting from where we are, where do we need to be? It is obvious that if humans as a species and individuals are to be given the opportunity to fulfill whatever potential we have, social orders have to be open to and supportive of this.

Democracy is essential as it alone allows feedback from the whole populace. The problem is that a democracy can only be truely demo-cratic when its citizenzy is. Modern democracy with all its flaws is still a baby, and many minds remain trapped in old authoritarian belief sys-tems and religions, or are primarily personally, not socially, concerned. This must change.

Every society confronts a tension between freedom and equality. If equality is forced (as communism supposedly attempted to do), free-dom is lost. The slogan "From each according to their ability, to each according to their need" does not address who decides both abilities and needs. Consequently, a small authoritarian oligarchy emerges that tells others how to be equal.

If freedom is given its run, which unregulated capitalism was supposed to do, the haves of the world have much greater leverage, becoming greater haves with the have-nots falling further behind. This creates a larger discrepancy that leads to an unfair, unhappy, unstable world with much squalor and violence. If one shifts from expecting equality to emphasizing equal opportunity, still opportunity is never equal because those with a better start have more opportunity. So an aware society has leveling devices to control the differential between haves and have-nots and offers opportunities to move up. Safety nets around basics are also essential to prevent people from hitting bottom. These are ways to bring more freedom into a social order, to prevent desperation and violence, and to create a favorable ground for social evolution.

The world has to reorganize in so many ways. We will focus on one social structure so deeply rooted that, if changed, a cascade of significant changes would follow. The way society structures sexuality and heterosexuality, and power and control between the sexes, is one of its basic pillars and forms the deepest foundation of men's and women's psyches and identities. We call the world's historic and still prevalent institutional structuring of sexuality, power, and the interdependence between men, women, and children the "sexual order," because unlike "patriarchy," the term is gender-neutral for a clearer analysis.

Human beings are a dimorphic species, meaning the genders are physically different. Given the mind/body interconnection, other differences follow from that—the extent of which cannot be known yet (if ever) because of heavy layers of social conditioning. Since men are overall stronger and more physically aggressive, ever since killing and violence became the cornerstone of social hierarchy, power has been structured differently between the sexes, with unequal, complementary roles. The post-agricultural "Might makes right" early male power hierarchies were overlaid on human dimorphism, institutionalizing and exacerbating biological gender differences.

Heterosexuality with its reproductive asymmetry has been hierarchically structured into two separate spheres as the foundation of civilization, with males dominant in both public and private spheres. (In some cultures women might have more or less of an upper hand in the home). This has determined the way power, gender roles, and intimacy between the sexes intertwine. In this imbalance of power and roles, women's power is emotional and sexual in the private sphere. Until recently, the public world outside the private family sphere where men controlled the institutions was called "the male world." Only a few men at the top of the various hierarchies dominate everyone else, but historically all men were dominant in their own private sphere until relatively recently. As opposed to the life-giving and nurturing powers in the female sphere, in the male sphere one leverages power through technology, production, and destruction (attack and defense). The bottom line of power has been and largely still is based on killing, which includes the threat and willingness to kill. Men individuate partly through competing for power, status, wealth, and sexual access (the latter often through being dominant).

Change has been occurring unevenly throughout the world, and of course not all societies, men, or women fit into the picture we're painting. Nevertheless, the hold of the traditional sexual order on the world remains extreme. It has been so all-pervasive that until sixties feminism loudly brought gender power imbalances and roles to the world's attention (again), the sexual order has largely been unconscious. It has literally created the world as we know it and gender identities—that is, how people think of themselves. It has been the unconscious "water we swim in." The sexual order was taken for granted, unexamined, and unchallenged; or if noticed at all, assumed to be an absolute expression of nature—especially by the men justifying and enforcing it. For us, an absolute index of the maturity of a society is how its women are treated, and how much of a role women play in institutional decision-making. Until men and women have a far more equal voice in the direction of a society, that society's evolution and thus its capacity to be a player on the global stage will be sorely handicapped. And for humanity itself to evolve, women need a much bigger voice in the world, which the world also needs from them.

Since male/female relationships, the family, and kinship are the foundation of every social order, the sexual order impacts everything, from the personal and sexual through the social and political. Given that the entire social system is totally interconnected, to change it involves radically changing society. This sexual order has promoted men gaining control over everything—nature, resources, women and children, sexuality, workers, slaves, and production—which is why many refer to it as patriarchy. Having been a primary force in the movement of history, for good as well as ill, it has brought us to where we are, and now it has come to threaten our very survival. The division of the planet into the two spheres of power of the old sexual order is no longer working. The current imbalance between men and women, with its conflicts, tensions, and confusion, is part of the global crisis that humanity faces.

Power in the female sphere is in the field of reproduction and nurturing, which is linked with the wife and mother roles. Thus women's power is largely sexual, emotional, and private, invisible to the world at large—and often even to women themselves. Although men had (and many still do) the formal and legal power in the family, men and children experience, and sometimes resent, women's control, which is often unconscious. Mothers form our psychic structures through their values, self-sacrifice, and patterns of intimacy and emotional control, which involve rewards and punishments like bestowing and withdrawing affection and approval and inducing guilt. This reproductive female sphere, where life is created and maintained physically and emotionally mainly by women, is the given upon which all human life and our future depend.

Although the role of mother is heavily idealized, women's work within the family is gravely undervalued, unpaid, and not socially rewarded. Even though the female sphere is the foundation for everything else, it is largely taken for granted and not taken into account—just as life itself is usually taken for granted, until threatened.

This role-bound, locked-in interdependency between men and women based on authoritarian worldviews, values, and conditioning has kept both sexes developmentally childish, emotionally and mentally. Men have been dependent on women for nurturance, sex, and sometimes intimacy; while women have been dependent on men for economic survival and physical protection (especially from other men). Traditionally woman was the "warrior's rest"—a protective oasis totally outside the male competitive framework, where man could go to let down his defenses and recuperate. This role varied from what amounted to being sexual slaves to pampered aristocratic wives and courtesans. Because marriages were arranged with no or little choice allowed, based on economics and modular roles instead of sexual fulfillment and passion, husbands typically turned to other women or males to fulfill their desires.

Throughout most of history, the two sexes have coexisted largely as if they lived in two separate but complementary psychic universes, dependent on each other but not really understanding or seeing each other—or even speaking the same language. (Freud reputedly asked in exasperation, "What do women want?") More than mere remnants of this division remain in most modern societies. Fundamentalist religions and some branches of Islam still perpetuate and violently enforce a rigid, cruelly oppressive, female sex role.

The two-sphered and tiered "heterosexual order" has led to two gender-specific, out-of-control "explosions" that are threatening humanity's survival. In traditional role-bound societies, women not having much recourse to possibilities other than motherhood has led to an untenable population explosion in the female sphere of reproduction.

The byproducts of the male sphere of production are violence, pollution, and destruction. The juggernaut of production and of applying technology to the rampant amoral use and sale of weapons, without any concern for consequences or repercussions, has engendered ecological disasters and mushrooming, uncontrolled violence. The lethal, symmetrical explosions of these two spheres—creating life and destroying it, and reproduction and the production of destruction—fuel each other, putting humanity at risk. Female reproduction and male production are both forms of creativity that take on life-destroying aspects. The circle is vicious and must be broken: Men's power and patriarchal religions keep women controlled by biology and roles, leading to overpopulation and anger that unleashes violence and warfare.

Population has been and is out of control in a biologically primitive way in the female sphere. Most women lack rudimentary control over their bodies, lives, and survival; many fervently desire the capacity to have fewer children. However, motherhood also appeals by instinct and by default to women lacking other options, as it provides easy access to love, meaning, identity, and often the only status available through having sons. It is accepted fact that by far the best way to reduce population is to invest in women's betterment, education, work, and family healthcare. Traditional male values measure masculinity by the quantity of children a man produces, but a deep-seated practical reason for overpopulation is that insecure parents without a safety net rely on children to support and care for them in old age.

Men's attachment to the power and privileges accorded them by the sexual order leads them to intentionally and sometimes violently enforce the split and lock it and women in place. This has kept most women in developing countries impoverished and uneducated—*de facto* prisoners not only of their biology, but also of men and the motherhood role. This is coupled with women's lack of education and internalizing and identifying with the outmoded traditional mentalities and sex roles that their security is (or was) based on. They are sometimes more conservative, fearful, and emotionally attached to gods, saints, and rituals of the old religious worldviews than the men. In many cultures women perform clitoridectomy on girls because this is essential for marriage, which is necessary for status.

The sexual order's ingrained pronatalist values condition people to reproduce unconsciously because "it's what's done" or for self-interest, rather than from aware and prepared choice. Many of the world's children are not desired for intrinsic reasons, nor valued for their own potentials. Historically and still today many children were born because women simply had no choice. Ours is the first modern era to offer a choice through widespread birth control, but the archaic pronatalist values still dominant in much of the world prioritize, often sacralize, propagating life in quantity over promoting and protecting the quality of people's lives. Thus even in so-called "advanced" societies, women still have to perpetually protect and fight for the right and means to control their bodies—the bottom line upon which basic freedom for women depends.

This constellation of factors produces more children than can be adequately loved, cared for, educated, hired, or than the Earth can support. Nor can the planet support the out-of-control production for consumption within the male sphere of advanced economies. Together, the two out-of-control, interconnected "explosions" are a grave threat to human survival and an ecological disaster destroying our planetary support system. We must find a new balance and interaction between the sexes, no longer based on the rigidly structured opposition and the old complementarily-unconscious roles of the two spheres.

Of course, these two gender spheres are not entirely separate. On the contrary, they are deeply interconnected in very basic ways: Clearly men are essential for reproduction and many participate in child-rearing. And men have the power and wealth to control the female sphere by making the laws and determining social priorities, policies, and agendas (in government and in tradition-bound families as well) that limit women's reproductive choices. Many women collude in war by supporting male power, especially if privileged themselves. Women benefit from male power—collectively, if their nation is a "have," and personally if their mate is privileged or offers security and protection. Women and children's status, security, well-being, and often very survival have traditionally depended on men's personal and social protection. Increasingly the breakdown of the family is leaving many mothers both single and impoverished throughout the world. But in spite of increasing gender cross-over (i.e., even though each sex participates and sometimes colludes in the other's domain), the sexes, sex roles, and child-rearing are still ordered such that on this planet today men do most of the violence and killing, and women create and maintain life— they bear the children and do most of the child-rearing, housework, and family maintenance—in addition to now also having to work outside the home to help support the family financially.

In politics, women's and children's issues are always of second- or last-order importance, usually not even seen as political. Perhaps this is partly because women and children are associated with the "private" female sphere. When political budgets have to be trimmed, the items and concern for women, children, and education are usually the first to go. Economics, defense, everything else, even going to Mars have always taken precedence. But now for the first time in civilized history, the female sphere, reproduction and childcare, has moved to the front lines in that it is threatening our survival—via overpopulation, environmental effects, and the angry uncared-for youth without options, many of whom are walking time bombs, or potential terrorists. On the other hand, the female role of nurturance (care) and maintenance (infrastructure and "clean up") has been sorely lacking in the male sphere of production, and this lack is now also a threat. In a socially evolved society that would offer more freedom to both men and women, the playing field of institutional power must be leveled. The most important first step to free women is for them to have control of their reproductive capacities. Without this women are at the mercy (or lack of it) of biology, accident, or the dictates of those who enforce, promote, and cling to the old "moral order"—now "immoral" in its effect on people, societies, and the world. Without the freedom of choice as a bottom line of freedom, women do not stand a chance to compete in the world of institutional power.

It is glibly said that "Children are our most precious resource" while an increasing percentage live in poverty. An evolved society and an evolving world would treat them as precious. Social evolution cannot occur without people engaging in conscious instead of unconscious reproduction and conscious child-rearing, with society doing its utmost to protect and foster the young's well-being. This includes social supports for parents to mitigate their sacrifices and stress, and re-visioning education to teach children how to think and relate better, instead of what to think.

Transcending archaic conditioning allows people to take on a more global identity and viable values. Healing the schism between the sexes frees men and women to support each other. Women's and men's combined focus, talents, insights, and very differences are urgently needed to deal with these extraordinary times. This means freeing women's time and energy to enter the public arena so they can use their special abilities and sensitivities to help solve our problems.

Humanity is at the frontier of an unprecedented social revolution—the potential for choice and control in one of its most basic and important functions. Freeing women from being continuously subject to a mysterious biology is a feat of the same magnitude as the discovery of paternity, which allowed men to become fathers and also transformed social foundations. But most of the world has not yet been reached by this revolution—because those within the old sexual order are attached to its power, privileges, religions, and beliefs. They cannot shift their authoritarian worldviews to see the dire implica-

tions of caging women (and men too) within its archaic and sometimes medieval beliefs. So most of the world cannot integrate the
true meaning and extraordinary potential of this liberation, which
is revolutionary not only for women as individuals, but for all of
humanity.

The sacrifice of women's individuation and potential to child-
rearing is the hidden foundation upon which the old sexual order was
built. Abortion is such a volatile issue largely because it challenges and
erodes the very underpinnings of society and the old moral order:
woman's forced self-sacrifice to her children and her "surrender to fate,
nature, God" (i.e., total lack of control over her life through her biology).
To overtly grant women freedom of choice undermines the sexual order's
roles, values, and gendered power hierarchies, and would change the
world as we know it. The more traditional the values, the greater the
hostility and moral opposition to women's conscious choice. The world's
major religions are the moral foundation of our planetary sexual order.
The breakdown of the old morality cannot be totally unwelcome, since
it is what is preventing the social changes necessary for survival that
conscious reproduction would bring.

Freeing women from being forced to have unwanted children would
also free many men who are forced to lead lives they really don't want.
The law obligates a woman to raise the children she bears and in various *de facto* ways to bear them against her will; the law obligates men
to provide financial support to children he may not have wanted, for
men too suffer from women's lack of choice and control. The traditional
sexual order, which prioritizes and often forces a narrow and warped
heterosexuality, is oppressive to other kinds of sexual expression.
Dismantling the old heterosexual order would free people to live as they
choose and with whom they choose, having the same rights as any other
citizen. Real choice is not merely about whether or not to have a child,
but also whom you can partner with, and be sexually involved with. The

archaic sexual/moral order retards everyone's development and freedom, limiting and handicapping social evolution.

The potentials brought about by choice in one of humanity's most important and basic functions, reproduction, have implications of enormous magnitude. Freeing women to partake in all other aspects of society if they so choose transforms basic social roles and structures. This opens the possibility of conscious conception and reproduction for humanity, which is new and necessary because so many social problems and personal tragedies stem from the lack of consciousness in reproduction and unprepared parenting. We are at the threshold of a new era where choice is necessary for conscious reproduction, and conscious reproduction is necessary to meet the momentous challenges humanity is facing.

Minions of the old order are so against abortion, which is still the bottom line of birth control, because truly free women would collapse their primitive worldviews and power—where even men on the lower end of the power hierarchy can still feel superior to and dominate "their" women. Their rallying cry as they send young men off to war to kill or be killed is "Life is sacred." (Beware of anything made "sacred," as doing so makes it unchallengeable, suspect, authoritarian—and usually demands self-sacrifice.) When overpopulation limits people's freedom and threatens the species, when women are expected and forced to self-sacrifice to the overall detriment of the world, we end this commentary with this thought: "Whose life is sacred?"

6. Images

The Passionate Mind focused on how the mind builds images of others that lock into memory, making real contact with others more difficult. In the present book, this discussion has been extended to self-images, including how they impact our behavior, sense of possibility, and identity. At the end of this chapter the commentary moves from personal issues to global concerns, showing how limited, rigid, primary identities are a major source of the divisions among people. Since narrow identity is at the core of many social problems, it's vital in these times of worldwide ethnic strife to recognize the relationship between image and identity.

Much of living is colored by the past and the future, desires and fears, memories of pleasures and hurts. Out of memories and expectations I create images of myself and others. So much of what I see is through a veil of images. When I look at you it's very difficult to see you, the living person. This is also true of seeing myself. If you flatter me, I like it. Even if I know you're flattering me, secretly I like it. If you hurt or offend me, I don't like it. When I approach you again I see you through the prism of flattery or offense, so I'm not in touch with you the living person as you are now, but rather with my own thoughts, with a memory of what you were. Of course, you do the same with me. As I respond to you out of that memory this triggers responses in you, often based on your images of me.

When I relate to you through my images of you, it's not only you I'm relating to but my own thoughts—my opinions, judgments, and feelings about you. Even in intimacy, much of relating is actually not direct relationship because we're not really in contact with each other. I'm relating with you through how I remember you were with me—if you pleased or displeased me. This is particularly true in families and couples, where emotions, expectations, and memories are heightened and more powerful. That's what goes on in much of relationship–images posturing in front of one another.

We saw in examining beliefs that to learn one must do away with outside authorities offering certainty that blocks change. One particularly insidious authority that is difficult to ignore, that has great pull, one that our life depends on, is the authority of our own experience, our past—the authority of our memory. Like fear, desire, and pleasure, memory is double-edged.

I'm not at all suggesting an attempt to forget or suppress memories. As with fear and desire, one cannot escape the past by running away from it or denying it. That's just thought trying to escape itself. Trying to do away with memory—dropping your story, your sense of self, as some suggest—in order to be more present or more spiritual is an ideal that can be carried to the absurd. To be totally confined to the present moment with no sense of past or future is to be cut off from relationship—even with oneself.

Just as the learning about oneself is cumulative, so too is learning about others. Memory is what allows people to get to know each other and a relationship to build trust and continuity over time. The question is not whether memories should be part of an interaction, but whether they are still pertinent—and if so, which ones and how relevant are they?

Problems arise when our images of each other are inaccurate yet so powerful that they block seeing and real communication. These images may have come from our experiences of each other, or from what others have said, from misinterpreting a mood, tone of voice, or facial expression—any number of factors that may or may not have accurately reflected who you were then, and essentially miss who you are now. Not only can memory be unreliable and biased, people change. But if you see how memories can be subjective filters that limit your perception, it's possible to pierce through them to be more fully in touch with another.

If you've hurt me or been mean or nasty to me, I don't forget this when I see you again. A slight or condescension can reveal how someone is seeing or judging you, which is valuable to be aware of. Perhaps it's a response to how the person perceived being treated by you, or it could just be the way they relate. Moving past hurt or anger doesn't mean forgetting it, negating your point of view, or not being guarded—nor does it necessarily involve forgiveness. It's natural and often necessary to remember and self-protect since you might get the same treatment again. When hurt by someone you care about, you usually want some kind of emotional resolution or at least to find out the cause. Otherwise, although you may resist it, when hurt there's an automatic urge to want to hurt back. But if you do want to stay open, a hurtful pattern has to be addressed somehow. In doing so, the focus is often more on the past than on preventing the offensive behavior in the future, which is even more important.

People will tell you to forgive and not to get stuck in the past ("Let go of your story," "Detach from your drama—it's just ego"), but if trust is broken it needs to be rebuilt. This is no easy task, especially if there's a deep sense of betrayal. People do change—but when words cannot be trusted, how can one know for sure? Trust cannot be regained through words or promises alone; it can only be restored through different behavior over time, which involves memory.

Although forgiveness as a spiritual ideal may make everyone involved feel better in the moment, it does not rebuild broken trust. Instead of moving the relation forward or resolving the issue, forgiving out of ideals tends to reinforce the unwanted behavior on the part of the other person. If "forgiving" is done in order to live up to an ideal, it can contain suppressed, denied, and unacknowledged hurt and anger that perpetuate unaware reactions and mechanical behavior on both sides. Covert moral superiority can be part of "idealistic forgiving" ("I'm more righteous than you who did me wrong and more virtuous too because I forgive you"). Here the one being forgiven can resent and react against condescension.

Since it's natural to self-protect, instead of struggling to forgive, a more realistic and safer way to think of "letting go" is to aim for a state when memories of the hurt no longer bring back the emotional moods and automatic triggers associated with it, such as thoughts that fuel anger. Even with trauma, if one puts blame and hurt temporarily aside and becomes curious about the total picture of what happened, this can move one to a new emotional place. Gaining a deep understanding of the dynamics that brought the pain about can bring movement in the form of release. The release is a freeing that comes from seeing, not from effort or ideals.

The images we've built over time include expectations, desires, and needs that influence how I see and relate to you. When people like each other, their openness is partly based on memories of feeling good together and the expectation of continuing to do so. We often develop unspoken reciprocal agreements with one another that attempt to keep things on an even keel. But it's more difficult for me to be in contact with you as a living, changing person if I really don't want you to change— at least not the aspects of you that I like. I don't want you to be too new or unpredictable; I want you to stay the same so I'll know you, so you're familiar and I can be comfortable with you, secure in our relationship, whatever that may be. If you change I may resist seeing you with new eyes, for your changes might push me to change or make our relationship more uncertain. So fear is in the background. And of course you do this with me, too.

Parents might be threatened as their child grows into adulthood, fearing loss of control and missing the influence and power they once had. Instead of trying to understand or keep up with this ever-changing, ever-new person, a disapproving or fearful parent might cling to memories of the child being young and pliant from a longing for the past.

We all have a wide variety of self-images, big and small, coming from experience and others' views of us; from childhood, society, and the many roles we play; images related to biology (gender, age, size, ancestry); images linked to likes, dislikes, preferences, emotions, beliefs, fears, desires, conflicts, talents and confidence, or the lacks thereof. Self-images can anchor habits and either motivate and inspire or limit me. They can spur me to realize my dreams and highest visions, or limit possibility by discouraging me from trying new and different things outside the scope of my experience, known abilities, and likes. Many of these self-images shift over time and are not locked into one's basic view of oneself. Some do lock in and to that extent, I become the self-images I create or internalize. These are the images I'm focusing on—not the ones that change with new preferences or that people adopt as part of a "social personality."

Self-images are among thought's biggest obstacles to seeing clearly. Thought can construct a background meta-program aimed at reinforcing self-image that directs what you think about and pay attention to. If I build a self-image out of the ways of looking at myself that I like or am proud of, this easily prevents seeing other aspects of myself that seem less praiseworthy. There may be things about myself that I don't like—such as wanting to punish when I'm angry—parts that dismay or upset me because they don't fit my self-image of being "nice." Wanting to be beyond pettiness, self-centeredness, anger, or jealousy can prevent me from seeing when I am. This makes effectively dealing with these traits almost impossible. Awareness can pierce through self-images that filter seeing. To observe the whole play of thought and image while it's happening, while living, so at that moment I'm aware that I am in part the images I produce—to see that is to *see*, which can bring movement.

Self-images related to our values, ideals, and worldview are of a different order—they can harden into core identities that, for better or worse, carry on for years or over a lifetime. Identity comes from how we think about ourselves, which can grow out of abiding passions and deep ongoing interests, or from such things as outmoded childhood or authoritarian conditioning. Narrow, highly conditioned identities not only divide people and groups but can create a conflict-ridden division in oneself because one cannot live up to certain values or cope with a rapidly changing world. This inner division is the source of much reactive, dysfunctional, and addictive behavior. An example would be a priest who can't live up to his vows of celibacy and pure identity and sexually abuses children. Betraying one's ideals comes from and reinforces this inner split where the idealistic side judges and berates the side that doesn't want to or can't live up to the ideals, while the "bad" side feels guilt and resentment at being caged, and in return sabotages or rebels against the "idealistic," often authoritarian part of oneself.

Guilt deeply affects self-images, and instilling guilt and fear in the young is easy, so they're two of the major social control mechanisms used by parents and society. Fear gets entwined with guilt—fear of disapproval, rejection, punishment, shame, and the fear of feeling guilty itself. Since guilt feels bad both in the body and emotionally, it's an internal self-punishment that people want to avoid. Avoiding it is partly what keeps them under control.

Although I think most humans have an inbuilt sense of fairness, a lot of the concepts in the conscience about what's good and bad are conditioned at an early age. People are socialized to assume that their conscience and feelings of guilt are largely trustworthy. Both guilt and conscience carry the weight of an internalized authority that's taken for granted as an accurate indicator of right and wrong. Deep-rooted values implanted at an early age before developing reason are more unexamined and conditioned than beliefs, because "provable" facts more easily erode beliefs than values.

So conscience, that trusted compass of right and wrong, is highly programmed by old values that often contain authoritarian conditioning and unlivable ideals. Such ideals can seem not only desirable but impeccable ("Everyone should love each other," "Self-centeredness is bad"), yet they contain notions of moral perfection and purity that negate part of what it is to be human. These values are guidelines for behavior that become part of your self-image—the ideal self that you want or try to be. Usually people are so identified with them that they unthinkingly assume their ideals are right and that the resultant guilt is proof of faulty behavior. Guilt acts like the indictment, judge, jury, verdict, and punishment all in one—without appeal. Many people automatically bow to guilt's judgments and surrender to its verdicts. But if instead guilt is seen as the sign of a gap, a discrepancy between one's ideals or self-images and actual behavior, one can begin to see the nature of guilt and how it too lives in thought. This changes its whole meaning and context, and guilt becomes feedback of a discrepancy instead of an unchallengeable condemnation with no recourse. This shift allows you to examine the ideals to see whether they're actually realistic and beneficial, or whether you're mechanically conditioned to buy into the guilt. You might discover that at times the ideals (and the self-images they perpetuate) need to be reexamined and changed—rather than the behavior.

Tradition—our collective past—is an immense reservoir of images that contains outmoded ideals, assumptions, and prescriptions. Since much of tradition is authoritarian, so are the images and ideals, which makes them largely useless if not outright harmful for today's world. Self-images that contain unlivable ideals not only produce guilt, they make it nigh impossible to see yourself clearly. Traditional images of spirituality, love, enlightenment, and ideals of moral purity are embedded in many people's minds as powerful filters that cloud seeing. If you're looking for someone "pure" to follow or emulate, it's likely you're involved in seeking illusory images. If I want to learn about myself, actually learn directly about what I am and how I work, then I must look at the images, the thoughts, the responses from memory, fear, and desire, and see how they work, because all this becomes part of me. I see how thought can shadow and remove me from the living moment, how it encrusts image upon image. The more encrusted I become as I get older, the more my habits and self-images are fixed. Habits in the mind and body are what cause me literally to stiffen, becoming more predictable and resistant to change.

If I become aware of how much of living and what is considered communication is actually the relating of images, I may look for something beyond or behind the images. So I look for the entity, the part of me actually spinning them out. Where is it? I want to be in touch with the real being behind all the spinnings of my mind, separate from my thought and self-images. Looking for the image-maker in me involves me in thought again, as I'm wanting something to be different than what it is. So many of us are searching to get in touch with ourselves, looking for the "real" me behind the layers of conditioning. The mind is very sly; it can build an image of not having any images at all. Trying to do away with images can be another thought or image, another trap in the bind of mind. Realizing that my images are subjective and fallible, with a tendency to get locked in, is an opening to change.

At issue here, which is controversial, is whether there is a self that thinks thoughts or no self other than thought's attachments to the memories of itself that it constructs. If you think, as I do, that humans are capable of will and intention and having some say in the direction of their lives, then thoughts and self-images do not come out of nowhere, nor are they totally a product of conditioning. Consequently, there must be an overriding part of the brain that to some extent directs what thoughts are produced. Yet if I look carefully at thinking or image-making, I find that the thinker is not disconnected from its thoughts or images.

If you observe yourself or others over time, there's what might be called a genetic "flavor" with a continuity through the changes that time brings that makes you uniquely you. The idea that the self is nothing but the accumulations of thought and the self-images it creates leaves no room for such things as the continuity of personality's unique expressions and the force of individual will in creating the future.

Although thought has mechanical aspects, we are not locked in and determined by them. We humans possess will and intention that can meet a new situation creatively, not merely out of past conditioning or ingrained self-images. There's an intelligence in us beyond thought that's a unique expression of who we are. We have insights and intuitions that are not thought itself, which thought works at translating into words and concepts in order to communicate. There is something within a person that can to some extent choose where to direct attention and what to think about. If you're conscious of your self-images, it's possible on occasion to uniquely break through their limiting lens and see that which makes you you, and not me.

This self that I'm always looking for manifests not only through thinking but also through willing, feeling, intuiting, and creating. To become aware of these aspects of the self, including the power and nature of thought and memory, is to get in touch with the nature of mind and oneself. Through an awareness of how the past works in you, it's possible in a living moment to break through its conditionings and touch that moment in a new and fresh way.

Question: Could you please talk about transparency, authenticity, and the social personality you mentioned?

Answer. Societies have implicit rules, etiquette, manners, and expectations around different levels of intimacy. Total transparency is rarely desirable in the social world. It isn't appropriate for casual communication and many other types of encounters—not only as one moves through life, but in intimacy too—so most people develop a social personality. When asked "How are you?" we're expected to reply "I'm fine," as people don't want a rundown of our problems or triumphs. In the social world we "put on a face to meet the faces that we meet."

Being authentic is not the same as being transparent. You can authentically want to keep something private or to make an interaction socially acceptable and smooth by choosing to be a certain way. In many societies, people have the acknowledged right to keep certain things private in social situations for their own or another's good. So they reveal only the parts they want to show. One can present a "persona" to the world for many reasons—including being deceptive for personal gain or, more commonly, merely conforming to what's expected out of politeness or a sincere desire to please people or make them comfortable and ensure that they like you.

A civil persona that protects people's boundaries and feelings is appreciated in much of social life, where total transparency is rarely appropriate, welcome, or even safe. People want to feel good as they move through their day, and hearing your problems or reasons for pessimism can be an unwelcome intrusion. Transparency leaves you vulnerable and can intrude on others. But the drawback of everyone presenting a carefully controlled and protective persona is that life is less interesting if no one says what they really think. You miss seeing people's deeper aspects that could make you want to get to know them better. So there are no formulas for how transparent or opaque to be in certain interactions.

Question: Is there a way to minimize what you call the building of images?

Answer: That, among other things, is what these discussions are about. Living consciously minimizes image-building because conscious interactions are "cleaner" and more clear-cut, with fewer misunderstandings, projections, assumptions, and the like that accumulate. This results in less emotional baggage and backlog, less relating through image, and less need to sort things out.

Question: Why do you say that the concept of enlightenment and being totally selfless is a bar that humans can't reach? Even if it's not reachable for all or most of us, doesn't it offer something to aim for that would improve humanity?

Answer: One can always debate whether there is or ever was a totally ego-less person. Certainly over the ages and now too there are people who present themselves as such, whether openly or insinuated. Even if such a person actually existed, the worldviews that put forth those concepts have had thousands of years to raise humanity to a better place. Yet here we are facing the possibility of not even surviving in the not-too-distant future. {Arguments showing why the very concepts of enlightenment and ego-loss as absolutes or a steady state are authoritarian constructs are too complex to get into here. See the chapter on Oneness in *The Guru Papers.*}

As to grand ideals that are unlivable being helpful for "self-improvement" by giving us a direction and something to shoot for, far too often unlivable ideals do quite the opposite. When people try to fit into a mold that doesn't work for them, they can become less conscious and less aware of who they are and how they actually work because they feel chronically inadequate or hopeless. Or they think they should make more effort to change by doing practices developed by those very traditions—it's a self-enclosed circle. Unlivable ideals usually result in guilt, justifications, confusion, conflict, or denial because they separate us from our humanity.

Who we are and how we relate are what brought us here. Solutions to the world's problems are not connected to having more or less ego, but rather to having a better understanding of ourselves—our self-images, identities, relationships, and how they affect what we do. We need more awareness of how what we're facing is a product of who we are. We also need to understand that the unlivable ideals that got us here are now dysfunctional as guidelines. Our self-images are entwined with our concepts of who we are and what we identify with, and thus care about. Since care is at the core of any solution—caring to survive, caring about others, about the web of life, the Earth—we need to enlarge the range of what we care about. Humanity's well-being and survival depend on realizing that our narrow identities limit the care we need to sustain a viable civilization. Since people care about what they identify with, expanding identity is one of the most rapid and effective ways to bring about needed change.

COMMENTARY:
From Image to Identity

Images of self and others easily harden into identities with a cluster of cultural suppositions around them that create divisions between people. Since we (the authors) see narrow identities in an interactive world of global impact as a major block to intelligently dealing with the many interrelated crises we face, this brief section examines identity and its consequences. We are moving the conversation from images to identity because as social animals our personalities are in part constructed by the social climate we find ourselves in, which greatly affects how we view ourselves and others, and how others view us. Images harden into the identities we utilize to define ourselves and others.

Identities move us more into the social sphere since they are related to and impact who or what we identify with, and thus to a great extent what we care about outside of ourselves. If you're interested in what your identities are, ask "Who am I?" instead of "What am I not?"—that is, how would you describe yourself? Here one gets into such arenas as family, nationality, religion, gender, age, region, occupation, tribe, political party, ideology, cohorts, and even friendships and differing worldviews. "I am a . . ." and you fill in the blanks. One could say, "I'm a heterosexual, Christian American male who believes in karma and whose main concern is taking care of my family" and so on.

In some spiritual worldviews the idea is to "Know thyself," which usually means looking within to see what you will find. But you are often told what you will not find. The Sanskrit concept *neti-neti* involves trying to pare away all superficial layerings of oneself. It proposes that I am not my thoughts, emotions, actions, relationships, etc., and if I were to look deep enough I would find a pure essence, a "higher Self" untouched by the corruptions of time. This is part of a worldview that promotes the unity of all existence. From the worldview of this book, diversity and individuation are what the cosmos, as a unity or unifying field, manufactures. This means that separate individuals like you and me are real—not on some lower level of existence, or an illusion, or a dalliance or amusement consciously constructed by some undivided entity. From this perspective unity and diversity are dialectically embedded, meaning that their existence reflects and is dependent on each other, with neither being higher on any scale. Consequently, if you really want to know yourself you must look at how you think, act, and relate, and what images and identities you operate out of.

Previous to the greatly enhanced communicative powers of technology that brought a world of accelerated change and globalism, people could remain relatively isolated from each other with identities wrapped up in local affairs. Many peoples claim to be God's chosen (usually oblivious of others claiming this too)—Hopis, Japanese, Nordics, Jews, etc. Race, religion, family, region, and tribe often have a different set of acceptable or sanctioned behaviors for different identities. A morality is a set of rules applicable to a specific group. There are different rules and therefore expectations within families than with fellow employees (for example). People are more comfortable with the familiar and give it priority in various ways.

The explosion of information technology has not only brought more homogeneity and cultural exchange, it also cracked through the isolation of regions, confronting people with the conflicts of diversity. The greater realization of the differentiation of power and utilization of resources between haves and have-nots, as well as differing cultural priorities and values, have moved many groups to reinforce traditional identities. The rules for gender identity for a traditional Muslim woman are very different than for a modern European woman. Consequently the information explosion has been double-edged, as it loosened identity barriers (particularly among the young) and hardened others in reaction.

Shared worldviews are a powerful baseline for shared identities. Worldviews have embedded in them values that serve to construct a system of morality for group interaction. The greatest changes in history occur when worldviews begin to crumble, followed by a breakdown of values. What ensues is what we call "the morality wars" where the world divides into those who tighten traditional identities (which tend to be role-bound and authoritarian) and those seeking a more pragmatic, democratic, and change- and feedback-oriented set of values in line with the demands of the times. We believe that the world is now engaged in morality wars that will impact, perhaps even decide our viability. The old order is crumbling because its worldviews could not handle accelerated change. In the United States this split is obvious between those identifying with the "certainty" and "security" of traditional religious structures, and the many others searching and hoping for some kind of breakthrough in consciousness that can bring meaning and a sense of direction toward viability.

The influence of technology, which is the motor behind globalism, has made human impact no longer local but global, with devastating effects on ecology, great impact on population, and worldwide economic upheaval. Yet most people's major identities are still local.

Hatred and violence between groups with different identities is one of the most intractable and challenging planetary problems. What to do with the traumas, suffering, anger, grievances, and vengeance resulting from historical or recent atrocities, oppressions, wars, religious and ethnic strife, injustices, and even indifferent uncaring? Sometimes they last for thousands of years and self-perpetuate in endless rounds of retribution. The place they reside and endure is in group identities that promulgate a righteous superiority with such ideals as patriotism, nationalism, racism, male dominance, and countless -isms–religious, political, ideological.

Many of the young have more multicultural identities, less limited to origin and ancestry than their parents. As narrow, limited identity loses its hold—its justifiability, sentimentality, and relevance—so does emotional identification with historical wounds and victimization.

Retributions and violence are perpetuated by emotional attachment to "group images" and values, such as how honor, pride, loyalty (whether deserved or not), and duty (to whom and for what) are defined. The more an individual's positive self-image depends on group identity, the more likely that identity depends on the group feeling superior. Concepts like honor that originate with an ethical component of integrity can become twisted into causing barbaric atrocities. This is especially true when gender and so-called sexual morality are involved. Examples: the legality of murdering or stoning adulteresses to death, or punishing or ostracizing women who are victims of rape, or Muslim fathers legally and with little compunction murdering daughters caught dating—all in the name of protecting or avenging family honor. Here a narrow family identity supersedes very basic and parental human care. When a religion identifies one group as inferior, it is tantamount to sacralizing oppression. In the past, many religions did so, justifying a wide spectrum of human abuse, including slavery.

Ego or self-centeredness is considered by many to be one of humankind's greatest flaws, especially by traditional religions and moral systems. Ego is singled out as the cause of greed, violence, and the blind uncaringness that have led us to where we are. The heavily idealized and sacralized image of a totally selfless being, whether a saint, avatar, or enlightened one, has constructed a bar of idealized virtue that the human animal cannot reach. Ego has shown that it can have destructive effects beyond the pale, but it is also the source of creativity, social need, bonding, and care. If caring about others did not make you feel good about yourself, there would be far less of it.

In our worldview that sees unity and diversity as equally real, ego is a core part of who we are, with all its benefits and drawbacks. So the necessity is not to try to eliminate it, which cannot really be done, but to make it work better for us. Identity is a greater social problem than ego. Identities bolster or flatten our egos and have narrowed our concerns. The problems with ego are hugely exacerbated when ego coalesces around limited identities denigrating or polarizing against those not identified with. Such identities create and depend on the outsider, the "Other." The very worldviews that denigrate the ego, preaching love and compassion, create identities that separate people, which is a deep root of violence.

Before one can fix something, it's important to understand the nature of the problem. Yet different worldviews have very different ways of analyzing and fixing a problem. Science focuses on technological fixes but has no intrinsic values in and of itself (other than the allegiance to the scientific method), although individual scientists have whatever values they do. Traditional spiritual worldviews in which selflessness is the ideal, or Oneness or the Void is the only basic reality, single out ego as the fundamental problem. Their panacea for everything is eliminating ego, or if that's not possible, squeezing or shrinking it as much as you can. History has shown that this strategy misses the mark.

In our worldview neither approach is the solution. Technology cannot solve the problem without values to guide and regulate it. Ego is here to stay and has an important role. The problem is not ego, but the narrow identities limited by the past and present that exclude others and do not change with feedback—identities that have not socially evolved to incorporate the changing world of mutual concerns that affect us all. To join together and solve our problems we need to take on the identity of global citizen as our primary identity, with our other identities being secondary. The world needs to create, adopt, and identify with pan-cultural viable values that aim at species survival and the recognition that global problems impact us all, and global solutions must have global values to sustain them.

People are a mix of using and caring. The nature of being a social animal is that we specialize; consequently we continually use each other for knowledge, skills, work, company, and—bottom line—survival. To date the way we have used each other and the planet has been short-sighted and narrow in its care and care-taking. Although "using" has a bad connotation, using and being "used" are in themselves neither right nor wrong—it all depends on whether care for who and what is being used is part of the situation. Use is a core part of our interdependence, much more so since specialization.

For people to broaden their identities to include the global, they must have hope for a better future; otherwise the past and its resentments will continue to define what they identify with and what has the main hold on them. Caring about how and what we use (including each other) is key to evolving socially.

7. Love

Love is one of the oldest and most powerful emotions and forces of our mammalian heritage. It is a unique and potentially transformative experience that opens people and the world in new ways, and can shine a brilliant light into your own being. Ever since Socrates, the phrase "Know thyself" has been a foundation for inquiry, learning, and maturation carried on by various traditions. Though many people try to do this through introspection or meditation, one cannot know oneself fully in isolation. We are social beings, so knowing oneself must include learning from how one relates. If you have never loved or been loved, a part of your being is unknown and unknowable to you.

In our worldview, love is a magical connector that is the cosmos' gift to itself, played out through those who can experience it. It can bypass obstacles and make life worth living. Though it contains a wild element that cannot be caged, much can be done to help it along. Love's benefits can be greatly enhanced by awareness of the dynamics of relationships and by understanding one's role within love's dramas. By taking an unsentimental look at love in this chapter, and what people do to shut it down, we hope to increase the likelihood that love's magic will be more encompassing in people's lives.

Although love is said to move mountains and make the world go 'round, clearly love has not been able to move our aggressive nature enough to curb violence and hatred, nor to bring about a viable world. Traditional concepts and ideals of love, although popular, are unlivable and block love's potential. The way the name of love has been used and abused, idealized and institutionalized—in religion, the family, and intimacy—is a root of the problem. A more realistic and viable framework can enhance instead of limit the ability to love, which can help humanity move forward.

Love has long been touted as the solution to our problems, but it often does not even survive in intimacy or committed relationships.

For love to flower, people need to see what obstacles stand in its way. Although feeling love itself is not cognitive, humans have ideas about everything important, and love above all has been highly conceptualized over millennia, for a reason. This has not been merely philosophical speculation. Not only have our institutions never made healthy relationships a top priority, unlivable ideals about love are a cornerstone of authoritarian moralities used to control people—throwing a wrench in the emotional architecture of our mammalian genetic heritage that is prone to foster bonding. This means that our enormous potential as social animals to bond, love, and care is a relatively untapped and unexplored resource. Our authoritarian heritage controlled us and kept us children, emotionally and mentally stunting humanity's potential to think, care, relate, and love.

The focus of this chapter is the arena where love and pain, desires and expectations, fears and resentments are the most intense—intimacy and the family. It and the commentary investigate how worldviews conceptualize love, and how they partly determine a relationship's success or failure. We also discuss the crucial difference between care and love, and care's vital role in arriving at a sustainable world. Care is more open to the mind's influence and understanding, so what one can care about has a much further reach than what one can love. And care brings less vulnerability than love. Care can be taught by showing interrelationships and consequences, while love can only be taught by loving—which limits its scope and does not always work.

This chapter on love aims to isolate and thereby help diminish the factors that shut down love and care. People want to break out of roles and communicate with more authenticity. Real communication is communion, which occurs when people transcend their subjectivity and personal dramas to really connect. Our hope as a species lies in extending the spirit of connecting to wider and wider arenas. So much energy is bound in relational conflicts that stem from outmoded structures. Relationships are a cauldron of transformation. People have an opportunity to create something new by couples becoming units of love and support. Although the focus here is on the couple, love can broaden into many different relationships, including with other species. We hope the perspectives we have arrived at spark positive change in your own thoughts and relationships. The magic of love is like quicksilver. You can't hold it or shape it—but you can allow it to seep through your being and transform you.

Within the human drama love ignites both the heroic and the tragic; poets continue to wax eloquently about its wonders and lament its loss. Love is one of the inspirations of existence. Its power moves the world by connecting people, infusing life with care and altruism. Its absence makes a life barren and lonely, and people more indifferent, even at times cruel.

Although the capacity to deeply bond is shared by other mammals, humans' special capacity to love with heart and mind is an extraordinary genetic gift. Human bonding and love are part of our oldest genetic makeup, embedded deeply in our biology within the highly refined emotionality and connectivity of our mammalian limbic system. The social fabric creates the foundation for our relationships, especially intimacy, which entwines and connects us through limbic resonance affecting physical, emotional, and mental development, motivation, neural networks, and body rhythms and cycles. Like other social mammals, our limbic system is designed to perceive and attune emotionally in close relationships, which our proper development (including that of our brain and our ability to talk) critically depends on. Whether our relationships are enhancing or detrimental in large measure determines our overall well-being, emotional balance, and even health and longevity.

Like other emergent qualities, love can only be "explained" genetically in retrospect. Evolutionary psychologists theorize that love originated as an aid to reproduction. This mechanical retrospective causality, which can neither be proved nor disproved, is the type of theory manufactured whenever real knowledge is lacking to bolster materialist beliefs. Through my lens, love is not amenable to scientific materialism, as it is not predictable. Love is a prime example of how, through evolution, existence enlarges experiential possibilities that help keep life and evolution both fascinating and flowing.

Most everyone wants to be special for someone, to love and be loved; and when love comes, wants it to last forever. The challenge lies in how to make this come about in a world where traditional roles that supposedly contain love and the worldviews that define it are breaking down. Making love last in a complex world where self-centeredness intertwines with loving takes a different level of awareness in intimacy. This and the predictable but avoidable ways that love gets blocked will be the focus of our inquiry.

All attempts to describe love's ineffable essence necessarily fall short. Its seemingly magical quality is neither cognitive nor even purely emotional. Love is an inexplicable, unique, and powerful connecting energy that lives in relationship. People have many ideas about what love means. The word itself is used in widely varying ways— to describe an emotion, an experience, a state, a living energy, a heart connection, a miracle, a magical spell, an infatuation, a power, a bonding, a concept, a drive or instinct, a spiritual ideal, and even a panacea. It's also used casually to express likes and preferences, activities, sensual pleasures, and excitement—"I love a film, a song, swimming, chocolate, Paris."

Like the proverbial "wolf in sheep's clothing," love is deviously used and abused by individuals and institutions to coat nefarious goals with seeming benevolence. Similarly to God and religion, love has been used throughout history for social and individual control, to mask and justify authoritarian agendas of power, control, and violence, bending love to its service through rights, duties, and roles. Religions have God give love for obedience and make obedience the proof of loving God. They promote "unconditional love" while loading it with conditions—the very concept places hidden conditions on love (that it have no conditions and be selfless). "In the name of love" is wielded like a carrot and a stick. So if you love God "He" will reward you, if not in this world, in the next— usually in the next. And if you do not love God properly, you will be punished in some way. Here "love" is used as reward and punishment, to ignite ambition and fear.

The softer, more appealing, "humane" version that Christ loves and will protect and forgive whosoever believes in him gave rise to a power transition that eventually put Christianity in ascendance. But this softening was only made possible through Christ's bloody sacrifice, by God ordaining and presiding over the acts of his only son being cruelly tortured and murdered. (This to show his own and his son's great love for humanity?) Thus love, cruelty, and violence are intertwined with sacrifice and enshrined as a sacred myth at the core of Christianity—Christ died horribly to save us from our sins. It is no accident that Catholicism promotes pain through forced motherhood, overpopulation, institutionalized pederasty, and fighting the use of condoms for AIDS. Too much of the world is still in the thrall of medieval, power-hungry, "pain institutions" successfully masquerading under the lofty language of love.

Ideals of love are used by those in control to promote and justify the self-sacrifice of individuals by placing "sacrifice" at the apex of patriotism and the sacred. Love for king or country is proved by being willing to die or kill for their sake. In the name of love we may be required to kill people we do not personally know or be killed. War heroes receive the highest accolades for patriotism, but if we criticize our country for not upholding its ideals we are often accused of not loving our country properly. This can be perpetuated because of the power of the mere word "love"—and because people want to associate it with something grand, like a king or a war.

The nature of being a bonding social animal is double-edged, as relationships are inherently a source of our greatest joys and deepest sorrows. Though a life without love is barren, love that starts with a heavenly soar can later make life miserable. Some think love alone could solve all problems—if only everyone could "Love thy neighbor as thyself." This and other promises that love is the answer have been around for thousands of years. But ideals of universal or even "brotherly" love have not even succeeded in making love last between brothers and in many marriages, let alone mitigated global hatred, violence, and warfare. Families both mirror and help create the world, displaying great extremes from supportive, caring nurturance to hatred, abuse, and violence. If there is an inbuilt genetic capacity to connect, why are many people having such great difficulty in doing so?

Love in intimacy between adults is what most of us are concerned about as adults, isn't it? When love comes, the rush of it, the bloom of it, it's a tremendous energy. When it leaves, I look for it again. I want to cultivate it, to keep it by my side always, to ensure that it will be with me tomorrow and next year, my whole life.

Although examining love could risk missing its essence, not to do so risks being blindsided by the layers of cultural conditioning and unrealistic sentimentality that coat it. Love, which feels like the simplest, most basic, vital experience, becomes complicated because it is not an isolated event unobstructed by concepts or its social context. Unfortunately, conflict and mistrust between the sexes, generating loneliness, have been inherited and passed on by how love has been idealized and institutionalized. It is conceptualized in ways that impact the ongoing nature of the experience. If ideals about love are unlivable, this distorts emotions and blocks love's potential by creating unreal expectations of self and others, pointing people down the wrong path. Traditional worldviews that feed our desires and create unrealistic hopes present unconditional love as the pinnacle of love. The concept permeates our culture and fantasies and is described in many ways, which boil down to love as total, unwavering acceptance. This can apply to mates, parents, children, and many other relationships.

These ideals float in the culture and condition the way people deal with love—especially in intimacy, romance, and the family. So I think I should feel love for my mate, children, and parents all the time and that they should do the same. But isn't that a fantasy? Doesn't it create huge pressure and conflict? "All the time" is just another product of thought, just another image to try to live up to—or to make one feel guilty and inadequate when one can't. There is no such thing as "all the time." The concept or idea of all the time that plays such a large part in most of our lives does not exist outside the mind creating it. The feelings of love come and go in any relationship. We want these feelings to always be there, but "forever" and "always" are ideas, products of thought.

The actual experiencing of the intensity of love only occurs in a living moment, no matter how long or short that moment may be. As it's happening, it can feel timeless and unconditional, without boundaries or emotional constraints.

But we also live in time, and timeless moments eventually pass. Once memory and expectation are part of the mix, a continuity occurs. Saying "I love you" means more than "I'm feeling these emotions now, and that's it." It has future implications that suggest some continuity's in time. If the relationship is mutually enhancing, as people move through time together their cherished timeless moments become part of memory, creating a historical continuity where love can keep recurring, growing, and deepening. Love then takes on a broader meaning than merely feeling it in the moment, just as happiness is more than feeling good in the moment; for both imply a basic ground of satisfaction that spans time. And both contain ups and downs and cycles within that time span. Though the actual feelings do come and go in the present, they filter into and are reflected in the temporal dimension of one's life in such a way that love is not merely a momentary occurrence. Another meaning of love includes knowing deeply, admiring, and valuing someone, as well as the memories of experiencing timeless love together and the realistic expectation of its reoccurrence. So it is within the scope of love's many meanings to say, "They loved each other throughout their lives."

Although the experience of love can feel timeless, without conditions, what is often ignored is that the experience only occurs in a given situation, which is very much in time and needs nourishing conditions for its continuance—a major one being spending meaningful time together. People do not experience a timeless moment in a bubble; they come to it with a past and with hopes and expectations for the future. Wanting the feeling of love to continue, fearing its loss, or being disappointed by a lack of reciprocity all inoculate time into a timeless moment, thus changing it. So timeless love is embedded in time. The experience is basic, primary. While in its spell questions of its nature do not arise; but the concept of timeless love is drenched with future considerations wherein one expects to love or be loved timelessly all the time. This confusion lies at the heart of the concept of unconditional love. The question is: can timeless love flourish through time? Love when experienced feels new; to keep recurring, the conditions must also foster newness.

When we're young and open, love may come in a rush of energy. Without a lot of encrusted habits, there's newness, freshness. Some people move from one relationship to another in an attempt to recapture that flash of newness. In this ongoing serial courtship scenario the mechanical push-pull elements of conquest keep repeating, while separations bring pain and a loss of innocence. Although each new beginning generates energy and interest for a while, the pattern eventually gets old and predictable, losing its initial delights.

We want those poignant, breathless, timeless moments as well as the continuity and security of having our loved ones around. Can one have both? Can love be cultivated? If so, how do I go about it? Parental love has its own unique biological and social expression, but love between equals does not flower easily when institutionalized, and there are no formulas for creating it. Since the conditions that keep the valence for love open change through time, the key is maintaining a foundation that allows love to keep regenerating—a foundation that itself changes, as do the people involved. One's life has shifting conditions that can open or close boundaries, that can build or erode trust. The context is not merely personal but includes the social—its values and whether there are social supports for parents and families, for example.

Ongoing relationships are like gardens: favorable conditions are needed to allow love to root, grow, and blossom. A love relationship is a life setting where the intense feelings and energy of love wax and wane as people change and grow both separately and together. Like a garden needs to be weeded, so the conditions for love need to be protected for love to continue to flower. Since knowing what erodes love helps prevent erosion, let's look at what obstructs and dampens it. Just as awareness comes not from trying to be more aware or match an image of it, but from seeing your subjective filters and how you block it, so too love does not come from trying to force it or match ideas of it. As social animals our inbuilt capacity to love and care is either thwarted or fostered by how we conceive of these qualities and how awarely we approach them over time.

As we've been discussing, a great cause of love's all-too-prevalent erosion is our ideas of what it is and should be. Over the centuries, love has been highly conceptualized and idealized by religions promoting self-renunciation as the pinnacle of virtue and spirituality. The problem with all spiritual notions of pure love is that they are one-sided abstractions that leave out the relational realities of love. This includes what occurs in time. Although love for each other may abide within each person as an ongoing ground of connection, in daily life the special experiences of merging with total absorption come and go as other priorities take one's attention. But true love is portrayed as unwavering, and so not subject to the fluctuations of time. Although love itself in a timeless moment seems not to make any demands at all, behind what appears to be total acceptance is a hidden desire for these powerfully transporting feelings to continue. So even here "pure" love is not quite as pure as it would seem—if by purity one means that the experience does not generate a desire for more, for attachment, or the fear of loss.

Love is often presented as pure giving without asking for a return, but joy is self-enhancing, which is a return. If giving did not give the giver joy or personal satisfaction, there would be far less of it. The confusions come from comparing timeless moments of what feels like pure love with no demands, with love as a living process that moves through time with mutual benefit and healthy reciprocity. This view of purity as devoid of ego and reciprocity stems from a false and harmful worldview dichotomy between love and self-gratification, altruism and self-centeredness, that unrealistically pits self-enhancement against care for others. This false polarization comes from villainizing ego and self-centeredness. Traditional spiritual worldviews mistakenly place egotism and altruism on opposite ends of a continuum as if they were mutually exclusive—so the more egoistic one is, supposedly the less altruistic, and vice versa. But they are not opposites isolated from and antagonistic to each other; on the contrary, they are embedded and often contained in each other.

Do I love you because you're so wonderful and special—because you're you; or do I love you because you ignite such powerful, exciting emotions in me? In your own life you can see that the answer is of course both, for they go together. The need to experience love is centered in the self ("self-centered") and is for the self, yet this need can only be met by breaking out of self-centeredness. Love is only fulfilling when I break out of myself and connect with you—by breaking through the boundaries of the very self that needs it. And that experience in turn feeds the self, so much so that one becomes attached to who or whatever brings it about. The seeming paradox is that to satisfy me, I have to break out of me. These conundrums are contrived, as love only comes when one cares about something other than oneself, and caring for others is self-fulfilling. Love is actually embedded in these two aspects of living—self-gratification and care or love for others. Part of the miracle of love is that loving others is inherently self-fulfilling. Fortunately for the world, love cannot be made to fit into rigid polarizing categories of selfless/self-centered, unconditional/conditional, altruistic/egotistic—and trying to do so distorts emotions and warps intimacy within entire cultures. This destructive concept of selfless love is at the root of the ideal of total acceptance, without expectations or demands, that wreaks so much havoc with modern couples.

The ideals of true love as timeless, egoless, and unchanging come from worldviews that make the unity of all existence the basic reality, with separation, boundaries, ego, and the like illusory or secondary at best. In these mystical worldviews, ego is made love's enemy. Collapsing everything into a basic timeless unity leaves little room for choice or for love to be self-enhancing—or evolving. Instead the spiritual ideal of loving unconditionally slides into concepts of "universal love" for all humanity, meaning loving everyone equally, without preference. But to love everyone and prefer no one is actually not to love at all. Love is a special relationship involving special attention. Attention is always selective, for us and for those we love.

A more realistic worldview that acknowledges the connection between individuation and merging, the spiritual and the mundane, self-gratification and giving, radically alters the basic context in which love occurs and what love in relationship means. Adding time and other realities of worldly existence and daily life to the picture changes everything. {This will become clearer when concepts of time within different worldviews and their implications are discussed in the Time commentary.} Once a love relationship is enmeshed in all the concerns, responsibilities, and chores of daily living, work, and child-rearing, many factors come into play. If love were always selfless, it could (theoretically at least) always be there, for what could disturb it? But selfless ideals do not work in relationships over time because the wants and needs of each person must be part of the total picture. Long-term relationships need mutuality and malleable boundaries for trust, which is essential for passion to keep rekindling.

Many spiritual worldviews that villainize ego and preach selfless love incongruently also preach detachment, but attachment is inherent in love and bonding. Instead of more detachment, humanity needs better forms of attachment. Since intimacy brings vulnerability to loss and pain, we need to learn to attach better to minimize its risks and problems. Although detaching from ego and desire is presented as more selfless, it is actually geared at protecting the self. Its purpose is to avoid suffering; as a defense mechanism it attempts to control negative emotions through cutting off life. Given that detachment and love are mutually exclusive, couples that bond believing that non-attachment is the path to spirituality have a predictably hard time—just one of many examples where detachment actually increases suffering through closing down to life. Detachment can be cultivated, but it is not selective; so once detached, many aspects of living other than pain, including love and care, are dampened or cut off. The goal of detachment cannot offer viable guidelines for attaching, which requires taking ego dynamics and two or more non-detached selves into account.

The ideal of detachment is part of an unlivable system of values that, like all unlivable ideals, breeds behavior that is the opposite of the ideals. Such discrepancies as supposedly detached gurus assiduously building fortunes are often mystified as "paradoxes" to defend hypocritical behavior. Detachment is entirely dysfunctional as a framework for intimacy. Claims are made that detachment enhances relationships, but valuing detachment amounts to valuing autonomy over interdependence and mutuality. If you care about anyone, you're attached to what happens to them; loving them makes the attachment all the stronger. Relationships that do not acknowledge, honor, and realize the inevitability of attachments do not work.

Self-denying concepts are traps hindering mutuality that also cage spontaneity, authenticity, and discovery. They inhibit communicating awarely and honestly about complex or controversial issues such as decision-making and power, and so-called negative feelings—anger, fear, mistrust, resentment. The latter and self-interest are seen as impure intrusions of ego, as are expectations and demands, which lead to that most dreaded phenomenon—control. Wanting some balance between getting and giving is seen as sullying love with crass egotistical concerns. "Measuring" is likewise disparaged, as is the desire for more appreciation or acknowledgement; yet dissatisfaction can be an important feedback of felt imbalance. It's almost a guarantee that the one measuring is "getting" less and the one disparaging it getting more—just like the one who resists change, who is happier with "the way things are," is usually the one with the most power in the relationship.

A new foundation for love is needed that allows people to take the self, specifically oneself, into account as part of the total picture—one that emphasizes fairness and balance instead of holding selflessness as more spiritual. As social animals interdependent for our very survival, we need each other in countless different ways and degrees. Whether or not intimacy is a universal human need, it is essential for a non-role-bound relationship to mature in ways that allow love to continue to flower. One of intimacy's great needs is to be seen, appreciated, and trusted by loved ones. These elements, especially trust, only occur as people get to know each other over time. So once again we see how time creates the background that can allow love's timeless moments to return.

Intimate relationships are a miniature universe containing all the things we've been looking at: beliefs, fears, desires, images, time, attachments. Through experiencing and exploring these things together over time, people evolve, transforming each other in enriching, interesting, and unpredictable ways. Real intimacy involves sharing the deeper parts of oneself. However, opening boundaries brings vulnerability, along with a greater need for connecting and trust. If there's need, then of course desire, fear, hope, and expectations that could lead to demands are there, too. You can watch it in yourself and in your life.

Although powerful, love, especially new love, can also be fragile. The more I fear losing it and try to keep it safe and unchanging, the more I risk smothering it. Love is an energy with a life of its own, not an emotion or experience you can control, making it come and go at will. Love has an uncontrollable side that is wild, flourishing in freedom and newness. Fear makes people try to hold onto love through promises. If I love you I ordinarily want and even need you to feel the same. Knowing that things can change, I may be afraid you'll leave me, or that our love may dim, or that you'll die before me—love can bring many fears. I'm not suggesting that any of this should or shouldn't be. I'm just looking at how fear intertwines with relationships and what often comes from that. Seeing the nature of all this brings an awareness that can prevent mechanical responses to fear.

Expectations are normal and necessary in life and relationships to keep the world running smoothly. They're like beliefs: one could not function, plan, or coordinate without them—that's how the brain works. Many expectations are beliefs based on past occurrences and habits that repeat with predictability. We expect the sun to reappear and countless other things. In relationships it's healthy to expect to be treated with decency and integrity, and wise to insist on it. Likewise, baseline expectations in intimacy are natural concerns that protect the context of love, such as being treated with fairness, care, and consideration—as opposed to expecting always to get what you want, to have all needs met, or never be hurt.

Some expectations are linked to reciprocity, which is essential in relationships. Unfair imbalances over time cause resentment, eroding trust and passion. Reciprocity and balance also protect the foundation for love. So ordinarily love does involve expectations, with an implicit need and possibly a hidden demand for some type of reciprocal behavior. If you say you love me, I expect attention from you. If you give me enough attention, well and good; if you don't, I feel unloved or insecure. If you look at another person, I may become jealous. In much of relationship there is an often-hidden *quid pro quo* aspect, which in intimacy is masked by the aura of sentimentality surrounding it. In some ways it's like a reciprocal trade agreement, mostly unsaid but expected. You do this for me, and I'll do that for you—give you attention, company, help, sex, and so forth. If you are my child, I also expect certain kinds of behavior; if I don't get it, I may withhold acceptance and approval. Although people usually do not like to look at this aspect of intimacy because it seems to sully its spontaneity and emotional purity, if not acknowledged and dealt with, it often erodes love. I'm not implying that anything is wrong with this—on the contrary, people have a healthy inbuilt desire for fairness and balance.

The problem is that love is overlaid with unrealistic selfless images and sentimentality that make taking oneself into account and striving for balance seem lowly and crass—especially to the one getting his or her way—making it harder to monitor and correct unfairness. Unmet expectations can escalate, turning into demands. Demands apply more pressure, which moves the relationship into a more precarious place, since it's harder to want to accommodate peremptory or angry demands. People may try to avoid this by offering to make a deal: "Make no demands on me and I'll make none on you." But expecting another or yourself to never make demands is a set-up that can leave people feeling angry or even betrayed.

Love blooms when not laden with unconscious, role-bound habits and expectations that make people feel taken for granted and unappreciated. Traditionally the institution of marriage controlled behavior through roles, idealistic vows, and laws. Its contractual nature created great social pressure to live up to the vows. In the sixties, ideals of freedom and autonomy within the countercultural civil rights, women's, political, and human potential movements, and the sexual revolution, brought reactions against constrictive roles and expectations—especially marriage and sex roles. Consequently, in the belief that people in love shouldn't control each other, many modern relationships operate out of an overall reaction against demands, which are viewed as a form of control. Combining democratic ideals of freedom with spiritual ideals of selfless love has perpetuated a cultural climate that continues to stigmatize demands and control, and often even expectations.

But trying to live up to the image that real love makes no demands creates enormous internal conflict because it's impossible to have intimacy without expectations. Expectations are neither right nor wrong—it all depends on the situation. Having some expectations met is essential for trust. Although demands can stifle love, so can refusing to honor a need for something important that is lacking. The fact is that we do have certain expectations in relationship and sometimes do make demands, especially with those who affect us the most. Since no formulas can deal with life's complexities, it's all in the awareness of how expectations and demands work—how they can either drive people apart or be integral to keeping them together. The really interesting thing is not to try to change or do away with anything, but rather to see how it all works; to see exactly how expectations and demands affect your relationships and when they are or are not appropriate. Then from the seeing of it, a movement can come that brings more real connection. Seeing how relationships actually work and the effects of what you do, as you are doing it, brings movement.

So I begin to live with my expectations and fears. I learn to see them in my relationships, in how I move with my mate, my children, and my parents. Demands are not only in the other person; they're in me, in my concepts of love and reciprocity. I listen to the sound of my voice, the demands I subtly make, and the ones subtly made of me. I see how my family life is full of role-bound and habitual, taken-for-granted demands that remove me from living and people from each other. To see it is to learn how you and I work inside ourselves and with those we're close to. If I observe how the whole thing works, if I learn about the nature of how we actually deal with others, the seeing itself brings forth a movement away from the mechanical conditionings of my genes and the past.

If I ask whether you value openness in intimacy, most of you would say yes, wouldn't you? If I asked how many of you believe that people shouldn't try to control each other, once again you would probably say yes, right? Because these two values each sound right, it's not immediately obvious that they don't work in tandem with each other. But they are in a sense contradictory and mutually exclusive—and therein lies the source of many relational problems. Valuing both of these things together in intimacy is crazy-making. Here's why:

Love opens up boundaries, especially when accompanied by sexuality. Most of us are unavoidably concerned with how we feel. When boundaries open, another person (maybe your child, your lover, a dear friend) can and does affect how you feel. In fact, the more truly open you are to someone, the more you care about them, the more they affect you. You know how much harder it is to feel good if your child is feeling bad and how you delight in their happiness. To the extent that a person affects the way you feel, you have a preference about what they do, how they feel, and a vested interest in how they behave—particularly toward you. Because love brings preferences and a desire to influence and protect loved ones, it's here that control comes in, often not consciously. An anti-control cultural context only makes it more covert and unaware, because it puts control and the fear of it in the mix of relations in a non-conscious way. Also, it's usually easier to see how we are controlled than how we control others.

Attempting to influence and control others is part of being human, whether for self-protection or to get one's way. (Either could involve thinking something is right or fair, less-than-benign purposes, or simply not wanting to be bothered.) The two main stances toward control are that one has a right to control or a right not to be controlled.

Since control is inevitable, especially in intimacy, and there are no formulas, the question then becomes: how best to deal with it?

This desire to control is not unique to relationships. Because people have a natural desire to maintain some control over how they feel and the direction of their lives, trying to control and manipulate the environment for one's own needs and purposes is a universal human trait. To be open to a person, the world, whatever, is to be affected by it, which means that one's feelings are somewhat out of one's control. Feelings are affected and to some degree controlled by what comes in from the surrounding world, whether welcome or not—all the more so if one's boundaries are open through empathy and care. To the extent that one is controlled by external factors, one also wants to control how, and how much, this occurs.

Reactions in the sixties against traditional and authoritarian roles ushered in an ongoing cultural "anti-control" phase in intimacy. But rejecting rules within traditional roles giving the "right" to control others does not make control disappear. This illustrates how a polarized negation (anti-control) is a reaction that often displays the very thing being reacted against. Reaction to the old still contains the old, because the old is defining it. Reactive opposition contains the same form in reverse, like a mirror or Escher image. If I react against my conditioning by doing what I think is its opposite, this is just another way in which conditioning mechanically manifests. (If I try to stop you from controlling me, I'm trying to control you.) Reactions are polarizations against the past shaped by the past that cause further reactions. A different way of doing things does not come through negating the old, but rather from seeing its nature and implications clearly. To see when our conditioning is inappropriate in the world now, including aspects of our genetic conditioning, to see this clearly without reacting against or negating it opens possibilities for a new response, a more appropriate action.

Control, power, and self-centeredness are usually justified by rights, rules, and the social climate. When accepted, roles minimize conflict by prescribing behavior and designating spheres of power. Sometimes tacit or unconscious cultural assumptions around rights justify control (related to racism, sexism, ageism), as in "I get to decide where we live because I make more money." Addressing control is a historically new challenge that emerged as democratic and anti-sexist values infiltrated private life, especially in any long-term relationship where roles are fluid. It's inevitable that at some point control issues arise (what to do, and who gets their way and how) and struggles around priorities and values. Since intimacy necessarily gives each person some power to move the other, avoiding addressing the realities of control ensures that control will go underground. Since power and control are a part of life, what matters is how one utilizes them—unconsciously, surreptitiously, or awarely, with as much transparency as possible. If people deal with control awarely, objectively, and fairly as adults, they can find effective methods that minimize conflict and hassle.

Control varies across a spectrum, with attempts to influence and persuade and ultimatums and threats at the extremes, and a wide variety of approaches in between, such as reinforcement and manipulation through reward and punishment, approval and disapproval, pressure, outright demands, etc. Like love and power, control has been highly conceptualized—pejoratively. This in itself is the source of much unnecessary difficulty. Even more disparaged than control, manipulation is associated with secrecy, premeditated deceit, and using others without their best interests at heart—but this need not be true. Those with less power—children, underlings, and historically often women—have to influence those with more power underhandedly (or using reverse psychology) to have some say in their lives.

Control, self-centeredness, and power in intimacy are very uncomfortable to look at or even acknowledge, largely because traditional morality makes people feel guilty for being self-centered, disparaging it as "selfish." "True love" is said never to control, that control has no place in love, that real love wants only the other's happiness. This one-sided view of a relationship is fertile ground for fostering imbalances and potentially even abuse. It's actually just the opposite environment that can allow love to flourish over time.

Although self-centeredness is at the core of many problems, it is also at the core of individuation, creativity, and the need to express whatever uniqueness we possess. As we've been discussing, many things in our nature are double-edged, with traditional values making one side into pejoratives instead of viewing these aspects of human nature somewhat objectively and with acceptance. This makes it impossible to understand and utilize the total package of what we are wisely, by seeing and using the positive side of maligned traits. Without denying that people of course can and do operate for the good of others, there is a self-centered core in all of us that tends to prioritize our own feelings. (I may greatly empathize with your toothache, but it doesn't feel like my toothache.) This is one reason why the prevalent ideal that people should not control each other is unlivable—it just doesn't work. Worth repeating: to the degree that I'm open to you, you can affect the way I feel; and I'd rather you made me feel good than bad, so I do try to move you in that direction.

After the first blush of connection, that early period of grace when love is easy and fresh, most relationships move into a more challenging phase of addressing issues of power and the realities of self-centeredness. One attraction of the new is that most problems in intimacy occur over time. When people eventually start jockeying for some control over their lives and what they want, this ushers in a new phase. Traditional ideals, roles, and anti-control beliefs prevent dealing with this phase openly and awarely. This is when anti-control ideals often are unconsciously used to control.

A better framework than pitting two supposedly autonomous individuals against each other, each fearing being controlled, is to recognize that a love relation over time has three elements that need to be considered—what's good for oneself, the other, and the relationship. Since each element has to be taken into account (not always or necessarily at the same time), part of the dance of relationship through time is "Who do I put first, me or you—or us (our relationship)?" The mistake is in viewing both love and control as located only in the individuals, instead of seeing that intimacy creates an interdependent relational system that is not totally in the control of either individual, where each tries to exert some control to get their needs or wants met. {See the chapter "Love and Control" in *The Guru Papers*.}

A typical place where couples get stuck is through trying to change each other, or resisting it. One person says, "If you really loved me, you'd try to please me more and do some of what I want." The other replies, "If you really loved me, you'd love and accept me the way I am, as I do you." The first retorts, "You only accept me because I accommodate you so much. But now that I'm trying to get some of my needs met, you are not really accepting me as I am. You want me to change the part of me that wants you to change, so in fact we now both want each other to change." Threatening to withdraw unless someone stops making demands is likewise a demand and an attempt at control. Not controlling is really another unlivable ideal because no one has absolute control over how open one is at any moment, and also because the future is essentially uncertain. Wanting to be loved for who one is and to love that way in return is understandable. Complete acceptance, either given or received, creates an emotional bath whose waters are compelling. But wanting or expecting total acceptance to be totally there all the time is to put futures on an experience that only occurs in the living present.

The degree of fear within relationships depends on how secure one feels and how secure the relationship actually is. If the relationship is not balanced, the person who loves or wants more will be insecure and easily threatened; while if both people are equally open, the fear is naturally less. Fear is a danger in love that can become a self-fulfilling prophecy. If I fear losing someone, I might try to tighten the reins of control through demands, clinging, or becoming obsessed with worry, which often drives the other away. Some relationships are built around fear with contracts, promises, and structures to fortify against change.

Contracts are an attempt to perpetuate one's present state through promises locked in by law to offer some security. Marriage is such a contract that is many people's projection of the sepreme commitment. The expectation for love and sexual fulfillment in marriage is fairly recent, dating from the eighteenth century. The shift in the middle class from forced marriages arranged by fathers for material benefit, to children being free to choose their mate, was a revolutionary new personal freedom. People began to marry for love, but with marriages and sexuality being highly structured and role-bound (including husbands having extra-marital sex and the lack of provision for divorce), couples ended up settling for comfort, convenience, and companionship—if they were fortunate. Companionate marriages are still prevalent today in those that don't end in separation, and in older generations.

The institution of marriage was never originally intended to be about love or sexual fulfillment. Romance and passion were often viewed as an unpredictable threat from outside because they did not usually exist inside. The contemporary desire for love, sex, and individuation to be part of marriage was whetted in the sixties. The challenge is how to make marriage something it was never meant to be—passionate, sexual, and evolving through time.

Marriage was constructed around social, financial, territorial, power, and inheritance issues, as well as protection for children. That it was not created for passion among equals is an understatement. Until quite recently with the rise of divorce, it was almost impossible to get out of. Even now when so many marriages don't last, it does offer social protection and its own kind of status. There are many legitimate reasons for getting married, including social and financial pressures and rewards and often punishments for not doing it. Marriage is still conceived of as the ultimate in commitment—or at least the closest thing to it. And for modern people here is where the danger lies. This is pointed out not to try to turn people against marriage but rather to help avoid its "pitfalls." Marriage is one of the oldest institutions and archetypes and has within it roles, rules, expectations, implicit feelings of ownership, contracts, and lifelong promises to remain certain ways. This leaves open the real potential of feelings of betrayal that are very hard to counter. Modern people often create their own vows to make marriage their own and to counter its archaic aspects. But this does not take into account the insidious power of the marriage archetype, not only how one thinks of marriage, including conscious and unconscious expectations, but also how others and society think of it and treat you accordingly.

Marriage is a contract with vast legal and social implications. The danger is that any contract for the stability of emotions is based on projections of future feelings, with a promise to continue to feel the way you do now. But no one can know for sure or totally control how they'll feel in the future. If promises of enduring passion lead people to take each other for granted, instead of ensuring and securing love as intended, promises can dull passion. As a cultural ritual, cementing coupling with such commitments can be a powerful experience. It can make you feel relaxed, secure, and loved—or complacent. A broken contract creates mistrust that is hard to heal and repair, for if an actual promise is broken, the sense of betrayal is much worse, especially if secrecy and lies are involved. So contracting for love is not a neutral or simple act—the contract itself has many ramifications that influence emotions in different ways at different times. Awareness can help navigate these waters.

Every society uses power and control to maintain continuity by ensuring that its structures, including structures of privilege, are passed on through generations. A cornerstone of all human relationships is the way that society structures power and control among men, women, and children. This is a pillar of society, at the root of the deepest psychic and gender conditioning. The family or kinship is the foundation of every social order. The very fabric of society is created by the public and private spheres of power and sex roles. How men and women mate and interact determines how wealth and power move across generations.

The so-called "battle of the sexes" with its age-old oppression and mistrust is partly a heritage of our dimorphic biology where men were physically more powerful and women needed men's protection (from other men). Out of these and other differences, men eventually created power hierarchies and made the rules, which included ownership of daughters and wives by free men of all classes. The way heterosexuality, the family, reproduction, and child-rearing were institutionalized into a separate, mostly isolated, private sphere with marriage and prescribed roles became the factory of "social reproduction" that reproduced people, family structures, social values, and psyches. This archaic "sexual order" dating back to the early kingships was essentially based on dividing the sexes into castes: female "reproducers" and male "producers." {The commentary on Freedom in Chapter 5 describes in more depth the sexual order—the way society organizes around gender, violence, production, and reproduction—and its global consequences.}

If a society can control people's sexuality, many other types of control follow from that. Since sexuality and passion have a wild, unpredictable side, civilizations attempted to preserve class and inheritance lines through controlling sexual behavior. Men's progeny were separated into legitimate and illegitimate offspring by creating two female castes—wives-as-property (legitimate reproducers) and non-wives, usually prostitutes of one kind or another and slaves. Laws gave husbands the right to kill adulterous wives and disobedient children. Ancient power divisions and gender imbalances still prevail throughout the world in differing degrees. This results in tension and confusion in the private domains of intimacy and identity. The dysfunctions between the genders are a significant part of the overall global crisis.

The social function of religion is to put forth unchallengeable values that conserve the social power structure. This historically involved reinforcing male power privileges and tightly controlling female sexuality, as women are the bearers of bloodlines. So demands, expectations, and taboos are part of traditional "family values" and roles. These values have been authoritarian, linking honor with duty, loyalty, and obedience. Social control was internalized through religious ideals of selfless love (mainly applying to females) being infused into the family. Family members are expected to stay open to each other "no matter what," unconditionally—a potential recipe for abuse.

Historically, the selfless/self-centered dichotomy splits differently between men and women, reflecting overall male dominance. Selfless ideals are held up for women to emulate through self-sacrifice within the family to husband and children. The self-sacrificing, devoted, supposed-to-be unconditionally loving mother is the epitome of the ideal of pure (selfless) love, without expectations, demands, or conditions. A mother's love for a child can come the closest to unconditional love, but that is not always beneficial over the long term, as this can disrupt the couple and give the child an unreal view of how the world and love work. Daughters were conditioned to put others first and feel guilty for not being selfless enough, while sons were typically conditioned to associate love with being served by a woman—a conditioning still unconsciously operative in many men today, causing resentment and mistrust in women.

Portraying unconditional love as love beyond measure or measurement makes it a standard against which other expressions of love are measured. So love that does not measure becomes the measure of love.

Men were conditioned to either rule or submit, with competing in the niches of the power hierarchies deemed acceptable. Men's historical dominance gave them permission to be overtly self-centered (especially in their private kingdom, the family) with the "male ego" still being prominent in world and private affairs. Man's role as lord and protector of "his" family included the expectation that he would be competitive, aggressive, and violent, which gave him permission to be so. This fit and reinforced male genetic wiring and predilections. Men and women's feelings and behavior continue to reflect this deep, diverse social conditioning.

Thus powerful archetypes emanating from the antiquated sexual order are part of the global cultural landscape shaping us today. They handicap our potential for intimacy by creating a double standard and distorting our ability to communicate honestly and awarely. There's more than a grain of truth in the adage "All's fair in love and war." Men who are the pinnacle of integrity, standing behind their word with men, casually lie to women, particularly around love and sexuality. (Common statement from men: "I lie to her because I don't want to hurt her." From women: "He's such a child; I have to continually bolster his ego.") The sad fact is that many people and cultures are still developmentally locked into the old sexual order. By oppressing women and warping the male/female bond, this keeps both sexes dependent and childish—a way of being that our planet can no longer afford. An adult relationship requires awareness, fairness, and balance. This includes the relatively new realization that although men and women are not the same in all regards, each is better at some things; and we are certainly equal in intelligence, courage, and what really matters.

I've been emphasizing how different worldviews have different values; this is especially true in realms of intimacy and bonding. There are three main conflicting value systems in intimacy that are not consciously articulated and cause much confusion and strife. Most religions place priority on the continuance of the couple through marriage. Traditional marriage is an anti-evolutionary, no-growth model, because it sacrifices exploration and individuation for consistency and permanence.

The second value system is a reaction against the authoritarian roles, rules, power, and control of traditional marriage, made possible by birth control and the ability of women to earn a living wage. Birth control and the ensuing sexual revolution unhooked sexuality from morality—particularly for women, so that an unmarried woman could have sex and not be considered by most as a bad person. Here the values are freedom, the growth of the individual, and autonomy—whether married or not.

Still today, many conflicts within couples are actually between these two opposed sets of values. Both value systems are one-sided; both contain unconscious assumptions that create imbalances, expectations, and impossible ideals, which inevitably result in resentments, conflict, and guilt. Neither is realistic for these times.

Is there a way of loving that can include wanting change that does not make the other person wrong or feel unloved? Most of us want to be accepted as we are—don't you? Demands or expectations that we change are usually not very welcome. Yet relationships either become habit-bound and stagnate, or they grow, mature, and change over time, which only occurs when people evolve.

Although there is no absolute security in love or life, some relationships are more secure than others, and some things predictably lessen security. Security can come organically through deepening bonding over time. Some relationships become so entwined and seamless that they feel totally secure, barring tragedy or death. This kind of security is a deep bonding that does not come through promises or contracts. Trying to force it or committing to it prematurely or through pressure can be counter-productive and rife with pitfalls.

The structures that held people together in the past that came from rules and roles laid down by society and religion are breaking down. All this has made relationships both freer and more tenuous, less secure. A more flexible bonding is needed that fosters continuity without blocking growth. It would have to encourage feedback and change instead of being based on promises and contracts not to change.

A third value system that offers a more viable approach prioritizes both the individual and the relationship, rather than polarizing them or putting one above the other. Trust and commitment here come from a process of taking each other into account and working out conflicts with as much objectivity as possible. Doing so with integrity creates a more powerful bonding than contracts or specific promises of content.

Although humans manifest their sexual and bonding proclivities in a vast array of ways, we seem to be largely a coupling animal, given the right circumstances. Coupling occurs within the same gender, but this does not eliminate much of what we have been discussing. There is a human element that moves beyond gender differences.

People do attempt to influence and control each other. From an evolutionary point of view, our brain is set up to control whatever we can for our well-being and security, and for those we care about. Our heritage of authoritarian control, roles, and abuse has stigmatized words like "control" and "manipulation," but the fact is we are manipulative animals. Our evolutionary success comes from our capacity to get what we need from manipulating the environment. The use and extension of control through power hierarchy and technology without stop mechanisms is the problem, not control and power themselves.

Transformation comes from the interplay of control and surrender. Keeping an ongoing relationship turned-on and vital over time is related to the willingness to be transformed by each other. Fortunately, if approached with awareness, control has multi-faceted positive aspects—including making the other feel cared for. If control is acknowledged as an ingredient of intimacy as it is in life, it can be addressed, utilized, and even played with to the benefit of each person and the relationship. It's one way that people can move each other, opening up otherwise unimagined vistas. Letting someone influence and even change you can be a source of newness and creativity, leading to new experiences that can be transformative for oneself and the relationship. If my partner did not make it clear what she wanted from me and why, I would have missed many of the life-changing adventures and insights that have made me a significantly happier, more aware person. Changing each other, influencing through blending differences and wanting change, is a path to an ongoing transformation of the ground of love, which allows the experience of timeless love to keep recurring.

Love is always marked by a freshness, an innocence, no matter how young or old the relationship. Love itself is a miracle. The blessing of love, which is a renewal, comes when it moves beyond the old and the habit-bound that can destroy passion. The real issue in intimacy is maintaining a life that allows love to keep regenerating. For the flame of passion to stay alive through time, a relationship has to grow and renew itself. This occurs through each taking the other's needs into account and valuing an honest exploratory approach to differences. It is equally important to not let resentments build or accumulate, which means being open to hearing difficult feedback.

Relationships, not only intimate ones, are the evolutionary cauldron we live in. The world has become so intertwined that humanity needs to evolve socially. In order for me to truly love you, I must see you as clearly as possible; otherwise I'm not in touch with you. I must minimize whatever images of you I have and the filters I see you through, including the filters of my desires and judgments. To do this my lens must undergo continual polishing. I must be interested in inner clarity in order to see the changing livingness that is you.

Getting to know each other means being open to feedback and using the inevitable problems and concerns of being together as opportunities to grow instead of negations to defend against. I must see you as a being in process, as am I. Feedback from relationships helps clean the lens of subjective filters and is a direct way that people get to know each other and themselves. We all have expectations within relationships; some are met, some not. What's important is not which expectations are met but the process used to decide—whether it contains transparency, consideration, and fairness. If real trust is built, people can help move each other to have experiences that enrich their lives and bring more awareness to both lives. Here one plus one can equal far more than two.

Newness is part of keeping passion alive over time. The challenge and paradox of our time for intimacy is how to have continuity, a sense of realistic security, and the freedom to grow—without recreating the old cage or being stuck in an unrealistic reaction against it. This doesn't mean *laissez-faire* activity of doing whatever you want when you want to. True freedom involves responsibility, which means the ability to respond to the new in the other person. A new way of seeing and working with each other involves making conscious what's unconscious in relationships. A new glue based on awareness and the mutuality of mind that comes from evolving together can bring a powerful emotional and sexual connection. Passion and sexuality can grow over time through the aphrodisiacs of transformation and true communication, which is communion. Opening up to each other's deep reality and influence is a major potential source of growth for individuals and the world. Aware relationships are a crucible of evolution that can transform men, women, children, and societies.

Personal and especially intimate relations are our most important arena for displaying many of the issues that occur in the larger social and political arenas. They are the basic foundation where people do or do not learn how to appreciate and respect each other and the world around them. This is where the possibilities exist for love, care, and awareness to mature and grow—a prerequisite for social awareness. As we have seen, awareness does not come from trying to be aware but rather from seeing where you are not. Love does not come from trying to love, but from seeing what's blocking it, which can free it to emerge.

Many of us, perhaps especially the young, are pioneers as new forms of intimacy are evolving. Love needed freeing from its traditional cages of unlivable ideals and concepts. Creativity and experimentation are possible now that traditional roles are losing their hold, but this has also brought more anxiety and much confusion. We all have fears, desires, hopes, and expectations for ourselves and those we care about. The issue is not how to get rid of them, but whether seeing them can bring more awareness into life and relationships. That is, can these feelings and their implications be seen with a clarity that allows you to step out of your habits and conditioning so that you meet the moment and your partner newly and freshly? This is where passion renews and becomes an unbeatable foundation for mature relations.

COMMENTARY:
Love and Care

Unlike earlier chapters with a more inward focus, this discussion about love moves into the social arena, where relationships play out the drama of what it is to be a human social animal. Humans share with other social mammals an ancient and sophisticated limbic brain with extraordinary capacities for emotional sensitivity and attunement—many yet undeveloped and unrecognized. Our exceptionality lies in being a thinking mammal whose sociability is greatly influenced by ideas and values. This chapter on love and intimacy contains revealing examples of how beliefs and values on core issues within different worldviews have implications and consequences that partly determine personal and social relations.

Traditional spiritual worldviews, both monotheistic and Eastern ones, create a destructive polarity between the spiritual and the mundane—which is tellingly often called the "profane"—and then trivialize any concern that they define as "non-spiritual." Unity worldviews, though professing to be non-dual, have a hidden duality between the spiritual and mundane, in which the "spiritual" is considered "more real" and of course superior, with no acknowledged interface between the two supposedly separate spheres.

In contrast, in *The Passionate Mind Revisited* the One and the Many, merging and individuation, unity and multiplicity (separation), are viewed as dialectically embedded in each other, with neither being more "real" nor valuable than the other, as they are not totally separate at all. Neither side of the apparent duality has ontological priority. (Ontology is the study of "being," or more simply "What, if anything, is really real?") From these disparities in worldviews, many differences flow—including the nature of love and loving, and what distinguishes loving from caring. As this chapter makes clear, our perspective acknowledges the reality and value of self, ego, time, expectations, attachment, desire, fear, demands, control, boundaries, measuring, self-protection, and other issues that come up between two or more selves living and loving together through time.

To say that unity worldviews do not effectively address the plurality of diverse, individuated selves or relationships between and among them—given that many consider the self and ego illusory—is an understatement. Because love is relational, involving more than one person, even though unity worldviews champion ideals of unity and love that sound good, in actuality they do not encompass the reality of the self or selves, nor the complex issues involved in separate selves connecting. Instead the unrealistic, dysfunctional guidelines put forth by a unity worldview mislead people, causing unnecessary havoc in an arena that in the modern world has become complex and potentially problematic in and of itself.

Worldviews are the source of values. Worldviews that negate the reality of the self, boundaries, separation, individuation, the importance of time, and thus change and evolution, cannot construct viable ideals or guidelines for relationships between two or more people, let alone for evolving, passionate ones. Unity worldviews that negate the value of attachment and desire claim to offer better values and a loftier concept of love—and therein lies the problem. They are too "lofty," supposedly on a higher, spiritual plane, above the crass, ego-involved, self-centered dramas that occupy so much of this imperfect world. A worldview that denigrates or trivializes this world and the self cannot help people live with their exigent circumstances. It points upward to an idealized sphere of being that is thought to be on a spiritual plane fundamentally different from the mundane existence where our lives play out. This makes people feel inadequate, as we inevitably fail to live up to such "high" ideals—because they are unlivable.

A disguised problem and "behavioral paradox" resulting from unlivable ideals of selflessness is that they are very self-absorbing and mostly about oneself. Do I love enough; have too much ego? Am I spiritual, detached, timeless, selfless enough; making enough spiritual progress? Do I (or my mate) love unconditionally? Sacralizing unconditional love puts conditions on love that it be unconditional and selfless, and so quantifies love by setting an ultimate standard by which people "should" measure themselves and their love. We know people who berate themselves and live in conflict because no matter how hard they try, they cannot open their hearts to the villains of the world—the Hitlers and Pol Pots. This is an example of the elevated (and impossible) "spiritual" ideal that if one were truly spiritually arrived one would love everyone and maybe everything.

Unity worldviews emphasize ideals of timelessness, selflessness, and detachment and tend in various ways to denigrate thought, which is said to create ego, artificial boundaries, and separation. So the apex of love is conceptualized as timeless, unconditional, without expectations or demands (self-less). Conditions of any sort are considered time-bound attachments of the self. The historic split between the spiritual and mundane is reflected in this simplistic polarization of selflessness and self-centeredness.

Traditional spiritual values have had thousands of years to "raise" and "improve" humanity and failed because living is not simply a relation between me and the cosmos, or between me and "God" or some conception of absolute being. Life is relationship—but mostly among things on Earth, between the self and others who are also individuated pieces of what existence manufactures, with real definable boundaries and different needs, agendas, and ways to express their uniqueness.

The "unconditional love paradigm" is unrealistic and detrimental, resulting in fairy-tale romantic myths and ideals. It is based on valuing detachment, for one is supposed to love and stay open no matter what, without attachment to one's own needs and desires, including self-protecting if necessary. But the fact is, if you do love or care about anything outside yourself, you really cannot be detached—for the more you care, the less detached you are. Care automatically brings attachment to what you care about—both to have it in your life, and for its well-being.

Maintaining a posture of equanimity, such that nothing that occurs can bother you, is an ultimate defense mechanism. If this is important to you, then by cutting yourself off you can to an extent detach from desires and everything else, except for one thing—the attachment to maintaining equanimity through detachment, or to the image of it.

Relations occur through time; and love in general occurs in relationships over time. The ideals of loving timelessly without expectation and being detached from input and outcomes are some of the essentially unlivable, anti-ego, "spiritual" ideals that brought humanity to where we are now—in urgent need of workable new values to guide deep changes. We live in a globalized world with seven billion other non-illusory selves where the outcomes of what we do will affect everything. We had better care about this non-illusory world and about what decisions we make—and be attached to making the right ones.

In dealing with our precarious and fragile position in the cosmos, a typical panacea sermonized is that love is the answer. What this generally means is that if only more people loved more, or better, more widely and deeply, more inclusively or universally, more selflessly and unconditionally, it would usher in a new state of global consciousness and our problems would be solved. Depending on the worldview, this "Love is the solution" litany is expressed and expected to manifest differently. In monotheism where separate individuals are acknowledged as real, the path to love is direct and personal, ideally spreading outward to others. "Everyone loving everyone" is the next level of consciousness that many are hoping for. In most Eastern religions, love, loving-kindness, and compassion result from attaining a state of ego-less unity, which bypasses specific individuals and opens one to universal love, so the ideal is to love everyone while being attached to no one, presumably without preference. None of this is new advice, as different religions and worldviews have recommended and preached the healing power of love and compassion for millennia. Yet here we are in a divisive world of poverty and degradation, fueled by anger and hatred that instigate violence, by power and greed indifferent to others' plights, with shortsighted carelessness toward those with "inferior" identities and toward the planet that sustains us.

We (the authors) do not underrate the wonder and power of love. However, love is not the solution to all our problems, especially in social and global arenas where the mix includes power and profit, politics and corporations, and competition/cooperation to gain and protect privileges. We experience love's energy as a miraculous and magical feeling that is essentially not in our control. It opens boundaries in a personal way, through some order of personal contact or connection between individuals or within groups. Although love is affected and sometimes distorted by concepts and fantasies, often to its detriment, it is not a cognitive experience or expression. Impossible to rigidly define, love is an emotion, an experience, an energy that permeates one's body and mind. It can have a cognitive component; mental and emotional alignment in couples can be a communion, an aphrodisiac, and a natural bond not based on promises. Mutuality of mind can open boundaries, cement friendships, unite groups, and be a glue in relationships.

Caring is a way to extend our emotional connective capacity beyond what is possible for love. Caring and loving, though not identical emotions, have much in common as they both open boundaries and make life worth living. Care is part of love; we care about whatever we love—but we can care about far more than we can love. Although love has the power to "move mountains," the mountains moved almost always involve another person or people. Love is anchored in the realm of personal interaction and cannot be cast out into the world like a wide net. People learn to love through being loved and loving, which narrows its scope, and doesn't always succeed. This makes it a vulnerable capacity whose full development and successful transmission are far from guaranteed.

One of course cares about oneself as a baseline and wants to feel good rather than bad. But as thinking social animals embedded within the fabric of existence, we experience caring as not exclusively about oneself or the things that directly affect one.

The capacities to empathize and imagine can more easily be extended into caring than can the emotion of love. Although partly emotional, care has a much larger cognitive element than love. The openings related to cognition come from understanding. This expansive aspect of care contains hope for humanity because care can be learned and taught by showing interconnections, implications, and consequences, along with the pain that carelessness can bring. We emphasize care for "humanizing" the social arena because it can range far and wide with the mind's awareness of what is occurring in the world, without needing direct personal contact.

Our minds and emotions have the capacity to rove into and care about other parts of existence that one is somehow connected with, or cognizant of, or fascinated by, or alarmed for, or even in awe of—like beauty or the cosmos itself. One can care about ideals and abstractions like freedom, justice, beauty, democracy, human rights. Through empathy, imagination, and values, one can care about global tangible events and issues, some of which affect us personally at some level, like humanity's survival and the chain of life, and some of which can be seemingly more remote, like the death of an unknown species, oppression, and abuse—child soldiers, the global abuse of women from honor killings, wife burnings, and forced clitoridectomy, to the sale of young girls into sexual slavery—all can be cared about. One cannot love these people whom one does not know, but one can care about what's happening to them and feel a visceral horror, deep concern, and a protective urge. Caring can spread to planet Earth, trees, oceans, cities, and also to people doing their utmost to live responsibly.

To live, we humans both use and care. We sometimes care about what and how we use, but often we use each other and our environment carelessly and even cruelly. The question humanity faces is whether we care enough about evolving into being aware caretakers to make the necessary changes in values and behavior to continue our evolutionary journey toward becoming a more adult species.

Is care as natural to human beings as the self-centeredness that the old moralities have long tried defeating to no avail? The old moralities have at times managed to control self-centeredness somewhat through guilt, fear, and the hopes and desires created by dangling coveted but unverifiable and even silly promises. Traditional spiritual ideals falsely polarize love and self-gratification, self and other by conceptualizing love as "pure" (self-less) and without conditions (that take oneself into account). The care promoted by these structures tie it to self-sacrifice, whose reward is the promise of personal salvation or some other type of spiritual reward.

If care is not natural to us but can only be forced through sacrifice to ideals, then we are lost. The fear of god's wrath, bad karma, hell, or a worse incarnation can no longer adequately curb the human capacity for destruction. The planet is in dire need of care-takers who do so not out of self-denial, which is the old paradigm, but rather out of care and natural intelligence that do not negate the self's concerns. To negate the validity and value of the self-gratifying aspects of care is to perpetuate the destructively polarizing and false separation that traditional spiritual worldviews make between self-centeredness and care.

If the capacity to care is an intrinsic part of who we are, then we do not have to force it in ourselves. What we must do instead is create situations that can nurture it and allow it to flower. It is here that we need an awareness of how our conditioning patterns, mechanical habits, and unconscious values and fears can create blind self-protectiveness that prevents involvement and care. The next stage of social evolution demands that we internalize a more global identity, exhibit more awareness of the nature and dynamics of power, along with more knowledge of the implications of our animal nature, and that we construct the pancultural values necessary for mitigating global impact. For humanity to grow up, we must realize that our future is in our hands and that saviors will not appear like the cavalry at the last minute.

We must somehow learn to care about treating each other better while becoming better caretakers of the Earth. We need to be emotionally attached to this world that some religions have written off as an illusion of one form or other, or as a cruel morality play specifically created to determine whether we are damned or saved. We need a sense of the preciousness and fragility of our planet and life itself. If life itself were infused with spirituality, it would be experienced with reverence and seen as the true miracle that it is. A shift in perspective that sees from a larger, more inclusive framework opens up the limitations of the narrower point of view and frees people to care for our planet and for others. From such shifts there is hope that the world can be made a place where human life with its strengths and frailties can flourish, and its uncaring and careless side will significantly lessen through a more enlightened awareness.

8. Time

Since time is all we have and how we use it is our lives, this chapter and especially the commentary are pivotal in understanding this book. Many of the ways in which this book differs from the original *Passionate Mind* revolve around the issue of time. The commentary puts forth our perspectives on time and worldviews and delineates the quandaries around time and timelessness, which helps illuminate other chapters. The talks in *The Passionate Mind* were part of a wave of teachings in the late sixties valuing Eastern perspectives on being in the now and showing the connection between time and thought—and how thought puts people out of the moment. Since then living in the "now" has become a mainstream concept, and a plethora of books urge people to be present by being out of time and thought.

We (the authors) find this view of time one-sided and misleading. Over the decades we have seen it sow confusion around the nature of time, thought, and what the "now" actually consists of, and all this points people in the wrong direction. The arrow of time is not just inwardly subjective as it relentlessly moves forward in the cosmos and in our lives. Our past is what got humanity into its current dilemmas, along with a failure to take future consequences into account. Since the past and future are part of the construction of any "now," trivializing them as mere creations of thought is not what the world needs at this crucial time.

This key chapter looks at two basic subjective ways of experiencing time, both having their place—being in time and being timeless. How worldviews conceptualize the nature of time and the values they prescribe for living in it are fundamental to how lives are led. How we think about time is an underlying meta-program at the core of the ways we live in it.

Most of us spend a great portion of our lives struggling with time. Either there isn't enough of it and we race around trying to accomplish self- or other-imposed goals; or for some, there's too much of it so that time hangs heavy on their hands. Like life itself, time is often taken for granted—until threatened or there seems to be too little of it. As we grow older, time gets increasingly precious and seems to race by faster and faster.

Normally people experience time as consisting of past, present, and future with a continuous yet indistinct flow connecting them. The movement of time from past to present to future seems elusive: although the present is all there is, the past and future are present in real ways within it. Here we are discussing the inward feeling of the movement of time. But where is the past? Where does it live in you? If I were to ask you to search for the past and find where it lives in you, where would you look? The important thing in these talks is to look at yourself, to see how you work. The past that lives in us lives in memory—in thought and in our cells, doesn't it? And what about the future? It too lives in thought. The future is thought in the present projecting past experiences into expectations, hopes, and fears—experiences I want or don't want to have.

People are capable of experiencing time in different ways. Our brains are constructed to deal with challenges that involve the future through a complex and sophisticated time-awareness, an example being child-rearing. With language expanding memory and causality, fears, anticipations, and goals all become part of the mix. We can escape the inner feeling of the passing of time through the subjective experience of time-lessness—another gift of our evolutionary heritage. So one can use time for becoming, doing, and accomplishing goals—or one can just be, without future orientations. We control or use time through memory and planning; we can also be immersed in whatever is presenting itself, temporarily unaware of past or future, which has a timeless quality that in those moments is agenda-free. Timeless "moments," which differ in duration, have something in common with the intense, effortless focus of a child at play.

Working toward goals generally involves controlling or being controlled by time, while surrendering to what the moment brings or to the immediacy of interest can move you to a more timeless state. Although "doing" (using time for accomplishment) and simply "being" often correlate with being in time and being timeless, this can be somewhat misleading, as you can be timelessly absorbed in whatever you're doing or thinking. When you're totally interested and immersed in whatever you're doing—which does not preclude thinking or cognition as part of it—then too you can lose the sense of time, and it feels timeless.

Being aware of the flow of time through schedules and obligations is using time for a goal, while timelessness subjectively seems to remove one from feeling that flow. Timelessness more easily allows what's happening in the living moment to move you. Using time accentuates control, and being timeless accentuates surrender, with life being an interplay between the two poles of trying to control what's going to happen and just letting it happen. Trying to capture and clarify the difference between the two states is somewhat elusive (as is the flow of time itself)—like trying to find the exact point where the past or future becomes the present. As subjective states they depend more on your relationship to what you're doing than on what you're doing itself.

Being in time and being timeless are two subjective states that are sometimes referred to as becoming and being, and also as doing and being—although the differences are not that clear-cut. So I'm using descriptions in trying to contrast being in time and being timeless rather than trying to lock them in as fixed concepts.

These two basic ways of experiencing living in time—being either in time (past, present, and future) or being timeless—each have their place. Since they're both human psychological states, each with a different internal feel, I describe them as subjective experiences of time to distinguish them from the ongoing, chronological time of the cosmos in which evolution unfolds. Chronological time relentlessly moves us through aging to different relations with ourselves and the world around us.

The experience of being timeless has many attractions, including a cessation of worry and a heightened consciousness of the livingness of the present moment. Many people have had moments of awe and what could be called ecstasy. What ecstasy really means is *ex-stasis*— being out of time. The ecstatic moments that occur when there is no experiencer separate from the experience are subjectively timeless. But timelessness is not necessarily pleasant—not if the now one is "in" or aware of is unpleasant or difficult.

For most of us, thought is an almost continual companion, keeping us company by silently talking to ourselves as a partially automatic process. It has taken most of us over so that it becomes much of who we think we are. Thinking is often presented as a hindrance to living because much of it is conditioned and habitual, which removes you from the actual livingness of the present. Some thoughts are loops that go 'round and 'round, mechanically repeating out of habit, fear, or unfulfilled desires, spinning in mental circles. In daily life aren't you usually thinking about what happened, or what you want to happen, or what might happen? To be either preoccupied by the past or projecting into the future, both of which we do so much, is to remove your attention from the immediacy and ongoing movement of what's happening within or around you. Sometimes this is desirable; sometimes it's mechanical. This separation, which lives in thought, changes the experience by coming between you and the experience. Techniques abound for quieting thought, which can be so appealing that many people spend a good deal of time practicing them.

When thought is quiet there can be a temporary suspension of personality, which includes ideas of who I am. Personality lives partly in thought and keeps recreating itself through remembering and projecting in time. What I am, in addition to my genetic foundation, is the accumulation of all my memories, thoughts, and experiences. To be living in memories and the anticipations they foster, as most of us do, can bind energy. It can be creative, but it can also shadow responding to the newness of life, to the immediacy of challenge, because I am not totally there. To see this relation between time and thought is really extraordinary and, as we saw with fear, it can be very freeing. When I am fully present in the moment, energy is unbound and I am more fully alive. It is through thought—which so often generates the sense of time—that I remove myself from the actual living moment. Why do I do this?

Again we go back to fear and pleasure, wanting and worrying, liking and disliking. Much thinking involves the pains and pleasures of memories and anticipations. Being in thought, thinking about what I'm going to do and remembering what I've done, sometimes gives me pleasure. I like thinking about the things I want to do and the experiences I've had, and how rich and full my life has been or will be. I also wonder about and regret mistakes I've made and worry about the future. Pain and sorrow come as I remember my failures and losses and realize what I will never get to do. I regret the could-haves, should-haves, and might-have-beens.

You may see this in your own life if you look. All this rumination removes you from the energy of the living moment. Time lives in that space between you and the ongoing now, bringing with it the potential dullness and even sorrow of missing life's unique moments. Being removed from what is dims the vitality of life, of perception and the vibrant connections within direct relationship. You can observe thought just as you can observe anything that's occurring, and catch yourself creating this separation.

Nothing is inherently wrong with being in thought—life is not necessarily more interesting or important than what you're thinking about. Throughout these talks we've been examining the aspects of thought that can be limiting and problematic, as well as thought's valuable functions. Thinking is part of living and experiencing. But so much thinking is repetitive, conditioned, and "on automatic." See it in yourself—see if that isn't true of your thinking. Catching your thoughts removing you increases awareness.

When looking at the relation between time and thought, one may want to escape it. I say, "I want to be in the now" or "I want ecstasy" (but all I really can want is an idea or the repeat of a memory). Or in seeing how the mechanical aspects of thought dull life, I may try to stop thinking to stop time. Here obviously is ambition—wanting a known or imagined state of being that I've either had or heard others wax eloquently about, or I fear not getting again. Much of what we've been discussing together—pleasure, fear, sorrow—lives in and creates the subjective experience of time. If I try to stop thinking I'm using effort to reach a future goal. As soon as there is a thinker trying to still thought out of an idea that it would bring more pleasure or more spirituality, the future crowds in. This puts me in conflict with what is because I'm desiring something else, which is neither fresh nor new. Those who become interested in experiencing something that feels eternal may try to do so by practices designed to stop thinking, which is endless. The eternal experienced at different moments is always new and cannot be captured by techniques or a return to previous experiences.

I'm not at all implying that being "in time" is somehow inferior, or that thought is a hindrance to living fully. Our complex relation to time allows us to extend into the past and future through thought—this is what makes us human. Looking at your own life, it's obvious that learning from the past and having some concept of the future are inherent parts of living. Our brains have evolved to think, analyze, and evaluate the present, past, and future, to remember, foresee, and plan. This has been our big evolutionary advantage—and will be again if we succeed in raising our capabilities to meet current needs. But however important thought is as a practical and creative tool, it can dominate our lives when it's not useful and inhibit other modes. Seeing when thought is appropriate and when it is not takes awareness.

I'm talking about a way of seeing, a way of being, an awareness that can observe what is (including thought) but is not thought itself. It's a type of meta-cognition that turns thought on itself to see how it works. Many of our ideas about the way things are or should be are highly conditioned. Preconceived ideas about how something is or ought to be can freeze spontaneity and creativity; then you're no longer living as an ongoing process. This includes how you see yourself, for when you say, "I know myself," you're talking of the past—not what you are, but what you were. Of course there's more than a thread of continuity between who you were and who you are and will be. But to believe you know yourself as a relatively unchanging entity removes you from ongoing learning and encourages a repeat of known patterns.

The structures and demands of modern living can make taking the time to be timeless seem difficult or a luxury to people struggling to cope with competing responsibilities and a tightly scheduled life. So the time to be on occasion timeless can ironically depend on thought valuing and prioritizing it enough to free the time to be timeless. In the modern world timeless moments are less familiar than in more traditional cultures, where long-term future orientations are not the major focus. An attraction of indigenous cultures is their different relation to time—their capacity to be more timeless, related to their minimal concern with progress and individual achievements.

The sixties motto "Be here now" was a valuable pointer to a different relation to time and way of being. The concept of simply "being" was a revelation in an achievement- and progress-oriented (thus time-bound) culture where simply "being" was considered "wasting time." Consequently, "being in the now" became for many an enduring prescription of an ideal way to be. Timeless periods are becoming ever more rare and alluring. Mounting fears and real and anticipated crises make timelessness even more attractive—and elusive. This is partly because in its popularized conception, the "now" is defined as being without thought, and ceasing to think about the future is a way to reduce fear.

Timelessness has long been touted by mystics as the gateway to spirituality and to "reality." Timeless, mystical experiences can reveal mind-altering ways of viewing existence outside normal consensus "reality" that can transform the way you see things afterward. The energy and intensity of these experiences is in a real sense beyond words and memory's normal grasp. Although such experiences may make one see the world in a new light, they do not give a pure, unfiltered lens into the nature of reality. They get interpreted through the worldview that the mind has, builds, or takes on to assimilate them. People bring their worldview to the experience, later interpreting the experience through it or whatever worldview they come to think better explains it. Christians have Christian mystical experiences; Buddhists have Buddhist ones; Hindus have Hindu ones, etc. Memories and interpretations of mystical experiences are constructions of the human mind and are potentially fallible, like all mental constructions. Since the sixties, in the West the ideal of being timeless all the time, or most of the time, or as much as you can, has become associated with being present to the living moment, what some call "presence." This ideal came out of worldviews that deem it more spiritual and promote it as the way to be. But even though this ideal has been somewhat secularized, it leaves out core parts of life and so is the source of conflict and confusion.

If being timeless or in the now becomes a goal, a sign that one is "high" or on a spiritual path, it becomes just another ambition, an idea about a preconceived state generating conflict with what I am now. Out of the confusion and conflict that such ideas bring, one may do prescribed practices to try to make oneself "live in the now," but that's only another formula, which is a form of conditioning that makes life more mechanical.

"Being in the now" as a formula for "the way to be" can also be used as an escape from unpleasantness in one's own life or the world, or used to justify ignoring future consequences. Under the guise of living in the now, one can bring more disorder and pain into the world. For example, one could carelessly and casually impregnate someone because "now" is really all that matters. Or I can feel superior to you who are caught in the "rat race," or dull myself with alcohol or drugs since all that counts is pleasure and immediate sensation. None of this has anything to do with aware living in the present, but rather with justifying uncaring, cavalier self-indulgence.

Although techniques that quiet surface thoughts can bring the feeling of timelessness, the question is when and how to use them, and whether they are furthering your life or serving as an avoidance, an escape from life's frustrations. Only you can answer this. Many people find such techniques a welcome antidote to a stressful life; others eventually find them a burden—one more thing they feel they should do because it's thought to be cumulatively "good for them." (We'll go into the benefits of stilling thought and the double-edged nature of techniques when we discuss meditation.)

Techniques to quiet thought can serve a valuable function in modern life by counteracting some of the great imbalances of a harried work and consumer culture that promotes scheduled lives and endless desires. This culture depends on people being driven to continually accomplish by a puritanical work ethic, which then makes them want to reward themselves for their efforts by buying things.

But however important, an antidote to an imbalance is in itself one-sided too when taken alone or prescribed as an ultimate way to be. Goals, work, achievements, etc., also meet needs and enrich life. The conventional view of "presence" tends to make surrender a tacit value, which is also one-sided for it leaves out or downplays choice, motivation, intentionality, will, and control. Here "being present" is conceived as surrendering to what confronts you, whereas life offers a wide spectrum of possibilities that you can focus attention on depending upon needs, interests, passions—what you want to be present to.

Since being and doing are each important and incomplete alone as a way of life, some kind of balance is needed. An aware life is a balancing act between being in time and being timeless, doing and being, control and surrender. The brain is constructed to think, which is often geared at doing, analyzing, and planning. There is also a non-cognitive, more intuitive part that can bring forth insights from just being that do not originate in thought—that, however, can only come from a being that thinks. The ability to experience timeless moments within the more usual flow of time is an important capacity, especially when combined with insight.

Passion brings a temporary abandonment of the self that lives more in surrender than control, but as mentioned, one can also be abandoned in activities that include thinking. Timelessness and thought are not mutually exclusive, contrary to some prevalent concepts of timelessness as devoid of thought. So the difference between being in thought and being timeless is not as clear-cut as tradition would have it. Thought and time interweave in many ways. Thought can create the subjective flow of time, but thought that's fully engaged (say in a problem or passion, meaningful project, or intense conversation) can feel timeless.

Timelessness can bring newness, unexpected insights and creativity, and at times peace, joy, a feeling of oneness and being closer to the eternal. This is not nor can it be a constant, steady state. Living in time well incorporates knowledge from the past and the insights, potential wisdom, and passion that can emanate from being timeless. A living awareness rides on the ever-shifting interface between the two subjective states of time and timelessness; a creative life depends on the interplay between them.

Question: I find all the different things I hear about timelessness confusing. Timelessness is supposed to be part of bringing balance into daily life. Regular meditation practices are said to lead eventually to timeless mystical experiences; but others say that enlightenment is just a heightened form of normal awareness. These don't seem very related to me and leave me wondering.

Answer: There are a variety of ways of being timeless, just as there is of being in time. Ever since the sixties when the "Be here now" ideal was championed by the counterculture, being timeless has been associated with being in the mystical "eternal now." There is also the implication that such experiences are always blissful, a gateway to a new life, a new world, and so on. In many spiritual groups promises of mystical experiences were dangled like carrots as an ultimate reward for joining in their beliefs and practices. Such experiences have occurred throughout history, but in the sixties they became more available through entheogenic substances. Seductive images of enlightenment and eternity, and even eternal life, led some to believe that a new millennium was just around the corner. Time and experience made people realize that not all mystical experiences are pleasant, and that they are often more about people's hopes than an absolute indicator of "reality."

Tantalizing images and promises arouse desire and sidetrack people from the more accessible timeless moments in daily life. Because mystical experiences are emotionally intense and of a different order than usual experience, they are often made superior or more real, while the more available timeless experiences get lost or ignored through being conflated with them. A common "mistake" fostered by the popularized concept of mystical timelessness is prioritizing it, while ignoring or making timeless moments in ordinary life less important.

Mystical experiences touch on different aspects of the universe and humanity and thus are not all identical. The most mentioned type usually involves removal of time and a usual sense of self, with a feeling of being connected to everything, including the source of creation. Contrary to the common idea that mystical experiences are the ultimate in rapture, they are not always even pleasant. This is partially because if you really come to experience that you are part of everything, this cannot exclude the horrors that we humans have done to each other. Interestingly, there are mystical experiences, seldom mentioned, where one feels eternally *dis*connected.

However special and revelatory mystical experiences are thought to be and at times may be, they rarely come from being sought, and do not give an unbiased touchstone into the nature of reality. We bring to them our worldviews, cultural archetypes, hopes, desires, and fears, and later interpret the experiences through these different lenses.

Question: I see the traps in trying to be timeless, but I still wonder how to have more of the timeless mode in my life. You said an intelligent use of time can help. Can you suggest ways to bring more balance in daily life?

Answer: Mystical experiences aside, the timelessness accessible in daily life can be missed if you have preconceived images of what it is or how you want it to be. Subjective experiences of time vary, depending on such things as interest in what's occurring, where we focus attention (which may or may not be in our control), emotions and mood, what we care about, and the ways we use thought—not to mention our work, schedules, duties, relationships, etc. Interest and care are special qualities that can draw us in to where we forget about time, but they are not mechanically brought about. As with the other perennial life concerns we're discussing, there are no formulas for living with time. Timeless moments using thought can be very powerful and extraordinary too. I am certain that Einstein had many timeless moments as he was grappling with time, acceleration, and the speed of light.

A key to timelessness is to have more open-ended time. As most adults lead highly structured lives, this can be a challenge. Although one can be timeless in any activity through "losing oneself" in it, surrender to what the moment brings, whether to what arises internally or externally, is also a potential avenue to it. For surrender, one needs leisure and unstructured time. As soon as there's a pre-established end point, the future crowds in. An open-ended conversation can be like improvisational jazz that could go anywhere, bringing newness, insights, and the feeling of timelessness. Some people find it easier to "let go" through techniques, practices, or whatever helps shift out of normal time frames—more on this when we discuss meditation. But this can be a trade-off since any kind of regular discipline adds more structure to your life. You also have to value being timeless by making it a priority to be without agendas some of the time. The question of timelessness in living is really how to keep interest, passion, and newness in life.

Question: What is it like to live awarely (at least some of the time) in a way that's not out of belief or a concept?

Answer: Awareness can bring more care, passion, depth, and transformation. It can be as ordinary as observing a bird on the wing, watching how habits affect your life, or noticing the way your mind works and how interesting it is to be the being that you are, alone and in relationship. Living in the present is really all one can do, but this is different from living awarely in the present. Likewise, the ways often suggested for "being in the now," such as focusing on what's in your immediate inner or external perceptual field, are also different from living awarely. Being aware in the present is really being aware, not only of sensations and the surface experiences confronting you, but also of deeper contextual relationships that you're a part of and that are also part of you. This enlarges the scope of presence to include what's happening outside your immediate experience.

Awareness is a turn of mind that influences what's occurring. If you have conflict, fear, regret, and endless desires and you live with them awarely, this can bring less conflict and more peace. Awareness makes living and relationships more interesting, deep, and transformative—always changing, as life itself is. There can be a sense of newness, adventure, renewal, and at times excitement in it. Since real growth, like evolution, is a movement into the unknown, you often don't know what's going to happen, so there can be less security. But how much security is there really? Although like life itself, awareness is not always easy or pleasant, it is interesting and growth-furthering and can counter our tendencies to be mechanical. Everything repeatable eventually gets old, no matter what it is. Although we are potentially changing beings, we're also creatures of habit, and habits can either further or hinder growth and well-being. Now it's more important than ever to be aware of which ones are no longer serving us. Awareness makes that discrimination possible. Changing times offer new challenges that can only be met through changing to meet them. Awareness can open you to the insights and energy of creativity that could change your life.

Question: The seeing or awareness that you talk of seems so fleeting! I feel I've had moments of it, but it doesn't last. I understand the impossibility of trying to hold on to it, and that wanting to be aware all the time is futile. Yet I feel pushed to do something. I've tried just observing like you say, but I realize I'm trying with a goal in mind. I'm not asking you what to do, just to comment on this.

Answer: When one gets involved in this type of inquiry, it's easy to get caught up in ideas about awareness and about oneself. It's not unusual for awareness to become an idea coated with images and preconceptions or another goal to achieve. Memory, where much of the "I" lives, can turn awareness into enjoying the self-image of being aware. This can dull you, for when you operate out of any image—especially of being an aware person—there's a tendency to repress whatever doesn't match the image.

Real awareness is not concerned with how aware I am or when I'm aware, for when there is awareness, it just is. The trick is to see clearly enough to discover when you're not aware, to see clearly when you're not clear. This seeing can move you so that clarity may come. Words on an ephemeral topic like seeing can be like smoke, disappearing afterward, seemingly without a trace. Instead of trying to hold on to what is being presented, it's best to view these discussions as planting seeds of a different way of observing that take root and have a momentum of their own.

Question: What about boredom—would you please talk about that?

Answer: Nothing interests me; I'm restless, dissatisfied. I want excitement or change, yet nothing seems worth doing. But the world is always moving, full of change and things to do. There are walks to take, music, reading, friends, whatever. Sometimes there is boredom, sometimes not—so something in you must be causing it. Boredom is not external; it lives in you. Most boredom contains conflict. It freezes interest and energy. Interest keeps you alive.

When you're bored, it's interesting to observe what's occurring in yourself. See where the conflict lives. It could be an indication of being out of touch with what you want. To see if this is so, you can try not doing things that you don't want to do and don't have to do, and reexamine "shoulds" to see where they come from—whether they're conditioned or appropriate. So often there are things one feels one has to do or should do but really doesn't want to. This squelches desire, curiosity, and interest—the fires of motivation. When one looks for escapes (and that's what much of being bored is) one cannot even channel energy into escaping, for the mind still dwells (sometimes almost imperceptibly) on what you're trying to escape from. You can observe that when you're bored, at some level thought is very active.

The very young are not often bored—at least not until they're programmed with "oughts" and "shoulds" or turned into spectators being fed the constant stimulation of technology. When we're young, a day is long and full; a week is forever, a summertime an eternity. As we age time seems to accelerate. When we look back it's as if our life has flown by. Why is that? Why does subjective time, inward time, seem to go faster and faster as we age? The young do not have the layering of conditioning that comes with aging. They don't live much in repetitive thoughts.

With aging repetitive thoughts increase, which are often fears or ruminating about the past, and time begins to fly. As adults, most of us live in thought so much. Our lives are so structured and locked in by necessities and responsibilities ("shoulds," whether imagined or real). We become so habit-bound, so automatic, that there is little actual spontaneous, inspired living. The more time one spends in habitual, repetitive thought, the more time drags—but in retrospect the faster time goes by.

Lack of interest can simply reflect lack of meaningful possibilities in your current situation. Maybe your life has reached a bottleneck, or you have outgrown old ways of being and need new outlets, meaning, and avenues to connect with others and the world. One of the great challenges is how to keep bringing newness and interest into your life.

Question: I find it valuable when you talk about the mind and awareness in general terms. Please talk more about the "binds of mind."

Answer: To completely see not only what I like about myself, but also my indifference and carelessness, my ambition and endless desire for "more," my aggression and feelings of superiority or inferiority, my fears, to see any of this is a seeing that has its own movement. When I see the dual nature of both thought and time, like fear and desire, I may get a strong desire to control them to get more of what I want, or I could try to make them leave through techniques. Yet doing either of these mostly perpetuates them. That's part of the paradox of the bind of mind. Whether we examine pleasure, desire, fear, freedom, time, or any other topic, ultimately we reach a bind, a seeming paradox, and anywhere we turn we seem to be caught. Trying to escape thought in whatever way one does is thought trying to escape itself. It's possible to get a feel for the nature of this seeming paradox—both of thought's importance and its limitations. This can make a shift in awareness come more easily, a shift that is not thought itself but that sees more clearly how thought works in oneself.

What we're doing here together is using intelligence in an extraordinary way—a way that is not simply thought nor an intellectual exercise. That is, we are using it to see itself, and the seeing can bring a movement beyond predictable or imagined confines. What is really important is not what I say, or agreeing or disagreeing. Seeing how the mind works in yourself is the important thing. The trick is to see how this whole thing works, which is to see how *you* work.

COMMENTARY:
It's About Time

A worldview reveals its relation to matter, mind, life, and evolution in its conceptions and views of time. This commentary on the Time chapter is key to understanding the worldview represented in this book. It discusses common conceptions about time and thought within prevalent worldviews and presents a different view of time and thought's relation to it. Because using humanity's special gift of time-awareness to deal better with future consequences is crucial for protecting the Earth and our survival, we must reexamine worldviews, beliefs, and ideologies that limit our capacity to effectively utilize our awareness of time. We as a species are running out of time. How long we have to rectify problems is uncertain. What appears almost certain is that time is limited.

What we do with our time and how we live in it are related to how we conceptualize it, which we (the authors) view as critical. This is why we have meticulously delved into the relationships among worldviews, thought, awareness, and time. That a shift in awareness is needed about who we are, and how we got where we are, is a major thesis of this book.

People develop or take on a worldview in an attempt to integrate their experiences into a belief system about the way the world works and the individual's place in it. Time and values are a core part of any worldview, so how you look at time and live in it depends largely on how you view the universe or "reality." People can be conscious of their worldview but often are not. In either case people usually think they're seeing "reality" in an unfiltered way as they become identified with whatever worldview they've incorporated. Religions, philosophies, political ideologies, and scientific paradigms are examples of worldviews that attempt to incorporate the big-picture meaning of the cosmos and human experience.

Worldviews organize, structure, and interpret perception and experiences, but not all in the same way. Some worldviews are handed down by tradition, some prioritize consistency, and others are eclectic, incorporating beliefs from different structures (like a Christian who believes in karma and astrology). Unless beliefs are integrated to be consistent with each other, contradictory identities can coexist as separate compartments in people's minds. Some people have different worldviews and beliefs for their different identities, which are like mental boxes. With a scientific hat on, one could be a hard-line materialist, and in another compartment also believe in a monotheistic, non-material entity.

Postmodernism undermined all absolutes, having picked up from anthropology the tenet that since beliefs and values are culturally relative, coming from different cultures and times with differing priorities, there is no way to determine whether one is more objective or closer to "reality" than another. Postmodernism holds that human subjectivity through discourse can only create stories or narratives from within their worldviews, with no overriding criteria for determining one as better or "truer" than another. Truth in the postmodernist view then becomes merely a human invention, not even an approximation of something objective—so humans cannot really know if there is any independent truth.

Postmodernism did succeed in eliminating all absolutes if you buy its arguments, except in one case—its own. It itself is an absolutist worldview, an absolute relativism—one claiming the absolute subjectivity of all human discourse. It flattens different views of truth to where it becomes almost impossible to make discriminations that are not summarily dismissed as purely subjective. This punctures truth-seeking, which easily moves to nihilism. Absolute truth and objectivity may not be available, but not to be able to say that something is truer than something else, independent of cultural norms, arbitrarily places an unreal and dampening limit on human knowledge and capacities.

This position had value in its deconstruction of the basis for authoritarian belief systems, but this was only achieved at the price of also undermining or dismissing anything non-relative, including all foundations for values and even reason itself, as either self- or culture-serving. This is detrimental to repairing the moral vacuum and confusion that postmodern thought helped create and even to our survival itself, given that pan-cultural values are sorely needed to guide and unite the world through what we hope is a transition.

As the attraction of this school of thought wanes in the current decade, many postmodernists have moved toward a pragmatic relativist conception of truth, which has its own unresolved problems. Unfortunately, postmodernism's long reign and now pragmatism's predominance have made truth-seeking unfashionable and truth-seekers defensive because truth is presented as an outmoded, naïve fantasy or pipe-dream. Instead of promoting much-needed truth-seeking and objectivity, the cultural climate created by relativists has conflated "truth" with "absolutes" and made the very concept of truth an object of condescension.

Another effect is that those who value and care about the truth (recognizing that fallibility is always a possibility) may have to justify and qualify the very word, toning it down to even use it. This is mildly reminiscent of how throughout history people had to hide "heretical," original, or non-conforming thoughts to avoid suffering ridicule, rejection, or worse. Whereas instead, a passion for the truth—which taps into our native curiosity and desire to understand how things work—is utterly essential if we are to find our way through crisis. This does not negate the "fact" that all human constructions of truth are potentially fallible and need to be open to revision through feedback. Nor does the fallibility of human constructs negate the possibility of finding truth. Humanity either is, or is not, at risk, and that is the truth. This for us is an objective statement of fact. Given the "fact" of our precarious state, to act as if we are not at risk is in our opinion objectively foolish.

We are positing that humanity's survival depends on people becoming more conscious, more aware of their subjective filters, which brings more maturity and needed objectivity. A first step is becoming aware of the worldview or views that one operates out of and the ways they filter information. Life's challenge involves refining one's worldview to be more in touch and congruent with what life presents us. It's obvious to us (the authors) that humanity is facing what is perhaps the most extraordinary challenge it has ever faced—our ongoing destruction of global life-support systems. The realization that humanity confronts an extraordinary challenge can make a person or group more conscious, functional, effective, and response-able—able to see the necessity for deep changes and creatively move toward them.

If you're not conscious of your worldview or are unaware of how it affects your relation to time, your values around time may help reveal it. Examining your attitudes toward time can be like looking through a prism that is able to reveal parts of the worldview you operate from and how it can filter perception and create ideals and agendas for living. Since different worldviews have different views and values around time, people usually value one time mode over another. Eastern worldviews tend to value "being" over "becoming," and so value the subjective experience of timelessness and surrender to it over experiencing the flow of time.

Both scientific and Western religious worldviews see matter, time, and life on Earth as real. Accomplishments and control over your life are valued and linked with progress, while just being ("doing nothing") tends to be considered wasting time or something done only on vacation. In monotheistic worldviews the eternal only pertains to the afterlife and to God, who manifested a separate creation, the cosmos, to exist in time. According to Western Judeo-Christian religious worldviews, the purpose of life and time is to serve as a morality test for God to reward or punish humans. In monotheism being spiritual is based on obeying God's rules, doing good works, and maintaining faith in whichever God the religion worships. In the Islamic worldview the past, present, and future are laid out by God—all is determined by the will of Allah so one surrenders one's will as one's own life is laid out too. (The word "Islam" literally means "submission.")

In many mystical worldviews (both Eastern and Western), the past and future "exist" only as projections of thought with no "real" existence outside the human mind, as it is only the ever-eternal now that truly exists. Here the "now" is viewed not just as "the present" but as a more profound way of "being" that is a gateway to "reality." Such worldviews value presence and mindfulness—meaning, being present to the timeless "eternal now." So if one has mystical predilections, the tendency is to value timelessness, which can feel eternal and peaceful, and to identify it with spirituality. In this view using thought, which puts you in the flow of time, is a practical necessity at best, as well as a potential hindrance to being "spiritual." Therefore, many spiritual practices are techniques for quieting thought and cultivating mindfulness to tame the out-of-control "monkey mind" that endlessly chatters to itself. Here controlling thought can become its own agenda—an agenda ironically created by thought.

The timeless ideal is part of a worldview that considers the basic reality to be the unity of existence, with all "things" totally interconnected. Boundaries and individuation are viewed as merely part of the illusion of separateness, or as a lesser order of reality within the material plane. Here spirit is conceptually separated from matter; although matter may contain spirit, spirit is viewed as being of a different and superior order. Placing spirituality on a "higher" plane than life as we experience it, in a superior, other-worldly dimension, creates (to our minds at least) a false separation between the spiritual and the worldly. Historically this split has been detrimental to life on Earth and is a core part of our crisis.

This spiritual/mundane split shows up in the seemingly non-dual Hindu *Advaitist* and Buddhist worldviews. In the *Advaita* worldview reality is essential unity (what we and others call Oneness), and in traditional Buddhism reality is a formless Void with the boundary-less interconnectedness of all the ever-changing forms that the Void somehow gives rise to. By making boundaries and separation less than real, both worldviews that claim to be non-dual actually create a hidden duality between reality and illusion. Both are involved in what might be called a unity fallacy—a fallacy because under the guise of unity duality is hidden between reality (unity) and illusion (multiplicity), mind and matter, formlessness and form, spirit and the world of seemingly separate entities. (See our critique of hidden authoritarianism in the ideology of Oneness in "Oneness, Enlightenment, and the Mystical Experience" in *The Guru Papers*.)

As a social reformer, Buddha eliminated the Hindu caste system and shifted the focus from Hindu metaphysics to his main agenda of ending or alleviating suffering. His reformation of Hinduism involved undermining its cosmology through creating a worldview that on the surface seems to be its opposite. But like other "protestant" religions, Buddhism harbors many Hindu beliefs in disguised forms (karma, reincarnation, and *khandhas* are examples). Although Buddhism eliminates Hinduism's concept of a higher Self by claiming there is no self, both worldviews negate the ego-self, calling it illusory, and both identify it as the main impediment to spirituality.

Since we're born with ego, villainizing it is structurally and functionally similar to original sin in Christianity. (This squarely places the basic human problem in intrinsic human nature.) The cosmologies of Hinduism and Buddhism are structurally similar. Hinduism's split between Oneness and Maya (the illusory Many) is carried over into Buddhism's split between the undifferentiated Void and illusory separation within the world of interconnected forms. Individuated life, time, and the self are devalued in both Eastern worldviews, along with the so-called "material plane" or "world of forms."

Given Buddha's agenda of dethroning Hindu ritual and caste hierarchy while spreading compassion, loving-kindness, and alleviating pain, he was more interested in negating Hindu cosmology than in creating a consistent one to replace it. Thus how forms could arise out of the Void and other such mysteries were left undefined and interest in such irrelevant abstractions discouraged in favor of teaching individuals detachment practices to end their suffering.

Just as villainizing ego is the East's abstract, more sophisticated version of original sin, karma as a cosmic virtue-measuring device is the East's more abstract, sophisticated version of an omniscient God's judgments. Karma and God both observe your every little thought and action and mete out appropriate rewards and punishments, and both prioritize self-renunciation. In both worldviews, these two concepts are tightly linked (God with sin, and karma with villainizing ego), as virtue is measured by how much ego or sin one manages to subtract from one's original defective state.

For both traditional Hinduism and Buddhism, time only occurs in the illusory world of *Maya* (Hinduism) or in the multiplicity of ever-changing forms. Being timeless is usually presented as superior to being in "mundane" time. The idea that one could and should be timeless all the time, most of the time, or at least more of the time than one is creates the behavioral paradox of using time to become timeless. Similarly, even the admonition to "Be here now" contains a usually unseen paradox, for it exhorts one to relate to time differently, which of course implies the future. These paradoxes are not merely an amusing play on words. They point to the important fact that whenever one side of an interwoven dynamic is peremptorily emphasized to the exclusion or devaluing of the other side, paradoxes occur. When one consciously values one side of a polarity, the other—the hidden side—displays itself in unacknowledged ways, revealing that the imbalance is untenable. This is why one so often sees these quixotic contradictions: desiring to be desireless, competing to be the best non-competitor, judging judgmentalism, being self-absorbed in trying to be selfless or in how selfless one is, etc. We sometimes call trying to escape the devalued side "the binds of mind," as these mentally constructed oppositions really cannot be ultimately separated, and the less valued side will somehow express itself.

Worldviews that keep people locked into outmoded beliefs are a drag on social evolution and maturity that we can ill afford. The most significant change in consciousness would involve the way we look at and behave toward ourselves, each other, and the world. For this one's attitude toward time is crucial. Accordingly, we wish to present a view of time that we think is more in line with the demands of the era. This view of time interweaves with concepts in other chapters.

Eastern worldviews that emphasize unity, and Western ones (including science) that acknowledge the reality of separate individuals, are all incomplete ways of looking at existence, even though each reveals an important aspect of the cosmos (unity and individuation within multiplicity). We have found that a dialectical synthesis bringing these two perspectives together is more representative of the way things actually work. It also resolves false polarities in the field of time.

By "dialectical" we mean that the two sides of a dynamic opposition are embedded within and dependent on each other—like creation and destruction, individuation and merging, control and surrender—rather than each element being autonomous. These polarities, including time and timelessness, define and thus are necessary for each other. By "embedded" we mean that seeming opposites (like competition and cooperation) create each other, as each side contains aspects of the other. For example, whether you see competition or cooperation depends on which level of engagement you're looking at. Teams cooperate at one level to compete better at another. We consider cooperation and competition to be in a dialectical relationship.

A dialectical worldview considers how unity and diversity are intertwined in the very fabric of existence and embedded in each other—with neither being more real, important, nor profound than the other. In fact, neither wholeness nor separateness could exist without the other. "Separateness" is not only just as real as "unity"—it is only through actually being separate entities that unity can express itself. Unity only exists within the many forms that multiplicity takes—not separately from them; both unity and separation are embedded within multiplicity. The unity embedded within individuated diversity does not negate the equal reality of boundaries and separation, which are part of individuation. Separation, boundaries, and individuation are not illusory, nor do they exist in some inferior way. Unity only manifests in the evolving forms of the Many (multiplicity) through time: So in a real sense *the One is the Many.*

For time to "flow" there must be movement, motion, which is change. Within evolution, something in relation to something else must change. There must be separate entities that move in relation to something else in time and space. Change implies diversity as well as the boundaries necessary for individuation and separation. Whether it be evolutionary development or simply a shift in physical location, change involves changing through time and in relationship to something else.

Unity implies an unchanging permanence. In a unity perspective where everything is interconnected, every single part affects everything else (like a mobile). This means that every individual movement is influenced and to some degree determined by the whole. The Buddhist concept of "emptiness" (the Void) as the ultimate reality is terminally static and timeless.

Change in the world of forms has a problem with continuity, for continuity implies some thing (perhaps a self) that is changing. Our sun, which is always changing by burning itself up (as are we) is still recognizable as our sun and will be for millennia. How much permanence is needed in order to acknowledge that permanence does have some reality? The Buddhist conception of change in the world of everyday life is also strangely static, for it seems to assume that what is changing is disconnected from what "it" was. Real change brings newness into the universe and is not merely varied and repeated oscillations. Real change only occurs when interwoven with continuity: In order for change to occur, there must be some "thing" that is changing. We see permanence and change as dialectically embedded. Change is in essence relational—either to itself or to something else.

In denying ultimate reality to permanence and continuity, and thus also change through time, Buddhists are unknowingly and quixotically denying the possibility of real change. This reveals how Buddhists can give reality to an underlying, unchanging Void while preaching that there is nothing but change. The concept of change that they put forth is as empty as their Void.

Where does evolution as a creative force come in? How to account for it if the really real is a timeless Void? And where do human will and intention that can affect the future come in? For those who believe in evolution, a simplistic unity worldview (we are all one) cannot work without casuistic convolutions to try to make it fit scientific facts. Casuistry is a way of protecting beliefs instead of changing them to align with new evidence. (Jesuits used casuistry to justify Catholic dogma by elaborate arguments that do not reach a conclusion, but start with one.)

We humans via evolution have been given the gift of experiencing both time and timelessness. What, if anything, does this say about the nature of existence from which we arise? An assumption we make (enlarged upon in the Evolution chapter) is that existence through evolution manufactures parts of itself that experience in myriad unique ways the nature of itself that is unimaginable in its totality to any individuated piece. If this has any likelihood, then the ability to experience both time and timelessness is a clue to what existence is about. It is our experience of time coupled with our ability to use symbols, think, and create generalities and abstractions that has given us a history to continually pass on. This eventually brought tools that allowed us to probe deeper into the workings of the universe.

Sometimes timeless moments allow us to touch into the feeling of being part of the source of all of this, which feels and could well be eternal. Other species probably live a more timeless existence than we do. Although some do to an extent take past and future into account, unlike us they do not concern themselves with notions about time itself. As far as we can tell, it takes a creature capable of abstracting with thought, with a history and language, to be able both to live in time and appreciate the timeless moments that occur. Many indigenous peoples live more timelessly (given a plentiful food supply) because their relatively more static cultures are not structured around progress.

If, as we think, spirit and matter, being and becoming, timelessness and time are embedded in each other, then being in time and being timeless are two counterbalancing modes available to human awareness. An awareness of the timeless state is only possible in people because they exist in time, for it too occurs within the flow of time. It takes awareness of the past and future to give a sense of continuity, and thus time, in a given moment. An experience is called timeless to distinguish it from instances when one feels the flow of time more. The word "timeless" only has meaning because it stands out as different in a context of experiencing time's flow. The inner psychological state of experiencing the flow of time and the experience of being timeless each need the other for contrast to be perceived. The concept of timelessness itself can only arise by comparing the memory of a timeless moment to other more time-bound ones. It takes a being who can remember, project, and think about the past and future to recognize a different state that feels out of time. Both modes are an essential part of living or at least being human. Like thought and non-thought, each is valuable and has an important role and appropriate function in the scheme of things, with neither being superior to the other. They each need the reflection of the other to have meaning and to reflect an aspect of how existence puts itself together.

Either/or thinking has difficulty with a dialectical synthesis that unites polarities because it assumes that one viewpoint must be more real and primary than the other: Seeming opposites are either "this *or* that," but not "both *and.*" Either/or thinking cannot conceptualize two seeming opposites being equally real and fundamentally embedded in each other. The way we're taught to think makes it difficult to see the embedded nature of much opposition because at first blush the two sides seem so absolutely different and opposite. If you look from a more inclusive level of awareness, you can *see* that they are not, but it is hard to *think* it.

Several other powerful factors work in tandem to reinforce the difficulty of holding unity and separation as embedded. For those who may have had a unity or Oneness experience, it often contains the quality of a sacred revelation of hidden cosmic truth. The "eternal now," which can seem to be all there is when thought quiets, feels timeless and more real, as if one has touched the essence of "reality"—even though one seems to move from one eternal now to the next. Given the nature of either/or thinking, for those who have had this kind of "mystical" insight and others who value unity, it's difficult not to make unity more important and more real than multiplicity. Even without these values, within the binary paradigm unity appears more encompassing, and in a fragmenting world the dream of unity seems to offer more hope and the possibility of an inbuilt solution. Multiplicity brings to mind the separateness of individuals, which highlights boundaries and isolation rather than their capacity to connect.

Then, too, the actual experiencing of unity is far more rare than experiencing oneself as separate. This naturally makes unity seem more special and profound. Moreover, strong emotions contribute to wanting to believe that separateness is an illusion or more limited reality, including the feeling that since unity seems eternal, the individual as part of this unity can be easily projected as eternal too. This assuages the inbuilt fear of death. The polarization in the world between spirituality and materialism, religion and secularism is partly a product of the prevalence of either/or thinking and worldviews. Two generic and opposing worldviews either place spirit in another realm or make the material world the only reality.

The proposed dialectical perspective can account for the nature of the subjective, internal experiences of time and timelessness. The unity worldview considers "psychological time" to be a product of thought as it plays in memory (the past) and projections (the future). So the thoughtless "now" is assumed to be more real than the inner feel of the flow of time. In our synthetic worldview both viewpoints are partially true: In a sense although the "now" is all that exists, it has within it the products of the past and the seeds of the future. So the past and future are not illusory. "Being" or "is-ness" has within it "becoming," and becoming at every instant displays within it "what is." The eternal ("timelessness") only displays itself in the field of time as each separate moment contains and expresses what some consider the eternal in its own unique way. Another way of saying this is that the "eternal now" only displays itself through the transformations and patterns within time.

Worldviews that present the sense of self (which includes an ego) as a construct totally built by thought conclude that the idea of a self that thinks thoughts is illusory, because there is no thinker (self)—only thought. In this view the brain is merely an automatic thinking machine. It's no accident that these worldviews (Buddhism being an example) look at spirituality as divesting yourself of ego and of the very idea (thought) that you are or have a self. In viewpoints where time and thought are defined as illusory, preoccupation with the past and future—

a future that will be different from the mind's spinnings—is seen as a major obstacle to being totally present. The living in the "now" ideal usually has an agenda that intimates it would be better to let go of the past and future, or at least not dwell in them, as much as possible.

Here the ideal of letting go of thoughts and the attachments that thought brings also becomes enmeshed in this agenda. Attachments, expectations, desires, fears, etc., are all a function of being in time, so that (theoretically at least) detaching enables one to be timeless. For how can you be attached and timeless? Attachment evoke desires and fears around continuity. Certain worldviews present detachment (or "non-attachment," the sometimes preferred articulation) as fundamentally different from and better than being attached. It's true that many past dramas and projections into the future come from thoughts and memories containing fears and desires, regrets and worries. Letting go of the past would be good if all that were meant by this is not getting caught in memory's mechanical loops, although this is not easy to do. But what is often meant by letting go is "detaching from your story," which involves detaching from your self, your identity, personality, and ego. The unity worldview maintains that your ego or sense of self is at the core of thought, preventing you from being truly present to "the only reality" there is, the now. Many "spiritual" paths aim at transcending ego, which really means trying to lose the sense of being an individuated self.

Although ego, personality, one's sense of self can at times be limiting filters that become frozen and inhibit growth, they're also an inherent part of being human. Without memory there would be little sense of self, but it is memory and the continuity of core aspects of the self that make us human. People who lose memory through brain damage lose the very fabric of their lives. One tragic amnesiac who lives entirely in the now with intelligence, but no memory whatsoever from moment to moment, describes himself as "condemned to live in the hell of the eternal now."

People say, "Be in the now because that's all there is." Though the present is all there is, thought too, which generates our sense of the past and the future, only occurs in the present. But as we've noted, it's equally true that the present contains the past and future in very real ways that do not involve thought. A seed containing a future tree is an example of the future being contained in the present. When we look at a star many millions of light-years away, we're seeing its past (what it looked like in the past), but the light emanating from it enters our eyes in our present. This is but one type of example of how the past is contained in the present. Thunder is heard in the listener's present after it occurs. So is one not fully in the now when hearing or seeing something from the past? Is that different from an internal memory trace from the past?

In humans too, one's past and future are not non-existent or merely the product of thought. Though parts of personality and the sense of self change over time, there are embodied and emotional aspects of the self that display a consistency through time. In one way it's true that everything changes, but what changes has a history that is structured into whatever it becomes and that ongoingly remains part of it. Past experiences actually change the cellular matter that one's "thinking and emotional body" brings to whatever now one is in. So the past does not live only as disembodied memory; past experiences live in the cells of the brain and body that thinks, remembers, and anticipates. This means that the past in a very real sense lives in and is part of the present you, as these changes occur through time within the unique structure that is and remains you. In short, the past is an integral and deeply meaningful part of the self. (Witnessing the later stages of Alzheimer's reveals how very true this is.)

The way past and present are intertwined in our very being represents the embedded nature that we humans manifest of permanence and change within the universe. We change, but recognizably so. If you observe a person over time, you see many changes, but through the years there is also something recognizable that makes people who they are—to themselves and to us. This is not only a physical continuity but one of mannerisms, preferences, temperament, and so on. People's genetic flavor, coupled with environmental input, develops over time to make them uniquely who they are. Their thoughts and worldview play an important role in this: when someone's worldview dramatically changes, so too do they in important, but not all, ways.

Like the past, the future is also contained in the present. Human will, intention, and desire, which are real factors that impact the future, all aim at a future while occurring in the "now." This partially constructs living moments, which become the next and then next present "now." What's important to see is that human will, intention, and action that aim at the future (in the present) are part of what creates the next present. Though our behavior and beliefs tend to come from social structures embedded in the past—and now determining and possibly destroying humanity's future—we are capable of novel behavior to meet truly novel and dangerous challenges. So how we understand the interconnections among present, future, and past can affect what we do or don't do—it really matters.

There are many possible ways of looking at the relation between the flow of time and that exact moment of livingness that we call the present. The present actually has no duration—that is, it instantly appears and disappears—and yet it's experienced as a continually uninterrupted flow. That there was a past and will be a future is necessary to make the present possible. The present contains within it the results, structures, and effects from the past that become part, though not all, of the living moment. The laws and tendencies that influence how the old and the new combine, as well as whether the inbuilt operators (laws, habits, patterns) are fixed or themselves evolving, is an interesting field of speculation. The past brings to the present its form, its shape, which comes out of what came before. Thus the present (and by extension the future) contain the products of the past, the old—these tend to be more

mechanical and causal. The past creates tendencies, habits, and is necessary for certain events to happen at all. We humans are alive today
and have civilization only because humans were alive yesterday and a
million years ago to create culture and pass it on.

The relation between the past, present, and future, however, is not
merely causal. The living moment has within it something else—something different from what the past brings. It is a *gestalt,* a unique con-
figuration that is not merely reducible to the sum of its pasts. The
present is the living, eternal miracle. That special and truly miraculous
moment of aliveness that is the present is inherently new. Each instant,
though often containing great similarities to the one before and after
it, is never exactly the same as others. That which is truly new in the
present comes as it intertwines with the future. This intermix of past
and present with the future becomes the next present moment. So the
future cannot be totally predetermined, defined, or predicted merely
by the past or by mechanical causality.

Cosmic evolution—that is, evolution in the broadest sense as an operator of change—works through the momentum of time. This is why many
who claim the ultimate reality of only the "eternal now" (with past and
future mainly being mere illusory products of thought) rarely adequately
deal with evolution.

When the past slides into the present it doesn't totally disappear.
Parts of it remain fossilized, like the fossils we find of extinct animals
in the present. From a geological perspective the present contains the
past embedded in matter (rocks), and from a psychological perspective
it lives less stably in the memory of conscious individuals, while the
present's possibilities (including human influence) construct a future.
The past, then, is not only present within the present, it partly influences the future's directionality and possibility. Both past and future
exist through the continuity of the ongoing present, which is always
becoming, instant by instant, something new. This means that past and
future, however different from the actual experience of the living

moment, are not illusory but are real in the sense that they are opera-tors within existence that make the living "now" possible.

This forward evolutionary movement, the one-way arrow of time, out of matter/energy created the galactic systems, the planet Earth, and then life, which led to consciousness and human thought. One might ask if the past and future are real, then where do they "exist"? One might as easily ask where the present, which does not seem to have a fixed point, exists. We think, as does much of science, that the best one can do at this time is to place the existence of the flow of time as a fourth dimension in the makeup of the cosmos.

Let's take as a supposition (one we think more likely than alterna-tives) that the only reason any life and intelligence are in the universe at all is because something in the way the whole of existence works aims toward it. That is to say that a vector toward intelligence is embed-ded in the structure of how existence puts itself together. In other words, the fact that intelligence evolved is not an accident or coincidence. If this were indeed true, it would mean that there is a teleological factor existent in the movement of time. (Teleology refers to the theory that the universe is not merely a function of mechanical causes, but has an element within it that aims or rather is pulled toward a purpose or result.)

This *telos* would reveal itself in the way the past and present com-bine to create the future. Insofar as the future is not totally determined, neither is the present that it helps create. The way "teleology" is usu-ally used means going toward an inbuilt, specified, somehow predeter-mined end or result. This is not what we mean—our conception involves an ever-evolving, embedded, unpredictable movement toward complex-ity of matter and consciousness that shapes and defines itself as it develops, and interacts with everything else. As the present moves seem-ingly seamlessly from moment to moment, this *telos* brings to the next present moment a directionality toward complexity. This eventually led to self-reflecting intelligence that can uniquely reflect on the wonder we are all a part of. Humans are not the conscious plan of some super-intentional intelligence. Rather existence is a context that through evolution moves to construct undetermined forms that display intelligence.

It is neither scientifically provable nor falsifiable (equally important) to posit (as we are) that self-reflecting intelligence evolved because there is something *(telos)* within the structure of the way things work that moves in that direction. However, the other alternatives assume that we evolved by chance, or that our occurrence is statistically likely over the long haul (science's two favored but likewise unfalsifiable theories), or that we evolved by the will of some outside agent or creator god. Given the extraordinary complexity that brought forth experiencing, making chance or statistical possibility the reason we're here seems to us far more remote and unlikely. This is especially so given the fact that at higher levels of complexity, new qualities and laws emerge that are not reducible to those of lower levels. How the qualities and laws emerge in essence is still not understood. Having the cause be some super-natural outside agent stretches unlikeliness to its limit.

Likewise, if synchronicity were one of the operators in the way the universe and *telos* work, it would also function in this interface of the past and future, that is, in the living moment. Synchronicity refers to the simultaneous occurrence of related events whose juxtaposition cannot be explained by causality alone, while a belief that they happen to coincide merely by chance strains credulity. One reason for this strain is that these so-called chance occurrences happen far too often for mere chance to be even a plausible, let alone the best explanation. But if a teleological factor were operative in the way things work, this would make synchronistic events more understandable. If events are not only causally manufactured but are also pulled or drawn together by another principle based on enhancing (say) connecting and complexity, this could explain those moments that we have all had of connections that seem to defy both causality and coincidence as an explanation.

We've been examining the two subjective ways that people experience time—being in time or being timeless—as non-evaluatively as we can. We'll now look more closely at the seemingly simple but actually convoluted question of what living in the present, the now, actually involves. Living in the "now" has become a very popular idea. The injunction to "Be here now" that was a rallying cry for the counterculture in the sixties came from the infusion of Eastern mysticism into a society hungry for new values, new experiences, and new meaning in life. It offered an alternative to the "rat race." For an essentially puritanical culture whose deep values warn against "wasting time" and laziness, this was heady stuff that gave permission to "be" instead of always being busy "becoming"—which usually translates into trying to become "better," however defined.

What "be here now" means is to be present or be mindful of the present: "Be in the eternal now—for that's all there really is anyway." The past and future live only in your mind, and dwelling there removes you from the potential ecstasy contained in the moment. In short, "be out of time; be timeless." The idea that the past and the future only exist in thought came from the East. So valuing timelessness was taken to mean detaching from the creator of psychological time, which was correctly seen to be thought.

Many popular books and seminars talk about a spiritual awakening that comes from being in total presence. They tell you to quiet thought in order to be "in the now" as much as possible, and they claim an ability to help people do it. Some extol the power of the now to cure all your problems and even the tremendous world crises. This belief is an example of how a worldview can influence ideas about time, thought, and the self, which have a direct influence on behavior—what people want to do, think they should do, try to do, and will or won't do. Quieting thought is said to detach you from your ego, ending the illusion of separation and allowing you to experience the interconnectedness of all things. The assumption is that if people would quiet thought and just be present, this would bring a radical change in consciousness (love and a sense of unity) that would enable us to solve personal and global problems. This is why many purveyors of unity worldviews tout presence as the only real revolution in consciousness, so radical that it will be a panacea for everything.

There are many problems with unity worldviews, including the fact that ego can't get rid of itself because it is integral to individuation. And the exhortation to "be here now," be present or mindful, presumes that there is only one present to be mindful of and one right way to be in it. This is an oddly narrow vision for the wide spectrum of existence and behaviors that one can be present to. Being truly meticulous with the meaning of "being in the now," one sees that everything that is happening is only occurring now. This includes people starving, ice caps melting, thoughts about the past or future—everything external and internal: if it exists it's happening now.

If there's no way not to be in the now, why all the concern? Does this mean that it's possible to not be in the now? If the present is all one can be in anyway, there should be no need to advocate being in it. The very interesting question is, then, what are all the admonitions really about? What is the underlying true concern? A hidden agenda must be involved in preferring some nows over others. People might say that although there's no way not to be in the present, there are many ways of not "being present" to the present. But an often-underlying worldview assumption here is that presence, being in the "now," only occurs when thought is silent and ego is in abeyance, and then the "real" now (devoid of human subjectivity) reveals itself.

Since many things are always occurring simultaneously in the present, including thought, one could ask instead a more relevant question: Which now should I be in? Which of the many possible "nows" should I pay attention to and why? Are some "nows" better to be in than others? If so, how is one to know which now one should be present to, or which is better—and who decides? So when one is "present," what present is it that one is present to? The external sensuous present of a flower, a sunset; an object of concentration (a flame, a blade of grass); daily chores (Zen's chopping wood, washing dishes); the internal present of one's thoughts, breath, heartbeat, or toothache; the social present of a conversation; or the probably distant present of suffering children and dying polar bears that can be in your awareness even if you are not directly thinking about them?

It is not entirely clear how much control one actually has over one's interest and attention, or over what to surrender to or attempt to influence. At every moment something different that's happening now may catch your attention or motivate you. That's why we ask which "now" do you want to be in: the thoughtless, pleasant, usually good or neutral-feeling "now" of sensations—a flower or sunset, a concentration technique, or your breath—or the social and global "now" that's challenging us and inviting us to care about and connect with others? Then there is the dangerous, more scary "now" of the evolutionary cusp we are "now" on, which includes your mind's awareness of the need for our powerful but untested evolving human potential to meet a wide variety of challenges: climate change, sustainability, social and gender justice, overpopulation, lessening the have/have-not gap, improving democracy. In this universe of ours, practically speaking, an infinite number of events are happening "now," and one cannot be in them all, so which do you choose—or let choose you?

Attending to sensations, objects, or to what's going on internally is commonly prescribed as a doorway to being in the now and to stilling thought, transcending time and the self. This is assumed to be the gateway to spirituality. In spite of considering self and ego as obstacles to unity, the focus in all this is incongruently totally personal. These all involve the individual alone. However, as social beings we all live in "social nows" and social circumstances with ongoing repercussions that greatly affect us—regardless of our attention being on them or not.

Given traditional spiritual values of selflessness, love or loving-

kindness, compassion, and interconnection, it cannot be an accidental oversight that the social present of intimacy, relationships, and
what's happening in the world is often ignored. When not ignored, the
social dimension is brought in through the ideal of "selfless service."
"Engaged Buddhism," which describes a modern approach to dealing
with social issues, seems to be an indication that Buddhism was previously socially dis-engaged. Being socially engaged means caring about
the future. One cannot truly care about anything without caring about
what happens to it and wanting it to be one way rather than another
(life over demise). If not being attached to results is part of unity and
surrender worldviews, where does the care and the energy for engagement come from? Since desire by its nature inherently contains attachment, how can one desire a better world without being attached to the
outcome? Wouldn't you rather have your children live well than die prematurely, and aren't you attached to the outcome?

Because ego is targeted as the core human problem, selfless service is supposed to be "ego-less"—done without attachment to results,
acknowledgment, gratification, or anything that feeds the ego. Helping
others and good causes is vital and gratifying. However, frameworks
and analyses that pinpoint the ego as the root of the human problem
have not and will not carry the world forward. They create reactive, ego-
assaulting strategies that contain the flaws of the faulty analysis. For
example, people will do more for others and the world if it gives them
satisfaction or some kind of reciprocity, even if only appreciation. To
make people feel their service is lesser if it's ego-gratifying is to put
them in conflict with their nature and possibly to arouse guilt.

The old orders of both East and West make reaching spirituality a
personal achievement, with personal rewards for doing so. The concept of becoming more "spiritual" is aimed at enhancing the person
in this life or the next. This is just one example of what we call "the
spiritual paradox": through self-renunciation one expects something
better to occur for oneself. This is actually a twist on an accumulation

mentality in disguise, in which one accumulates spiritual merits through self-renouncing deeds or practices. If spirituality is based on renouncing, then the more one renounces, the more spiritual one is presumed to be. This quantifies both renouncing and spirituality. People who do such renouncing usually believe that ultimately they will somehow benefit. Not to mention that a self trying to be selfless is (paradoxically) very self-absorbed.

Hidden in the mindfulness "Be here now" agenda is a value structure that implicitly makes some here-and-now moments better to be in than others. The idea that being in, say, sensory awareness or in the beauty of a sunset is better or more profound than, say, thinking about the rent or the painting I want to do is itself a value judgment made by thought. Ironically, the worldview and values that judge what "now" to be in are created by thought. It could only be thought, through its worldview, memories, and desires, that decides which of the very many nows do not qualify as "presence" or as worthy of it.

Underlying many practices are the same assumptions and prescriptions contained within mindfulness worldviews. Originally one agenda was opening the individual to a mystical experience through a withdrawal from the input and concerns of this world—at least temporarily. Some practices are concentration techniques to strengthen focus. Here, as with any "diet" aimed at reducing input, what is eliminated is more important than what is ingested. Techniques that train the mind, like different kinds of physical exercise, can be beneficial in different ways.

But many traditional practices, especially those purported to lead to other-worldly spiritual dimensions or experiences, have the hidden agenda of getting practitioners to eventually incorporate their worldview. Even people initially resistant to the beliefs, through getting involved with the practices, tend to soak in the beliefs through other practitioners and through the teachers' preparatory guidelines and interpretations of their experiences. The practices are usually accompanied by teachings that eventually seep in (providing the encompassing worldview), and the practices have been designed to create experiences that reinforce the beliefs. This whole circular process can become another form of conditioning, with subjective mental filters that cloud instead of broaden awareness.

For us, being present involves more than simply paying attention to what's going on in the immediacy of one's sensory range internally or externally. It has many facets, including the past and future. It can include the meaning underlying a conversation or gesture, or the more invisible but nonetheless present social situation one is in, as well as the epoch and evolutionary contexts that may seem remote but are part of our day-to-day life. A critic of the enlarged present that we place in the broader scheme of "what's happening now" could reply that these are invisible suppositions that just live in your mind. We could just as easily say that all of it lives in the mind, including one's ideas of what real presence is. This does not address what for us is the fact that what is present in the world in every living moment has many facets, and valuing one over another, or one way of "being present," is itself a function of thought.

To limit what the "here and now" consists of in a predetermined or formulaic way necessarily has an agenda—usually one intended to promote the experience of unity at the price of presence in this world, including the world beyond one's immediate sensory range. When what we know to be present is not in the forefront of consciousness, it still lives in the mind *now* in the brain's complex retrievable memory networks, which does not make it any less present. Disqualifying thought and ideas in favor of sensations or the immediacy of direct experience peremptorily cages the present within narrow personal, physical, temporal, geographic, and highly conceptual confines.

Furthermore, who is to say where the boundary between "here" and "there" is—or even if there is one? Since consciousness itself is not localized between one's ears, all such boundaries are arbitrary cut-offs produced by thought. Negating core parts of the present that we live in and that affect our lives creates an imbalanced view of reality and an other-dimensional, strangely limited view of spirituality that leaves out the world. This is why we assert that spirituality needs to be brought back down to Earth.

What you are "present to" or mindful of depends on how far and wide your awareness and care extend, as well as your values, worldview, agendas, practices, and what you focus on or surrender to in the moment. Being engrossed in something that interests you or that you really care about feels timeless but does not necessarily exclude thought, action, and initiative.

Unity worldviews tend to designate thought as the obstacle, nuisance, or even villain that keeps one away from precious timeless moments and "higher," more elevated "spiritual" states. This stigmatizing of thought has carried over into the dangerous tendency of conflating automatic, mechanical, and even either/or thinking with all of thought, and considering it the very essence of thought. Here thought can be trivialized as a necessary expediency only useful for the "lower" mundane, practical aspects of living. The necessity of using thought pragmatically for living in chronological time is usually acknowledged hastily, as an aside, because the reality of chronological time, history, and evolution, and thought's role in them, cannot be adequately accounted for by the timeless, unchanging, anti-ego, "unity-of-everything" mental constructs. Yet it has been creative and critical thinking and problem-solving that have vastly enlarged our scope of understanding of the universe, allowing us to ponder in new ways the meaning of it all and our place in the scheme of things.

The devaluing of thought and the consequent attempt to detach from it does not stop people from thinking—sadly, it merely hinders thinking clearly. The meditation commentary shows that trying to disempower thought is really thought trying to contol those aspects of itself it doesn't like, so as not to be disturbed. Our brain does have conditioning and conditions itself, with a tendency to go on automatic; this frees other parts of the brain to attend to other things, innovating and improvising responses. Our brain also has binary aspects and thus a natural predilection to go on automatic toward either/or, binary thinking. We can also think and be trained to think and perceive dialectically.

Surrendering to the ebb and flow of sensation and emotion and even thought—through not attending to their content—not only incapacitates reason, interpretation of feedback, and critical thinking (always a secret agenda of authoritarian belief systems), it also eliminates the human dimension of meaning from experience—which has huge implications for conditioning behavior. Such a "surrender" makes it impossible to interpret experience and feedback, which is where growth comes from.

When the future, the past, and time itself are presented as essentially products of thought and therefore categorized as either illusory or on a lower level of existence, this is not only counter-intuitive, undermining reason and self-trust, but it is seriously misleading and also dangerously wrong. The denigration of thought, which leads to muddy and often self-serving thinking, is the exact opposite of what humanity needs in *this* now. We need much better, more strategic thinking coming from care, intelligence (which includes thought but is not identical to it), and causal analysis with intuitive foresight. Instead of constricting awareness to an arbitrary, narrow, internal band of the "now" focused on and revolving around an individual's surrender to the panorama of their inner flow and sensory input, we need to broaden and expand awareness to include many more things that are not in our direct field of perception but are still happening now—such as potential future consequences of our past and present actions, which are in embryonic forms in the pregnant now.

Excluding thought and the larger world from "presence" excludes much of what is important in life. We do not think a meaningful and relevant view of spirituality is about personal achievement, nor does it exclude our world. We see spirit embedded in the world and in the evolutionary momentum that made us, and that we are a part of—it runs through us. It is the underlying energy that moves us to creativity, curiosity, and the pursuit of meaning because it is the energy that moves the evolutionary process. Most of us have felt moved by an energy into creativity or even a shift in relation to life. In different times spirit manifests differently. The phrase "spirit of the times" captures how individuals can either participate or not in that momentum. This spirit can move through a person or a group, opening boundaries, but it cannot be kept, acquired, or possessed. In these times the call is very clear; more and more people are hearing it. It is a call to evolve socially and connect in new, more viable ways. Many of us can feel this deep in ourselves.

Connecting is a dynamic, active, living process that involves individuals opening their boundaries—but not indiscriminately—to care and love. Connectivity can be a source of insight that can move us beyond our perceived individual limitations. Circumstances that favor connecting are needed and we think arising. Given that everything is presumed to already be interconnected, unity worldviews do not really allow for connecting, let alone offer viable values that foster it and are relevant to the tightrope we all walk between egotism and altruism. Thousands of years have proved that the major agenda of these established religions—getting rid of ego—is a misguided and futile task, neither possible nor desirable.

We call unity worldviews where interconnection is a static, timeless concept of everything being connected "the mobile theory of existence": if any part moves, the whole of existence is affected and affects everything else. Here even a butterfly's flight would somehow affect everything else. This not uncommon assumption is held because the believers have not seen that pushing the belief that "Boundaries are not real" to its end conclusion results in an extreme that borders on absurdity. It is far more likely that not all information passes through all boundaries because existence contains different levels of complexity of organization, with "levels boundaries" separating them. In living organisms boundaries open and close, which occurs in time and takes time. In a real sense making boundaries unreal makes individuation and connecting unreal, as it takes separate individuals to connect.

Our collective world includes commonalities and differences of thought that create a diversified yet shared climate of reference to global issues that underlies our daily activities. The social and political climate of democracy or dictatorship, prosperity or oppression, peace or war, celebration or dangers, affects our lives. If your country or the world is at war or suffering economic depression or natural disasters, it's either in the foreground or background of your awareness. The broader the reach of your concern and empathy, the more that global concerns live in you and are part of your reality. Care brings the "there" "here," so even to say "Be *here* now" contains assumed boundaries and cut-offs from the rest of what's happening in the broader social and global here and now.

It is essential that we become more conscious of being Earthlings, as has happened on a few occasions—when everyone watched in awe as the first rocket was launched into outer space, then again with the first man on the moon. The whole planet celebrated entering the new millennium together hour by hour, around the clock as the midnight hour moved from place to place, with each country contributing or performing in their own unique way on television—a powerful planetary experience. We as a species need more to celebrate that can bind us together.

More recently, nearly the whole world rejoiced with enormous relief when the first potentially global president of the United States was elected to replace one hated far and wide who wreaked global havoc and brought the world down in eight years by an incredible incompetence matched only by shameless nepotism that filled the coffers of his cronies at the world's expense, all coated with religious certainty. A true man of the past. This came at a time when the concept, ideal, and reality of democracy was gravely undermined and even seemed nearly vanquished by the forces of authoritarian reaction in the country that founded democracy in modern times. The global damage that one government administration in one nation can do and the resulting worldwide economic crisis make clear how interdependent the world now is.

Much of the appeal of stilling thought is related to the nature of the thoughts and feelings that one has. If one's thoughts feel good, there's naturally less impetus to quiet them. However, much of thought is habitual loops stuck in conflict, fear, feelings of inadequacy, and various types of discomfort. Quieting disturbing thoughts can give welcome, usually beneficial respite. This is all the more true if one's life or country is oppressive or if the world is in turmoil. Throughout history in difficult times, with no real possibility of improvement or changing things, in the face of much suffering sages have advised withdrawing into oneself to detach from the world and its pain as a way of coping and feeling better.

In Eastern worldviews, practices for detaching from thought and desire gave individuals some inner protection from and control over their emotions, thoughts, and attitudes. Emotional control through detachment as a self-defense mechanism was the only control then available to many.

Now too is one such deeply troubled time. The now without thought can indeed feel better if "better" means less fear, or more good feelings, or even more internal peace. Being timeless without troublesome thoughts can be an antidote to the pressures of modern life, a revitalizing balancing of the nervous system to better face the world or day. Techniques for quieting thought can be a valuable arrow in your quiver as part of a repertoire. Being quiet with oneself, whether in nature, sitting, hearing music, or lying comfortably, can help you relax, become more centered, and counteract the imbalances of civilization and unhealthy stresses of modern life. This is very different from holding silence and timelessness as superior, revolutionary, or more spiritual than thinking or "using time" to do things. Instead of simply acknowledging that trying to quiet thought can be motivated by needing respite and wanting to feel better (a healthy desire), it's being touted as a superior and special way to be all the time. Prescribing silencing thought as the solution to personal and social problems, not to mention a grand strategy for survival, comes from old ego-bashing ideologies that have not and cannot work. The ways we humans have used thought have gotten us where we are, and it's only thinking better, more clearly, and awarely that can get us out of it.

The question then also becomes how are you in the now, and what difference does it make? When the agenda (sometimes hidden even from oneself) is really to minimize and internally still the layerings of the present that are not comfortable, this can inhibit one's ability to be moved by them and to deal with them awarely. (More on this when we discuss meditation.) Trying to be timeless through silencing thought can easily become an escape mechanism from what's happening right now in the world that is frightening, uncertain, and dangerous. What passes for being in "timeless reality" can actually be "time out from reality"—depending on how your worldview defines "reality." If the hidden agenda of feeling good by withdrawing into the self to escape less pleasant "nows" is popularized as an effective way to meet world challenges, this is a tremendous deflection from the needs of the times.

To denigrate thought as merely coming from ego is to do it and the ego great injustice. The ego can become just as involved with saving the species as it can with winning a chess game, or healing a relationship, both of which require thought and insight. Detaching from the self and approaching time through limiting the now to what one is personally confronted with is a bad survival strategy. Although it might bring some quality moments, it does not improve the quality of the world. Aside from misleading and distracting people from the awareness and unfettered thinking needed to address urgently pressing issues, it frames the problem obtusely and points people in the wrong direction. It's confusing, dysfunctional, and dangerous to prioritize timelessness by denigrating thinking about the future—a sorely needed skill that must be further developed to be vastly more far-reaching instead of tethered and stigmatized by old ideologies.

It's possible and fruitful to look at the different problems that both Eastern and Western cultures are facing as connected to the imbalances created by the either/or thinking within their worldviews (which also places their worldviews in opposition). The East in its yearning for the eternal ("being") has developed practices to help individuals turn inward, on occasion connecting with an energy and power larger than themselves. But holding life and the individual cheaply has been and still is inherent in this worldview, which has brought great poverty and human degradation, matched by fatalism. The West is exemplified by the way that science values progress ("becoming"). This has given us great technical mastery, leverages to power, and many material advantages—including a longer life—but has also fostered the isolation, alienation, and hedonism that accompany the spiritual vacuum within a consumer society. In reaction to modern ills and fears, a fervent religious revival of outmoded authoritarian worldviews is burgeoning in many places. All these are major factors putting us at risk.

The fact is that we live in time, for even when we are in those timeless moments, time passes. Time is a very real dimension of human existence. The human mind evolved to remember and learn from the past and anticipate the future in order to, in some degree, manipulate the present and to have some say in what the future will bring. While planting a seed, in that moment one can be totally involved in the act of planting. Yet one still hopes and knows from the past that doing so will probably bring the desired flowers. This capacity of having memories of the past and anticipating the future has been a major evolutionary advantage—and could be again if we can make it match and guide if not control our technological advances instead of being run by them. But our capacity to anticipate the possible consequences of our actions is extremely undeveloped for what is required "now" in this new, fast-paced, technological era. We must now develop that capacity more than ever to keep up with all that we've set in motion. We need a new relation to time, and to spirituality, that includes truth-seeking and connecting. To detach is to detach from care. We need to care about the repercussions of what we do and be attached to getting better at care-taking. For the overall betterment of present and future personal and social nows, we crucially need to be more aware of how we live in time, with thought, while looking for whatever truth and objectivity is available.

Our home on Earth can no longer be taken for granted. Worldviews that see this world and life itself as a lowly springboard for a spirituality whose main function is to test and measure self-sacrifice are obsolete. Instead of focusing on "higher" states or spiritual-seeking as self-gratifying entertainment, wishful thinking, or self-absorbed, self-justifying, only seemingly self-denying fantasy, our connection to spirituality needs to be brought down to Earth. This means seeing that spirit infuses life rather than exists in some other realm.

Greater awareness of the past and future will make us a more conscious part of the evolutionary process. The Earth is now crying out for care-taking. A spiritual relation to time must involve the many facets of care: caring, care-taking, taking care of, being care-full—which puts the future front and center of our concerns (future consequences and possibilities), for one cannot care for anything without caring for its and *the* future. In order to take care of something one needs to understand it, to identify the past and present causes of problems, and to discover solutions based on causality and future implications in order to plan effective strategies for the future. All of this involves good clear thinking, care, and insight. This is the evolutionary challenge we're facing. As future possibilities are contained within the living now, how we as a species use our minds, thoughts, emotions, and intuitions to envision and counter the long-term consequences of our actions will either construct or not, help or prevent, our chances.

9. Meditation

This chapter can be viewed as a meta-meditation—a meditation on the nature of meditation, examining its many aspects, relevance, and implications. The topic is timely because of the need for a consciousness shift, which is critical if we are to move into adulthood as a species. Meditation is often presented as a way of exploring the nature of consciousness, bringing greater clarity and wisdom. Being conscious is a core part of being human that each of us can tap into through our own self-reflective capacities and experiential feedback. Though meditation can help in this process, it can also reinforce the conditioned habit patterns that filter the way information is perceived, internalized, and acted upon. Whether meditation expands the mind or conditions it, broadening or constricting awareness, largely depends on the worldview (with its assumptions, values, and goals) that stands behind the practice. This includes how the practice is taught and what effects it is designed to produce. We approach our inquiry by examining the benefits and potential of meditation, including its hidden drawbacks.

For millennia cultures of the East have focused their explorations inward, while in the West cognizance of an inner approach to understanding has been limited—that is, until its twentieth-century upsurge in the mainstream. The West has put enormous emphasis on understanding through science and external routes, studying the world and people as outside observers. Since Freud the West's way of going within has been psychotherapy, different in practice and intent from the East's. The external scientific focus gave our species ever-increasing power through an understanding of the physical, mechanical, and predictable aspects of the universe and ourselves. Its strength lies in creating a process that is self-correcting. Science is a feedback model that is challengeable and changeable. As objectively as is possible, it uses reason and values derived from repeatable experiences that are both verifiable and falsifiable, presided over by the overall agreement of specialists. It proves itself by prediction, control, and workability.

But what about the unique, the creative, the spontaneous? Can a human being or the universe be totally understood by reason and science alone? Are love, care, emotions, and beauty reducible to an equation the mind can create? Or are there realms of understanding that come from a different place?

The strength of the Eastern inward approach to understanding lies in being able to touch directly into what's going on inside oneself. Since a human being is a miniature universe, manifesting an expression of what evolution produces, self-awareness enables one to directly experience aspects of the way the cosmos works, in a personal, unmediated way. To the extent that one can touch into both the complexity and the simplicity of the inner workings of one's own being, one can experience patterns of impersonal universal processes.

The great danger of the inward approach to understanding lies in how easily fear, desire, beliefs, preference, and attachments reinforce subjectivity. It is so easy to tell yourself what you want to hear and be blinded by your mental projections and emotions. If going within is colored by my wants and images from the past, or by my beliefs and values, or my deepest fears of death and dying, then what I see will itself be tainted with the very subjectivity I hope to transcend. This is the great paradox and weakness of the inner path. Unlike science, going inward is not easily correctable by feedback, as one is almost always looking through one's subjective filters, which includes a worldview that is generally taken for granted. With spiritual practices in particular, this obstacle to true clarity is compounded by the fact that one may also be looking through the worldview filters of teachers who design and prescribe the practices.

Traditionally, the emotional bond between seekers on an inner journey and their teachers was the link that helped counter the dangers of getting lost in the mind's projections and endless capacity to create its own world—with itself at the center. But relying on a guru to correct one's subjective biases and conditioning creates a different danger: out of the need for certainty, security, and feeling protected, it is so easy for the seeker to create a subjective world with the guru at the center. Here, under the guise of looking within, one can in fact be merely internalizing another person's viewpoint. The methodology of another person being one's mirror is invaluable and irreplaceable—but mirroring only works long-term in the context of the basic equality necessary for mutual feedback. Since gurus are considered perfect, they have no one to mirror them. Few teachers (even those who do not claim perfection) are really open to having an environment of equality with their students. In fact, it's even more impossible if a teacher is authoritarian, because there can be no equal, two-way exchange with real dialogue or feedback. Then there's no real teaching—just another unchallengeable authority who cuts off learning because you get involved in or seduced into belief and suspend your own inquiry.

We believe that looking within oneself and at the external world, including what other people are thinking and doing, are two different and complementary routes to exploring the timeless questions "Who am I? How do I fit into the scheme of life, and what is it to be human?" In this chapter we distinguish between meditation practices and a meditative frame of mind, the latter being akin to the kind of awareness explored throughout these discussions. We hope that this book can aid you in delving into the deepest regions of your being.

M editation in its different forms has moved from being an Eastern spiritual import to a mainstream Western practice. When people meditate, what do they want and seek? Many use meditation to alleviate tension and stress in a manner that can be more interesting and healthy than many other means, with the idea that it can lead to something deeper. Because books, gurus, and meditation teachers often paint extraordinary pictures of experiences and transformations possible through regular practice, many choose to meditate as a spiritual path. Most types of meditation aim toward something else, so people meditate usually for some reason, whether physical, emotional, health-related, or for other benefits: centering, stress relief, relaxation, insight, exploration of consciousness, and as a spiritual path. There is some intention or desire in the process, at least in the background, even if it is simply to feel better. One reason meditation has become popular is because people want something predictable that will help them have more control over thoughts and emotions, which is appealing. Meditation is usually presented as a way of shutting off the extraneous "noise" that life continually bombards us with, including the noise of our endlessly chattering minds.

When the mind is engaged, interested, learning, playing, exploring—that is, enjoying what it is doing—there is little motivation to quiet it. But for so many of us, when not being filled with external stimuli and interests or relating, the mind is busy with conflicts, duties, fears, and desires. Life gets mapped out with responsibilities and work so that one's time seems not to be one's own. Turning inward and seeking a quiet place in oneself can be a counter to a frenetic life. For some people, meditation may be their only peaceful time alone. In addition, meditation connotes for many an activity that offers access to different states of being, consciousness, awareness, presence, and profundity that are said to be cumulative through regular practice.

All meditations are exercises of the mind, and like physical exercises, different ones do different things. The mind can become calmer in a wide variety of ways, from being in nature, listening to music, being in the flow in sports, fishing, weaving, etc. Most meditation practices involve quieting or silencing thought, although some try to get you to think differently. Methodologies vary widely: witnessing sensations or whatever your inner panorama is displaying; focusing on breath and the body or affirmations; visualizing a person, emotion, or symbol. One type of meditation even promotes repeatedly imaging your heart's desire, be it money, world peace, or a Ferrari.

The simple act of trying to relax reveals the nature of a typical "bind of mind" that we've been discussing. Wanting to relax while tense is a desire to be a way that you are not, which is a form of inner conflict. Of course struggling to relax is counter-productive, increasing tension—similar to trying to fall asleep when you can't. Trying to still thought is just more thinking so (similar to trying to relax) it cannot be done directly. Behind the effort is the hope (a thought) that it will help you in some way. The mind can't relax through trying or effort, although techniques that refocus the mind can be effective. Since the mind and body are interconnected, another route to quieting the mind is through relaxing the body—whether through exercise, body techniques, massage, or touch.

Knowing how to get out of ordinary modes of thinking is valuable. Since the human body and mind have mechanical aspects, they can be approached mechanically to bring certain predictable effects. It's possible to quiet your mind mechanically and gain some control over mental habits. A mechanical technique involves repetition, which is a form of concentration, with specific instructions as to how and where to put your awareness in order to gain certain results. You can say a word or *mantra* over and over again (*"Om,"* "Hare Krishna"), count prayer beads, follow your breath—anything, it doesn't matter—to bring at least a surface quietness. Many other practices and concentration techniques can shift the nervous system, ranging from visualizations, affirmations, and autogenic training to complex machines like biofeedback units.

You can also see most any vision you desire, as the mind is both powerful and very facile at eventually spinning out anything it wants—whether visions or feeling certain qualities or energies. You might experience altered states, timelessness, and even a sense of being connected to a basic universal source and even all beings everywhere. If you want to experience heart openings, oneness, loving-kindness, or compassion, one way this might come is through focusing on loved ones. Imagining and remembering them can make you feel more open, a broadening that can be expanded through concentrating on it. Remembering a joyous experience brings back pleasant feelings, creating mental and emotional openings, including the release of neurochemicals connected with the experience. Some practices are of a different order—more of an art that involves mind/body awareness, such as yoga, t'ai chi, and martial arts—or chanting, which like singing is beneficial and uplifting with energizing, clearing vibrations.

Our bodies have layers of mechanisms that build habits, much of which we are not conscious of, but that deeply influence the thought patterns we habitually repeat. If thought quiets, this can influence the underlying patterns and bring relaxation or centeredness—and on occasion insight. However, if meditation is primarily used as a stepping stone to a preconceived idea or notion of where I think I'd like to end up, this mental framework means I'm still involved in thought, even if the thought is in the background. If I'm involved in trying to quiet myself, isn't thought telling me that doing so is a good thing? This is yet another example of what is meant by being caught in "the bind of mind."

Look, my mind is very noisy. If I observe the nature of the noise, which is thought, I see just what we have been discussing together—fear, ambition, conflict, beliefs. I see what a distraction the noise can be from things I value more, how it can court sorrow by shadowing the moment. I say to myself, "Wouldn't it be nice to be still?" So I try through techniques to quiet myself. Yet a mind ambitious for quietness is a noisy, busy mind underneath.

If those of you involved in meditative techniques observe carefully what you are doing, I think you will find that often a part of you is watching and waiting for changes to take place, for the promises to be realized, for the goodies to happen—like taking an aspirin and waiting for it to work, or waiting for a cocktail or a drug to take effect. Through one technique or another a temporary stillness may ensue, but the noise— and the conflicts, concerns, anxieties, or whatever the content of the noise is—eventually returns. That's one reason people practice meditation daily, like regular physical exercise.

All mechanical meditative techniques have limitations, which doesn't mean they're not helpful. Like many tools, they're double-edged; they can be useful or dulling. If your son is noisy and you give him a toy, he'll become quiet while the toy is absorbing him. When he loses interest or you take the toy away, he cries out for a new toy and becomes noisy again. Likewise, mechanical approaches can be helpful for changing mental states or toys for mental projections. I'm not implying that anything is wrong with techniques or agendas or a desire for something different. If approached with awareness they can bring learning, as mental and physical exercises are prone to do.

Mantra meditation is a good illustration of both aspects. Repeating a *mantra* or anything long enough can calm and refresh you by removing you from your usual concerns, stresses, and habitual ways, which makes you feel better; yet it also contains the problems of living. *Mantra* contains ambition to achieve or repeat a state, as well as a belief that it's good for you. Since *mantra* repetition removes one from ordinary habits for a time, it may be possible to see one's patterns and conditioning more readily, or it can be an escape from what you don't want to see. So *mantra* is double-edged because it too is conditioning that, like all mechanical things, can remove you from a more aware relation with life. In terms of awareness, the real use of any repetitive practice is to see the nature and limitations of the practice. Seeing the limitations within a practice does not limit its benefits. The mechanical gives you mechanical results; to see that is to move beyond it. Seeing techniques as tools for gaining certain results frees you to do them or not, depending on your needs and interests.

In this day and age many of us are quite exploratory and experienced with different psychological and "spiritual" viewpoints and styles of meditation. We go eclectically from one form of stimulation to another, from experience to experience, workshop to workshop, teacher to teacher—all of them possibly offering something valuable. And out of accumulating so much varied experience, we become more knowledgeable and sophisticated. However, people seldom realize the importance of a worldview in influencing how they internalize and interpret the experiences. This is all the more true if one is a spiritual seeker, which is a category all its own, with particular sets of beliefs, hopes, and desires, as well as pitfalls, paradoxes, and limitations. Many seekers move from guru to guru, from one belief system to another, always searching for the best path or something deeper and more meaningful, afraid of missing what is said to be the most important aspect of life.

Many meditations were and still are presented as a path to a way of being that is or feels higher or better or more spiritual. It is vital to be aware that all meditations presented as a path to greater spirituality, awareness, loving-kindness, enlightenment, *samadhi, nirvana,* a better next life, whatever, all have a worldview that the respective meditations are designed to promote. This is so even with meditations that purport to be ideologically neutral. Usually being on a higher path involves a worldview containing the belief that eventually eliminating or at least controlling what are considered the baser parts of being human—such as envy, hatred, jealousy, cravings, ego gratification, and the like—is the gateway to spirituality. Because competition often contains aggression, it too is to be eventually transcended.

Traditional meditations have in common the goal of something called ego loss, and a worldview that sees ego as an obstacle to spirituality. Seeking ego loss is part of the spiritual paradox, for it is the ego itself that seeks ego loss because of beliefs that not having an ego would be a better state to be in. The very concept of ego loss as a spiritual path comes from thought, and also from the ego itself because it involves the desire for the seeker's particular advancement. That's just another source of separation involving images and a presumed "spiritual" hierarchy.

Actually, to be on a "higher" path is a highly competitive activity because being "higher" necessarily requires a hierarchy of values. Whoever is at the top of the hierarchy (whether a person, a teacher, pope, guru, prophet, or self-proclaimed interpreters of sacred texts and traditions) determines which values are sacred. Where you stand on the hierarchy determines your progress and value—whether measuring yourself internally with your ideal self-image or externally with others. When there is a hierarchy of spiritual accomplishments within groups, this brings either overt or covert competition as to where on the hierarchy you stand and who determines it.

Another common behavioral paradox in the so-called spiritual world is that spiritual competition can become all engrossing and self-absorbing, even though the spiritual ideal is invariably to transcend ego and self-centered behavior, including competition. The spiritual leader who determines rank on the spiritual ladder is of course dominant, which seekers expect and want. This is fundamentally no different from other forms of dominance, except in spirituality it is more hidden, or at least the dominant ones have to appear detached from needing or enjoying the dominance. If you're a businessman, it's fine to be competitive and recognized as such. But if you're on a spiritual path, you're not supposed to be competitive and proud of it—it's not spiritual, so it has to be slyer and more hidden (often even from oneself). This creates an unfortunate inconsistency: by the very nature of having a worldview that negates and denigrates the ego with the resulting unlivable values, spiritual practices that claim to increase awareness instead actually increase unconsciousness in those very domains (competition, power, control, dominance, and self-centeredness) where awareness is most needed, resisted, and lacking.

As typically happens with unlivable ideals such as ego loss, they create behavioral paradoxes: to win the spiritual competition you have to appear to be the most modest and non-competitive. Unlivable values breed their opposite—hypocrisy, corruption, and deceit. Like a moral "arms race," both gurus and politicians have to appear the most self-less to successfully compete with others doing the same. So many people follow—and elect—the best hypocrites, performers, and liars. (This is a serious problem in democracies with influential religions that promote unlivable ideals, since hidden self-interest is harder to regulate.)

To be hungering after spirituality is not essentially different from hungering after anything else, though we usually place it on a higher plane. It's like trying to cultivate humility—the "I'm very humble" persona of course means "I'm better than you who aren't." True humility is never cultivated and cannot be. Real humility comes only when I truly see that I am basically no different from you, no better in any ultimate way than anyone. No matter how great my achievements, no matter how externally significant I appear, the fact is that I'm really no different from you in very fundamental ways. From that knowledge comes real humility. It comes from seeing yourself, which requires being interested and willing to look at what might be very different from your self-image. Of course we are also very different. Difference is essential for individuation. Yet we can accept, appreciate, and cultivate whatever our special talents or attributes may be without putting them at the apex of a hierarchy of value, with ourselves on or near the top. When differences are made grounds for superiority, they become identities that separate us and fragment the world.

Most meditation practices aim, through quieting thought, to give people more control over their thoughts, emotions, and how they feel. This is so even if the avenue used is one of surrender to whatever their mental and emotional flow brings. Of course, when space is made by interrupting usual networks and patterns, the mind does not actually become empty. It should be self-evident that when thought does "still," when one is not actually thinking, thought merely stops being active temporarily and is no longer in the foreground of consciousness. Then, depending on what one is paying attention to, other experiences such as sensations, feelings, breath, or the body replace thought, either intentionally or by coming to the fore on their own.

An empty mind is only empty at the surface. That is to say, thought's basic structures and habits are not really eliminated. Stilling thought just shifts focus and patterns, changing the brain's energy and activity levels, brain waves, and so on. It does not change thought's core cognitive frameworks. Stilling thought can bring insight that affects thought's structures but does not itself necessarily do this. As with sleep, the mind is not emptied of its contents in meditation; its memories, accumulated experiences, and knowledge about the world and oneself remain intact, as well as its beliefs and values, and its cognizance of relationships with others. So the mind brings its entire cognitive structuring to the meditation as sub-stratum and retains it during the meditation, regardless of what thought is or is not thinking.

Spiritual practices in particular are all devised from within a world view and its values, which determine the nature, goals, and methods of the practices. Newcomers to the practice bring one worldview or another, an open or closed mind, with interest and possibly doubts, but they are not a blank slate. They are then instructed how to do the practice, what to look for, what to expect, and how to interpret the experiences that the practices are devised to create. If practitioners already hold the accepted worldview, the practice reinforces it. If not, eventually the practice along with group influence usually induces them to take on some or all of the beliefs. If the practitioner does not "convert," this may or may not interfere with the practice.

Worldviews are often either taken for granted or invisible to the holder because they seem like reality. Consequently, a blind spot develops, with huge ramifications in many spiritual practices: when thought stills, the worldview continues to largely determine the very nature of the "mindfulness," what one is mindful of, and the conclusions and beliefs later drawn from the experiences.

The human mind and human relations thrive on having or creating meaning. Awareness is not just being aware of one's immediate surroundings; it involves correctly interpreting the intention behind a glance or the import of consistent environmental changes. Establishing meaning involves mental acuity over time, and most types of meditation purposely delete meaning from their methodology. This denies the need to interpret experiences through a broader lens than meditation—which increases the danger of becoming more unconscious.

In the control/surrender dialectic, Eastern spiritual worldviews all value surrender over control. Whenever one side of an embedded relation is valued more, it is a sign of imbalance that gives rise to unconscious "behavioral paradoxes," which are incongruities between an ideal and the behavior. {It's also a sign of authoritarianism and spiritual hierarchy as described in *The Guru Papers*.} Eastern meditation practices are generally designed to prevent thought from controlling you by surrendering to whatever arises.

Even Buddha's goal of eliminating or reducing suffering is in effect the desire to control it. The method he recommended, detaching from attachments and desire, is likewise a means of self-control. So at one level Buddhism uses surrender to detach you, while at another level it actuality increases control—as self-protection from suffering. People are taught to surrender to the inner flux and flow of thoughts and feelings by simply witnessing them as they go by. This practice is guided by instructions on how to ignore and detach from mental and emotional contents so as not to get caught up in (controlled by) them, which necessarily negates the meanings of the content.

Meaning is thus discounted and is considered along with ego, the self, and one's "story" as an obstacle that blocks experience of the pure, ever-changing flow of consciousness. As a result of discounting the content (meaning) of thoughts and emotions to avoid being "grabbed" by them, whatever is repressed in meditation can keep recurring because its meaning is never understood or resolved. Discounting meaning is related to another imbalance in the Buddhist worldview within the dialectic of change and permanence (continuity). Buddhism posits change as the underlying reality. The resulting "behavioral paradox" is that only focusing on change, without meaning, creates continuity in the persistence and recurrence of unresolved issues. Saying "All is change" is both a method of detachment and a conclusion that verifies the worldview. A closed circle.

Although many people find meditation worthwhile, lest one assume that meditation is always only beneficial (as is the predominant view), note that some who have meditated consider themselves casualties. A significant scientific literature exists on the damage that meditation has caused. It shows that for every study that "proved" the psycholog ical and physical benefits of meditation, other scientific studies (not mentioned in "spiritual" literature) have found the opposite. Furthermore, almost always the experiments with positive results (actually most experiments) are done by believers in meditation—a fact that even the laudably scientifically-minded Dalai Lama laments, acknowledging that it undermines credibility. Other scientists deem many of the exper- imental designs to be unreliable and not replicable (thus unscientific).

In addition negative, scary, or unpleasant repressed parts of oneself can arise in meditation, sometimes with lasting effects. Mental and emotional content has surfaced during meditation that exposed people to things they were not equipped to deal with. This is all the more true if someone is emotionally vulnerable or unstable. Since meditation by its nature negates analyzing and interpreting the content of what the mind and emotions bring up, some American Buddhist meditation teachers recommend using psychotherapy as an adjunct to fill medi- tation's lacks and repair its harm.

The devaluation and negation of mental and emotional contents is a form of mind control (in both senses of the word), under the guise of "surrender," that can limit the self-understanding and overall aware- ness of long-term meditators. Meditation may or may not be a source of intuition and insight, depending on the worldview and agendas you bring to it. However, meditation does not necessarily make you more aware; it can even dull and decrease awareness so that one gets further mired in the projections of one's own mind. Although this can happen from any type of meditation, it is more likely when a spiritual framework or agenda is involved since this introduces more desire, images, hopes, and expectations—along with the accompanying binds of mind and potential disappointments.

If one meditates within a worldview that teaches not only how to do it, but interprets what happens in it for the meditator, one's awareness will be circumscribed by the limitations of that worldview and its teachings—including its potential flaws, blind spots, authoritarianism, and obsolete aspects. This is not to say that "flow," witnessing, or other forms of meditation are not valuable in many ways, including bringing deep insights. I'm just suggesting that it's prudent to be familiar with the range and possible limitations of negating meaning and not to assume that meditation automatically enhances awareness in living.

As a modernizer and reformer of Hinduism's hierarchy, dogma, and cosmological speculations, Buddha reputedly admonished people to trust their own meditation experience over teachings and teachers, and to challenge dogma. Change and modernization within Buddhism over millennia imbued Buddhist teachings with the spirit of anti-hierarchy and reform. That hierarchies of power still predominate within Buddhism and its sacred texts testifies to the fact that no matter what a founder says, organized religions petrify the beliefs of the founders and other revered "masters" by making them sacred, and adherents of the religion always manage to create hierarchies that profit those on top. However, more than other religions, Buddha's critical spirit and reformist vision gave permission to modernizers over millennia to renew and reform Buddhism from within. Because religious authorities continually create power hierarchies based on interpreting ossified sacred scriptures, vigilance in the spiritual arena is ever necessary (just as it is vital to democracy). Although Buddhist practitioners are told to trust only their meditation experience, the practices are taught by telling people what experiences they will have, how to interpret them, and what they reveal about the nature of reality.

The current Dalai Lama officially gives science priority over Buddhist dogma whenever they conflict (unlike the pope), courageously challenging the blind faith and superstition especially rampant among the uneducated in Asian Buddhism, where people pray and make offerings to Buddha as a god and magical being—many never even having heard of the Four Noble Truths.

With this in mind let's look at Zen Buddhism, which many thoughtful Western seekers have turned to for a relevant spiritual tradition. I focus on Zen because it is considered one of the cleaner spiritual traditions and the least frilly, most down-to-Earth form of Buddhism. Zen has a long tradition of *roshi*-reformers clearing its worldview of dogma to bring back a simplicity within awareness. It originated in sixth-century China in Ch'an Buddhism, where metaphysical speculation was discarded (as Buddha had done) to teach that salvation is an inner enlightenment that comes in an instant, in a sudden conversion obtainable here and now, as it came to Buddha. Japanese Zen adopted this spirit of hostility to scriptures and much that had become traditional in Buddhism, stripping Buddhism of dogma and overlays. Instead Zen's teachings and practices were geared at promoting instant enlightenment. At one level, the goal of Zen is to bring students to the realization that it is only the "pristine moment" that allows for *satori* or a mini-*satori.* This is said to come only when ego is suspended, which is what the practices aim at.

Buddha replaced the Hindu *atman* ("higher" or absolute Self) with the doctrine of *anatman* (no-self). He denied the reality of the *atman* Self as well as the "small" self that Hinduism pronounced an illusory obstruction to *atman.* Since Buddha experienced what he called his enlightenment in meditation, he taught this practice so others could experience it too. In so doing, he shifted the focus and goal of meditation away from the Hindu goal of realizing the universal *atman* in oneself in order to have better reincarnations and ultimately get off the Wheel of Life. His practices were designed instead to help people experience and understand his doctrine of no-self and to undermine their sense of self through detachment—in order to free them from suffering.

If there is really no self, then ego is an illusory construction of thought, and ridding oneself of that illusion is the prerequisite for enlightenment. This worldview assumption became the goal of many Eastern practices. As Zen is *renunciate,* its traditional forms promote unlivable ideals of purity through self-renouncing. Claiming to be more pure than other forms of Buddhism, it easily falls into the spiritual competition trap of equating the most renunciation with the most spirituality. So at one extreme Zen is rigid, harshly austere, authoritarian, anti-body, anti-pleasure, and ego-bashing.

In Japan the harshest, most ascetic Zen monasteries are considered the most spiritual. They promise ego loss with practices geared at breaking the ego and the will through extreme physical deprivations and suffering (even though the ultimate agenda of Buddhism is to quell suffering). Breaking the spirit and will is equated with breaking the ego—an ancient version of mind control and brainwashing. Those who obey the most fervently, meditate the longest, eat the least, get up the earliest, wash with the coldest water, and shrink their egos to the will of the master are the best students. The few who become masters in turn demand complete obedience and likewise break people down through deprivation and punishment. (Often gurus teach what "worked" for them since that's what they know.) Zen too, in its guise of doing away with religious rituals and dominance, is much like all the other routes to enlightenment in practice. During a two-hour visit with the head abbot of a famous Zen temple in Kyoto, a continual stream of young acolytes and students crawled in and out to serve us, backing away with their faces touching the ground.

As a contemporary context for meditation, Zen aims at spiritual awakening through reinforcing the dominance of the teacher. You go to a Zen master. (Obviously any structure where some members are called masters automatically sets up a dominance/submission relationship, especially when lineage is made important.) You go to a man versed in Zen and ask, "Zen master, tell me what life is really about. Tell me about my real self and how to find it." Then the Zen master may do one of those charming, paradoxical things one reads about: laugh at you, tell you to listen to the sound of one hand clapping, hit you with a stick, or send you away on a Zen mission. When you return he'll do it again. Or he'll tell you to go sit facing the wall for an hour a day; then for two hours a day. Then you'll come back and he'll tell you to do it for three hours a day—so say Zen stories.

Why, when you come to him with a question of great intensity, why does the Zen master laugh at you or hit you with a stick, or any of the quixotic things the masters in Zen stories do? What is he saying to you? The answer isn't complicated, really. He's telling you of the absurdity of your coming to him and asking him questions that you can only answer by looking within yourself. Of course you keep coming back to him until you see the absurdity yourself; then you finally stop coming. But why doesn't he just tell you this directly? Why doesn't he just say, "Look, no one can answer that question for you. You've got to find out for yourself." Why doesn't he just say that? Perhaps that is how he learned from his master and he is "doing Zen" somewhat mechanically; or perhaps he knows or suspects that you won't believe him—instead you'll just go to someone else who will tell you what you want to hear. And when you do that, you're lost. So at least if you keep going back to him, maybe you'll have a chance. And that, essentially, is the game of Zen.

Although the focus of Zen is supposedly to do away with structures, on another level Zen creates its own mystiques and mystifications, supernatural legends and lineages. You hear stories where the Zen master renounces his masterhood, or Buddha fights the creation of

Buddhism. Ninth-century Zen master Lin chi warned, "If you meet the Buddha on the road, kill him." But one is also told how this or that Zen master is the reincarnation of some famous past Buddhist saint or is part of an unbroken lineage, while on the other hand these very same reputedly reincarnated masters challenge the reality and continuity of the self (and of everything)—so what reincarnates? And how can a lineage, which creates a spiritual hierarchy, be passed on, especially since *satori* is an immediate spontaneous occurrence? How can there be a lineage of spontaneously enlightened masters? Buddhism does have convoluted answers to all this, but the point of Zen was initially to cut through metaphysical convolutions and spiritual hierarchy, not create more of it. In spite of its claims to the contrary, Zen overall has succumbed to its institutions—failed to get rid of structures, titles, spiritual lineages, hierarchies, and other trappings of power. Such are the incongruent double messages within much of Buddhism, which are justified by calling them "spiritual paradoxes," while criticism is deflected by portraying these confusing acts and messages as spiritual teachings, like koans.

In using Buddhism as an example I want to make very clear that I am referring to traditional Buddhism, not the almost countless variants that modernizers are constructing. Anyone involved with a discipline like meditation or yoga for any length of time eventually personalizes it to fit. Given that Buddha's focus was psychological, not creating theoretical dogma, Buddhism lends itself to continual reinterpretation and renewal. Some Buddhists do not have karma or even spirituality as part of their worldview. As part of a much earlier effort in China to reform Buddhism by discarding metaphysical speculation and scriptures (that led to Zen), the sixth-century teacher Bodhidharma reputedly taught "Vast emptiness; no holiness." This says to me that he accepted the concept of the Void, a core Buddhist worldview, but not the spiritual trappings that much of Buddhism had even in his times.

These days especially, people eclectically construct worldviews to fit what they think is true. However, no matter how far afield Buddhists' personal revisions take them, there remains a "basic Buddhism" that includes the Four Noble Truths and the agenda of alleviating suffering that is at the core of the Buddhist worldview. If what I say does not fit your experience of Buddhism, and if you are one of the eclectic modernizers, I hope that this cursory view of traditional Buddhism may have some relevance for whatever track you're on.

All spiritual structures, all paths, all attempts to organize spirituality eventually become power-driven hierarchies where the real concern is maintaining power. This destroys the freedom of all concerned, as their structures repeat the known, ignore new information and the unknown, and stifle the creative in living. Please don't believe me. You have to find it out for yourself.

For centuries organizations and religions have kept us children, because as children we are very manageable and willing to give up adulthood for our spiritual hopes and desires. We are given spiritual entertainments and practices as toys to keep us occupied that sometimes alter our states, which we are told means that we are on the right path. Many spiritual teachers, if you surrender totally to them by making them the new locus of control, can in fact alter many of your conditionings rather quickly—except for one. It is among the most basic conditionings, a meta-program affecting everything else: people's authoritarian conditioning to give their power away to someone who claims with certainty to know what's best for others. This tendency stems from self-mistrust inculcated through failing to live up to unlivable ideals, such as selflessness—another closed circle.

Buddhism, especially Zen, reminds its students to be mindful, which means be attentive to what's around you and what you are doing. This is another way of saying "Be in the now." There is much talk today of "being in the now," with the assumption that meditation or some practice will lead you there. As we saw when examining time, the present is richly multi-faceted, and there is no way not to be in it. It contains the seeds of the past and of future possibilities, as well as the social con-text we find ourselves in, and all the other ways existence is displaying itself "now." So the real question is not "How to be here now?" but "Which here and now are you in?" {Chapter 8 and especially the commentary on Time go deeply into time and timelessness and the hidden quan-daries within the ideal of "being in the now," so just a few of the issues will be touched on here.}

The "now" that meditative practices put you in is your internal land-scape—the now of your breath, sensations, heartbeat, visualizations, a disconnected stream of consciousness with the shifting panorama of emotions and thoughts, or whatever states and openings arise from this, such as on occasion the glow of feeling at one with the universe. Suggestions for mindfulness as you move through daily life are to be present in the beauty of a flower, a bird's flight, the exquisiteness of the moment, where the focus is on the sensory now.

The common thread in all these techniques is the goal of quieting thought. The "now" that many meditative techniques aim at removing you from is the now of your thoughts, not only about the past and future, but about your life and what's going on in the larger world. Since thought cannot be stopped through trying directly, the practices are designed to do it indirectly, through detaching you from the content or distract-ing and replacing thought with something else—hence concentrating on sensations, breath, mantras, objects, walking slowly, and daily activ-ities. Some people find that temporarily removing themselves from the external world and daily life—with its conflicts and the accompanying projections and emotions spun by thought—allows them to approach life with more calmness, centeredness, and clarity.

This can happen, but again I ask which "now" is one attending to, and what is one being mindful of? Both meditation and being mindful empha-size a certain kind of witnessing. ("Don't try to make whatever comes up go away; just observe it until it passes; watch the flow go by without getting involved.") Witnessing is devoid of meaning and interpretation, as they both involve thought. This is another excellent example of the dialectically embedded nature of control and surrender. As I "mind-fully" (which could ironically be defined as "thought-lessly") surrender to whatever presents itself to the sphere of my perception, I am also controlling my emotional states. Interestingly, the dictionary definition of "equanimity" emphasizes calmness under stress, self-control, and imperturbability. What this amounts to is not being bothered by the vicissitudes of life—an understandably desired oasis from the out-of-control world most of us find ourselves in. Taking "time out" sometimes helps revitalize you to meet challenges; sometimes it deflects.

But this "immediacy" approach to a narrowly and arbitrarily defined "here and now" means that what one can be mindful of depends on where one is. Being in the beauty of the forest or in the dangerous hostile territory of a war zone do feel and are extremely different and call for different approaches to the now. In either case, being connected to your environment is valuable, but for different reasons. If you happen to be in the "now" of war, you had better consider future consequences that are part of its now. Is unperturbed equanimity or engaged initiative more valuable when fighting for your life or needing to feed your child or pay the rent, or dealing with any of the often-unwelcome exigencies that come one's way? Some say that you can do everything better with equanimity, but this is just another unlivable ideal. Many extreme occurrences not only demand full attention, they also require unmitigated will. Equanimity is often confused with being centered, but its actual meaning involves control. Centeredness enables one to respond in a total way to living situations; it is not an ongoing state nor is it about control.

The meditative frame of mind is a quality of awareness that is usually not brought about through mechanical means. Although quieting thought can bring worthwhile results, these are different from what I call a living awareness. None of them, no technique, ensures that the quality of awareness that I sometimes refer to as a meditative state of mind will come in a given moment. Calming and relaxing the mind can loosen the intuitive and the creative, but when that occurs it's a gift, not a guarantee. Quieting thought is double-edged, as it can remove you from seeing the layerings occurring within the living moment. Even more importantly, the elements that most determine the value versus the detriments of quieting thought are the worldview and value system of whatever approach to "being here now" one adopts. The framework that promotes it and prescribes practices can program you to devalue thought, and along with it to discount the meanings, implications, and repercussions within one moment for the next moment or the future, for your life or the world.

Living moments as they move out of the past into the future are not isolated *quanta;* they are connected, with each having some influence upon what the next moment will become. As every living moment exemplifies aspects of what could be called the eternal and is also the template for the next moment, so each moment offers a potential depth and breadth for expanding one's awareness. Lest this sound a bit mysterious: I operate under the assumption that everything there is, was, and will be are examples of what existence produces and, to an extent, how it is done. So every moment displays aspects of the processes of creation and destruction and is part of the momentum of evolutionary change.

Quieting thought through technique—whether concentration techniques, which involve effort, or supposedly "surrender techniques," such as paying attention to whatever presents itself (this is concentration in disguise, as it takes focus to pay attention)—are not the kind of meditation I personally find interesting, nor do I find that such methods facilitate the kind of awareness I've been talking about. Concentration is a narrowing of the spectrum of awareness, which actually strengthens the very thought that is supposed to be quieting, for it is thought that is doing it. In concentration there is always one who is concentrating—a separation from the act itself that is thought. Since increasing the mind's abilities has value that could lead to important and unexpected outcomes, training the mind to concentrate is valuable too. Most activities including reading, sports, science, competition, and cooperation require some concentration. However, awareness does not come through concentration techniques; there are no techniques or formulas for becoming aware.

Even when thoughts cease to recur for a time, usually a non-conscious or even a conscious meta-program is saying to itself, "When a thought or an emotion occurs, use this or that method/technique to stop it." This could be as simple as labeling it by saying to yourself, "I'm thinking again," or just "thinking," "anger," "envy," or whatever is occurring and letting it drift away. Or you are told to simply notice that you're thinking, or whatever, and go back to your breath or *mantra.* Any meta-program directing attention is concentration, even though the program may be to surrender to this or that. (One always surrenders to something.) These meta-programs, actually thought programs, which are supposed to help free people from thought and its mechanical aspects, are mechanical forms of thought that instead condition the mind with negative thoughts about thought. It is possible to surrender in meditation and let the flow of your inner panorama take you where it will. This too shows the dialectic between control and surrender, for what you are surrendering to is being controlled by whatever your mind happens to create.

There is a difference between meditation as an activity that you do and a meditative frame of mind, which is a widening of the spectrum of awareness to be more inclusive, with no techniques or programming. This occurs without effort or force from just looking—a looking that is guided by interest, not goal-oriented or with techniques designed to bring a certain type of experience. So depending on one's interest, one can have preferences as to what one attends to. But just as interest is a gift that is not always in one's control, neither is preference.

This meditative frame of mind is alert, receptive, and in a real sense a curious state that is attentive and even passionate about seeing "what is." This passion contains intentionality to see as objectively and clearly as you can, including seeing what filters awareness. Curiosity and intention differ from desire, as desire has an object, while the intention to be aware has no specific object, like awareness itself does not. This frame of mind is not a separation from the world or necessarily without thought. To exclude thought based on a judgment (a thought) that thoughts are not worthy of attention is itself a use of thought that is self-negating—again a "mind bind" that disqualifies itself as a credible judge. One's thoughts are part of what is and can be approached by a meditative mind that is really interested in how one's own mind and the mind in general works. If you find that thoughts are repetitively looping, a technique could be used to temporarily shift the pattern. However, the way thought patterns itself is also a part of what is and can be an interesting inroad to learn about your conditioning.

Quieting thought through meditation techniques may on occasion allow the meditative state of awareness to enter, although there is no guarantee it will come or return. It is more likely to come when there is a real interest and a sense of urgency to see or broaden one's perspectives on "what is"—that is, what's happening, what's going on. It is not a constant state and not always comfortable, but it seems that access to this meditative state of mind increases as you see how it can open you to new and deeper perceptions and understandings.

I think this is a bit different from what we ordinarily envision when we think of meditation. You may listen to people who come from thousands of years of authority with centuries of tradition behind them, and they will tell you something quite different. They will tell you that meditation will lead you to the eternal now (as if that were different from where you are right now), into bliss, joy, spiritual states, unity with everything, enlightenment, eternal life, or a better reincarnation.

The concepts of these states are laden with millennia of glorifying descriptions and have as much baggage as the words "God" and "spiritual." They conjure up a removal from life, or something at least bliss-fully beyond the ordinary, even super-natural. Such states became the stuff of legend and have been kept alive throughout the ages by spiritual teachers who, to this day, must claim access to them for credibility and to compete with others making similar claims.

People get enamored with so-called spiritual practices that promise spirituality—as if it were the accumulation of credits. This is all the more true if they hold or take on a worldview that says they can "become more spiritual," which means possess it as a trait, as if spirituality were a personal accomplishment. (In spiritual parlance, "I'm going to meditate until I get enlightened" illustrates this belief.) In today's more mainstream language, "enlightenment" is often replaced by the ideal of constantly being "in the now," which is sometimes presented as "the only true revolution in consciousness." This verbiage disguises old spiritual worldviews and values as new.

Spirituality, if it has any meaning, is neither a personal acquisition nor an ongoing state that one can arrive at and remain in. Spirit does not live in old religious structures or texts; it lives in living people. If, as I see it, spirit moves the evolutionary process that we are the products of, then as individuals, spirit lives in us. And on occasion we can connect with a larger sense of spirit if we connect with the evolutionary spirit of the times.

Often meditation practices become another way of emotionally self-protecting and controlling oneself. This is not to say that self-control is wrong if you realize you're doing it, how and why, and its implications. But when the practices emanate from a worldview defining them as "spiritual," and leading people to believe they will become more spiritual through doing them, this is a form of mind control. It limits rather than increases overall awareness of one's own and life's dynamics. Instead it entices people to get lost in their desires, whether for enlightenment, eternal life, or endless bliss. Whenever images of spirituality are otherworldly, or related to disguised rewards for years of practice, these are sure signs that spirituality has been separated from life.

A curious mind passionate for exploring and truth-seeking is a meditative mind. It leads to a more engaged, responsive, creative, and interesting life, which is its own reward. You may believe tradition, and it is difficult not to because of its seductive images, which we have been conditioned to trust and accept as "the wisdom of the ages." Those who promulgate tradition have weight and authority on their side; they dangle the carrots of people's greatest hopes and deepest desires. You may believe them or you may believe me—but to do either is not the point. You can only find out for yourself what meditation and the meditative state of awareness are about. The important thing is to look at living and see for yourself; then you'll know, and you won't have to be told. You'll become a light unto yourself, which is what this inquiry is all about.

What then is this meditative frame of mind? It brings more awareness as a way of living, of being, that is its own reward. It is not a stepping stone to get somewhere else; it is not a possession; it cannot be owned or accumulated. It is not something that one does repetitively for a certain period of time. There is no way to practice it. The meditative frame of mind involves an awareness whereby in that instant of seeing there is no separation between seeing and what's seen. This does not mean that the observer is the observed in the literal sense, but that in that moment there is no division. The quality of attention that sees "what is" is neither a removal from the world nor is it simply passive. Although without effort, it can be a profound activity that is a direct confrontation with that which is happening, containing within it aspects of the eternal. Every living moment displays basic forms of how existence constructs itself.

In the process of examining ourselves during these discussions, instead of looking for reputed states we've heard of through others or by reading books, what we have been doing is allowing a meditative state to perhaps enter by coming into direct contact with ourselves. The meditative frame of seeing who and what I am at different moments involves many elements of being human that we have been examining—pleasure, conflict, expectation, fear, desire, belief, and ambition. Instead of running away from, or trying to increase, decrease, or eliminate those aspects of ourselves that we have been conditioned to like or dislike, the meditative attitude is truth-seeking, interested in seeing deeply how I as a person really work. This opens greater degrees of possibility that can move one beyond the conditioned responses of being largely on automatic. Seeing the nature of one's conditioning and on occasion transcending it frees spontaneity, which is a source of creative living.

So what is one to do? People ask what is the best path? A path is where people have been before. But there is no path, no pre-determined or pre-scribed way. The meditative mind blazes the frontiers of the unknown, which is pathless. It requires a passion for whatever truth can be gleaned. This is true seriousness, which is not taking oneself seriously or negating the humor of living. It is a seriousness that involves care and attention. I must care about finding out what I am and what it is to be human. I must be interested, curious. How does one start? One starts by starting, by looking. There are many things one could look at, internally and externally. An interesting place to look is where you might differ from your ideals, and where your ideals came from. And what are your fears, your self-images, desires? What makes you feel superior or inferior?

This passion for truth, for exploration, is what I call meditation in action, in living. The looking, the absorption in experiencing the living moment, is the meditation, and this creates a possible movement into the creative, the unknown. This doesn't aim toward moving anywhere in particular. If you're aiming toward something, you're aiming toward the known. The movement that comes with increased awareness can move into the unknown, and when this happens there is no effort. The energy for creativity that crests on the unknown can threaten established beliefs and supposed truths—of others or one's own. So it challenges our notions of security, which institutions and belief systems have built up over centuries. But especially in these times, there is no real security, and all the securities of insurance policies and the usual things we cloak ourselves with are beginning to crumble, as is the very world around us. Certainly, if one is rich or in a wealthy country there is more possibility of being shielded from crises—or there was. Now the crises go beyond protective barriers. There isn't any such thing as absolute security—not in relationships, the economy, health, and now not even on the Earth. It is more dangerous than ever not to see what is, to be out of touch. It may be more comfortable for a time, until the denial itself creates more problems.

What we've been doing here together, one can do alone or in relationship. Occasionally a removal from our usual environment or being in nature changes one's viewpoint so that one can observe things with more clarity. It is the clarity, the awareness that is the essential ingredient. To be aware, alert, responsive, and responsible is to be an adult. To be totally here is to be totally in relationship. As I get to know myself I get to know that what I am is a being in relationship. Fundamentally what we are is a part of an energy system. The awareness that I'm referring to is a moment-to-moment occurrence that can at times bring a seeing of both the connection among and yet the separation of all things, the embedded nature of unity and diversity. The meditative state is not a denial of the self or removal from relationship, but rather a seeing of the nature of oneself—and others—in relationship.

The meditative frame of mind is the essence of an age-old process of transformation that can be creatively adapted to the needs of the times. It helps break through the habits of mind that bind us, opening up new ways of relating to each other and the world. It also brings sensitivity, response-ability (in its literal sense), and the flexibility that allows us to assimilate change. In the coming years, we need to further develop these capacities to meet the uncertainties of the times. The time of our adolescence is ending. If humanity is to respond to existing challenges, adulthood is necessary. A meditative state of mind can be an adjunct to a new and needed evolutionary awareness.

Awareness is a key that unlocks the door to dealing with the unknown. Conscious evolution is actually about broadening awareness, which does not simply mean being present in the now in a totally accepting way. It also includes being truly responsive to feedback, and foreseeing consequences for the future (in the now). Others have said that awakened consciousness involves a total surrender to "what is," or to put it another way, to seeing and surrendering to the perfection within the living moment. For me, surrendering to that so-called perfection includes the fact that I (and many others) don't think it is perfect and want to make the next moment better—and that's perfect too. It's not only perfect—it's an essential and powerful driver in how human evolution works. Wanting to change things, to make them better, is an inherent part of being a conscious participant in human evolution.

Cosmically, it may not matter at all if we humans survive or not. But there is deep in me a hope that we can rise to the challenge by living up to our potential. I feel a passionate concern and care for my species because in spite of all our "warts," I find us the most interesting and (when at our best) the most beautiful creation on this planet.

Question: How did you arrive at your view of meditation?

Answer: Many years ago I once heard a man talk named J. Krishnamurti who spoke of seeing things as they are. He presented a method of looking and what he said struck me deeply, although I didn't at first totally understand it. As a methodology it made a deep and lasting impression on me, and I began to look in the ways he suggested. I took him literally when he said, "Don't believe me," and I didn't. In time as I began to look, I saw that it was his method of inquiry that intrigued me, not his conclusions, which I felt contained many traditional spiritual perspectives that did not resonate with me. I had already been influenced by many great philosophers in my training, but his way of looking was new for me and brought changes in me that were new and surprising.

Through his method of self-inquiry I began to see more clearly. I found that being able to internally experience the structures of my thoughts was an amazing new route to self-understanding that gave me the handle I needed to move forward. Then one day it happened—the whole thing just opened up and was there, the nature of thought and meditation. It can happen quickly, simply from looking, or it can be more piecemeal—"aha" here and there, with surprising insights. Whichever way, after the mind turns in this direction and begins to look, it is very difficult to not look this way because there is a directness in looking that is hard to ignore. This led me on an odyssey of discovery where I eventually found that neither Eastern nor Western worldviews quite fit my experience, which led to writing books explaining why.

It is possible to come into contact with that energy of creativity that cannot be named, with the mystery within existence. Doing so is not a function of the projections of mind, or of spinning webs of thought. One sees that it is something totally beyond structure, something that does not come from the asking for it. It is totally different and beyond all the imaginings of mind, which is why mind alone can never get you there. All one can do is open the window, then the breeze may blow in. That's what the meditative state of mind is—the opening of the window to seeing with a clarity that can on occasion pierce through the filters of subjectivity.

How does one look? One looks by looking. It does not involve practice, for practice is mechanical. Nor does it involve effort, for effort always removes you from what is. What we have been doing together is not a marketable commodity because it cannot be described or made a formula or technique. It doesn't bring what most spiritual seekers are seeking. The traditional notion of enlightenment as a state or a possession is just an idea—an image of bliss promulgated in the East for millennia. If I call myself enlightened, I'm talking about the past: I am in memory, and out of memory I build an image of myself. As soon as I have an image of myself as an enlightened being or anything else, I have shadowed the living moment and removed myself from growth.

A meditative awareness is a way of looking, a turn of mind that just looks at what is going on. I can see the prevalence of injustice. This might motivate me to try to do something about it, but in order to be successful I must first see clearly its nature, and how and when I participate in it. This all brings awareness that can move into real change.

Question: You say this looking takes no effort. Examining my life, it seems that any time I moved into something new, great effort was required.

Answer: When moving into something new it can feel like great effort is involved, but the effort really comes from hanging on to the residue of the old—the old pleasures, securities, and even at times relationships—or not knowing what you want to do. I may see that the necessary movement requires the focus of will and intention, which can feel like effort. This inquiry can take a great deal of energy. Many of us equate energy with effort, but they are not the same; there is also confusion among effort, focused energy, and will. If I see clearly that being a doctor is the way I want to help people, this takes focused energy over time. I can have times of fatigue, discomfort, and uncertainty, but if the vision is strong it carries me through.

Have you ever watched children play? There is enormous energy there, enormous attention, but no effort. No one is forcing the child to play, not even the child. What we have been talking about has to be like play, in the sense that you must be really interested in yourself and how you work. Real interest contains passion, which is effortless. Our efforts are often designed to control passion, out of fear.

It takes no effort to see "what is." Say I put you in a room with a flower in the center of it on a table, and I put a sensing device in the flower to record whenever you look at it. Then I tell you that if you can stay in the room for a month and not look once at the flower, I'll give you a million dollars, enlightenment, or whatever you want. How much effort will you have to exert not to see the flower? It's there; in order not to see it you must be constantly on guard. So it takes great effort, great guardedness, not to see ourselves, not to see what's going on in the world.

We fear that if we give up effort, we'll vegetate and become dull. If one sees, without getting caught in self-judgment or self-pity, that one's life is stuck or stagnating, that deep recognition can spark a flame that causes movement out of it. If you see clearly that your life is isolated or boring, that awareness can bring newness. Seeing clearly makes one responsive to the new, which is the creative aspect of life. Real awareness is not a removal from life, but life as creation.

COMMENTARY:
Control through Surrender

Over the past two decades many neuro-physiological experiments have shown correlations between behavioral acts and physiological states in the brain that point to the mind being subject to emotions, tensions in the body, and habitual ways of processing information. However, to date there has been no true understanding of just how firing synapses, chemical and enzyme releases, incoming wavelengths, and the like translate into color, sound, emotions, and experience in general. Without a limbic system in the brain there would be only the most primitive emotions, and without limbic development no emotional communication between people and other mammals. We would have something similar to a cold reptilian mind—people with stunted limbic systems are called psychopaths. What is clear and obvious is that our mind depends on having a brain and is also affected by the other parts of the body. Yet the actual location of the mind remains something of a mystery. Is it between my ears, behind my eyes, located in the brain matter in my head or scattered through my systems? The location of the mind does not really fit into the space-time coordinates of what we call the material world. Still, without a brain no mind displays itself.

Meditation involves influencing and affecting the brain/mind connection. But what is affecting what, and who or what is doing the affecting? The simplest answer would be to say and believe that the physical causes the mental states, because if it's a one-way street, the human predilections for will, intention, and the possibility of real choice become mere physical causations ultimately explainable through science and physical means. But if (as we think) the mind contains will, intention, and even desires that are not totally reducible to physiological mechanisms and can themselves affect changes in the physiology, this would mean that it is a two-way street where the mind can change the physiology, including the brain, which can lead to changes in emotions, thoughts, and even worldviews.

A magnet generates an electromagnetic field that is not located in the magnet; but no magnet, no field. This is a good but incomplete metaphor for the brain/mind relation whereby the brain can be viewed as the generator, the mind as its field. The brain and body generate the mind, which can in turn affect the brain. What this means for meditation is that intention that aims at quieting the mind circles back to affect the brain. It is not surprising then that intention and quieting techniques cause measurable differences in the brain.

Meditators, especially long-term ones, describe a spectrum of results and benefits. (To meditate for many years there must either be some perceived benefits or an ongoing hope that if one does the practice long enough, eventually some wonderful and special occurrence will happen, or both.) Meditators' descriptions vary from "I meditated for many years and nothing much ever happened" to a wide range of recognizable effects. Some say that clearing the mind of its somewhat mechanical chatter can bring feelings of wholeness, centeredness, or connectedness, and on occasion insight, or some movement toward creativity. Some have visions or experience energies, while others say they feel more spiritual or loving. Those who have meditated to do away with their ego or so-called negative emotions like anger or fear with the hope of becoming enlightened are invariably disappointed, for after all those years of trying they still have an ego as well as the full spectrum of human emotions—although they may have different mental habits in responding to these emotions.

From an evolutionary point of view the human mind is constructed to think. This has been our major evolutionary advantage. It is possible through techniques to empty the mind of conscious thought for a period of time. However, the often non-conscious layerings of memory, deep structurings, and holographic networks of synapses remain intact. The interesting irony is that most practices geared at emptying the mind fill it with many thoughts and interpretations. A meditation technique is almost always embedded in a worldview or a way of viewing the world that contains implications and prescriptions about how to meditate, and what results it should bring if done "properly."

Most meditative techniques aim at stilling the mind and detaching the person from thoughts. Each meditative system has overt or covert values that either state or intimate why one would be better off doing so. In a historical era where the social order is breaking down and values are shifting, thoughts and feelings of inadequacy, anxiety, helplessness, and hopelessness are rife. Reprogramming techniques do work at a certain level to detach people from what they do not like or are uncomfortable with. Consequently people can and often do feel better and more relaxed or peaceful after having done them. Techniques do not, however, protect against the relegation of these unwanted aspects to a non-conscious level that does not disappear. One reason Jung was suspicious of Eastern religions is that he felt one could not and should not transfer them (whole hog) to the West.

As a case in point, we would like to use Buddhism as an example of a way of looking at the world, having both implicit and explicit values and *vipassana* "insight meditation" as a practice embedded in Buddhism. We'll examine the way the formal practices are currently taught, not necessarily the way people actually do them. People get information from many different sources and eventually make an ongoing practice their own, not necessarily taking on its traditional worldview. Some Buddhists don't believe in karma, or ending desire, or the no-self doctrine. We try to present a lens that you can look through to see if it has pertinence for you and can shed light on what you're doing. If what we are saying does not fit your experience, if nothing else we hope our thoughts might give you something to consider.

As explained in the chapter, we use Buddhism for this type of query because it is more open to modernizing, revision, and reform than other religions. (Buddha taught that everything can and should be doubted and challenged.) A meditator is supposed to trust the teacher long enough to be taught the practice; from then on experience in the practice is supposed to become the point of reference, as opposed to what teachers or others say.

According to the traditional Buddhist worldview, there is no real self. The concept of having or being a self is nothing but the construction of thought that strings together memories that give the illusion of there being an essential self with a continuity of experiences. When the concept of change is abstracted out of the permanence/change dialectic, creating the belief that there is no real permanence within life, the idea that there cannot be a permanent self naturally follows.

There are different traditions of *vipassana* and ways of teaching it, but they are all designed to provide experiences of Buddhist beliefs about the self and universe. The meditation is geared at teaching people to break up the linearity of thought into bits and pieces and to perceive them the instant they occur. Getting good at this means you are able to get quickly into the maelstrom of the bits and pieces of experience, which is a kaleidoscopic ever-changing flow that in that state seems endless and timeless. At this micro-level one is seemingly totally detached from content, meaning, and interpretation. So this state is presented as being more basic, more pure, more ontologically real. This experience is used to verify the no-self belief and the "truths" of

Buddhism and its cosmology in general. Along the way one is also programmed to believe that getting the predicted experiences proves the
truth of the worldview that stands behind the practices. This is totally
circular. The worldview constructs the techniques that support it. That
differing meditations justify different worldviews in actuality only
proves that with practices designed specifically for the purpose, the
mind is sufficiently malleable and powerful to give itself experiences
that it strongly desires and has been preprogrammed to have.

We do not question the ability of the human mind to train itself to
do this. The mind is so powerful that it can eventually give itself any
almost any experience it wants, given the right techniques. Nor do we
question that various benefits such as deep relaxation, altered states,
energy releases, and insights can come from that state. But we do question the Buddhist interpretations and values that are overlaid on this
experience.

Vipassana group retreats usually require silence and no external
input from reading. But they have compulsory lectures on the Buddhist
worldview and ethics, which include guidelines on how to meditate,
what to expect, predictions and interpretations of the meditative experiences. The rationale given for the required talks and small group sessions is that people need guidance and direction. For us, what guidance
really means is programming in Buddhist beliefs and shaping the experiences before, during, and after the sessions, while people are vulnerable and open to influence.

Emptying the mind of conscious thinking can allow something new
to come in, but it also can allow belief systems to be reinforced or a new
one to be superimposed by different means of persuasion, by a revered
figure, group influence or pressure, or an alignment with one's hopes.
In *vipassana* part of the "guidance" includes affirming some of the
basic tenets of Buddhism through putting forth what we call a reduc-
tionistic fallacy. Reductionism is the mistaken belief that one can understand something best only through its most basic units, because these

basic units are more real than other expressions of reality instead of just different. Looking at the nature of *gestalts* can illustrate this.

Other completely different interpretations of *vipassana*'s "bits and pieces" experience are possible, having to do with the nature of gestalts and levels of complexity. The word "gestalt" refers to any pattern or integrated structure that has specific properties that cannot be derived from or reduced to its elements. In other words, a gestalt is a higher-level whole—an entirely new pattern or entity—which is both greater than and different from the sum of its parts. An organ like the human brain cannot be understood through focusing on the individual cells that comprise it. A brain is made up of tissues, but it is not merely the sum of its tissues. The meaning of the sentence is not merely the sum of the individual words. The way the tissues and words are organized creates the new whole. The very feeling of being oneself, who one is, is a gestalt, one's identity. So if you break a sentence into bits the meaning disappears; and if you break thought into bits the self does temporarily disappear. This is a bit like saying a chair is less real than the particles that comprise it, or that a dismantled brain or liver does not exist because it can be dismantled; that its true reality is to be broken apart. After a meditation retreat or just doing it alone, the meditators are recognizable as the same people by others, and even by themselves.

A human is a whole entity, a gestalt, that although changing through time keeps a recognizable flavor and continuity. We are all isolated within our unique experiences. That actuality and our genetic makeup create our selves. If Buddhism is right about the self being merely a mental construction, where do will and intention come from? Using a technique to break up the stream of consciousness into disconnected pieces, and claiming that this verifies there is no real self, is like using the indeterminacy within quantum mechanics to "prove" that causal laws at a different level are not real.

Vipassana is a particular type of meditation geared at breaking down experience. Then in conclusion it says, "See, after you break things down, you have nothing left except what is broken down; so only this is real." This kind of meditation is also used to prove Buddhist ontology (beliefs about the nature of "being" or ultimate reality), which gives reality to emptiness over content, and to change over permanence. Content that involves any kind of meaning is always a whole, a gestalt, which is always more than the sum of its parts. If you break the parts up, the meaning found only in the whole is of course lost. People often use the fact that a meditation "works" as "proof" that Buddhist beliefs about the self and nature of the universe are true. But "works" only means that the mind is very malleable and the practice does what it was designed to do, as they were told it would do.

All this proves is that if you focus on bits and pieces, you end up with bits and pieces. Buddhists, like everyone else, come to their meditations with whatever beliefs they have, and they interpret the memory of what was going on in their meditations through these beliefs. Buddhist beliefs are conclusions, and as is the case with all beliefs, they filter and bias perception in the direction of justifying themselves and dampening exploration. None of this proves that the gestalts are not as real as their components. To try to understand either human experience or cosmic reality in this fashion—by breaking it down into bits—would be like trying to understand a whole human being by only looking at its cellular structure. Even more to the point, it would be like trying to understand what a computer does by only looking at its digital aspect. Here you would see an endless series of zeros and ones and nothing else.

If you were to take, for example, the feeling of envy, or anger, or hurt down to the most micro level of thought and sensation, you would not end up feeling envy at that moment. This, however, does not make the feeling any less real or durable. But it could easily be a way of attempting to escape and negate feelings that one is uncomfortable with. At this micro level everything seems to be insubstantial and in flux; there is nothing to hold onto. This is also true at the quantum level in physics. Yet regularities and patterns occur at many different levels that are not explainable at the quantum level. To limit one's understanding of (say) evolutionary processes to the principles of quantum mechanics would be absurd and impossible, because the very nature of evolution is to create levels of increasing complexity. Reducing any whole object or gestalt to a micro level would also leave out the world of daily life we live in and need to care about—which is precisely what the hidden agenda of renunciate religions is about: renouncing one's self as illusory carries over to the world.

In the change/permanence dialectic, Buddhism stands heavy on the change side. But reducing this dialectic and the universe to the either/or idea that "All is change" just because it is so at the micro level leaves out meaningful evolutionary change at more macro levels. Any potential meaning has within it some complexity. Interestingly, *vipassana*'s reductionism, like all meditation techniques geared at stilling thought, negates content and meaning within and after the meditation practice.

The Buddhist idea of "emptiness" (the Void) as the ultimate reality is obviously static. Change is in essence relational, that is, there must be something that is changing, either in relation to itself or to something else. The Buddhist conception of change in the world of everyday life is also strangely static. For there can be no real change—only "flux"—at the micro level. Real change brings newness into the universe and is not merely varied and repeated oscillations. Real change is dialectical and only occurs when interwoven with continuity. In denying permanence and continuity any reality, Buddhism quixotically denies the possibility of real change. This reveals how Buddhism can give reality to an underlying unchanging Void while preaching that there is nothing but change. The concept of change it puts forth is as empty as its Void.

The only exception to "All is change" is the Buddhist belief in the permanence of the truths of Buddhism (the Dharma); the permanence of the value of their meditations; and the continuing and seeming permanence of many Buddhists' identity as Buddhists. Then of course there is the absolute permanence of its basic empty Void—for how could it be anything else?

The deepest kinds of human conditioning are a function of the patterns and gestalts that are internalized. These conditionings can be bypassed by focusing on a micro level. Thus giving more importance to the micro level can detach you from these macro states of being. The great dangers in giving the micro level prime import are twofold: An emotional impoverishment can occur that the person will not even be aware of due to becoming attached to the control over one's mental and emotional states that meditation brings. (This control is not absolute, as unwanted "attachments" have a way of sneaking in.) The conditionings that occur and continue to form on the so-called macro level of daily life will be even more below the surface than before because now one has a bias against acknowledging their importance or even reality, out of wanting to feel or believing that one is beyond them.

An influential Burmese *vipassana* teacher in his lectures tells people that they should meditate all the time, as much as they can, whenever they have a free moment, waiting for a bus, whatever, that it's the best way to be spiritual. If people were actually to do this, or think they should, or even want to, he would be controlling their minds in daily life—a deadening form of mind control that is counter to awareness. Another Buddhist belief is that the last thought people have before they die totally influences their next incarnation, and that the ultimate purpose of meditation is to empty the mind to have that last proper thought. This belief is an insidious form of conditioning, geared at making people afraid of not meditating. But if there is no continuity of self or personality, an obvious and legitimate question is "What reincarnates?" Underneath often not-conscious meditative guidelines that promote quieting thought are agendas that are themselves constructions of thought.

The cultivation of detachment easily creates more baggage. Many systems of meditation since coming to the West now claim to delve deeply into the unconscious, eventually eliminating its power over the psyche. The idea that meditation techniques eliminate or bypass unconscious motivators is naive and shows a lack of understanding about how the mind works.

The idea that whatever insights appear in one's meditations are free of unconscious aspects leaves no real way of refuting the possibility that meditators are seeing what they want or have been programmed to see. Buddhism does present ideals of how to be and gives techniques to get there. This context can create the wanted experiences in meditation, and also suppress those that do not fit. For the power of the mind is such that it has insidious and endlessly clever ways to hide from itself anything that does not fit into its mental frameworks and self-images. This is further compounded if one holds one's ideals to be sacred or spiritual, as this greatly increases the unconscious collusions that justify suppressing whatever isn't considered spiritual or in line with the ideals one cherishes. Thus if I am trying to conquer fear and desire, if I believe that attachments are hindrances, if I look at my self-centeredness as something to be done away with, then the likelihood is that I will indeed keep those aspects of myself that do not fit my aspirations, self-images, or images of spirituality as hidden as possible from myself.

Meditative techniques often create more conscious control over thought patterns and emotions, thereby creating more possibilities of subconscious denial. An example of what we consider unconsciousness on the part of some who teach *vipassana* is their saying the meditative technique contains no ideology, precepts, or agendas. We assume that they believe this is true. It seems then that they are unaware that the way the techniques are presented is another obstacle to "pure witnessing." (The idea that one can "witness purely" doesn't take into account the accumulation of experience that the person comes with.) The very idea that meditation is a path to spiritual realization is an agenda. This view, which implies that spirituality needs to be achieved through practice, makes it into a future attainment and in so doing divorces spirituality from life.

All these prescribed techniques are mechanical formulas for shifting consciousness that function like a "meta-program"—that is, a master program that controls other programs and shifts the very way the mind programs itself. The formulas are presented in such a way as to make them unchallengeable. There's always a prescribed method to the witnessing—whether it be with eyes open or closed; following the breath; detaching from the content of thoughts and feelings; scanning the body; going through and not resisting pain; or breaking down fluctuations of the inner panorama into the smallest possible bits. The methods either emphasize control (concentration), surrender (not resisting anything), or some combination of them. All of these techniques contain a hidden agenda that comes right out of the Buddhist belief system that the mind and its preoccupation with itself, its fears and desires, must be tamed. Interestingly, one motive behind surrendering to the flow and detaching from one's desires is the desire for equanimity (self-control). The desires for equanimity and to end suffering are just desires, and if one is somewhat successful, one then becomes attached to keeping it that way.

Traditional meditation techniques contain covert agendas that promote a view of spirituality that values unity and merging over individuation. Here thought is considered the hindrance to merging. And so most meditative schools, even the ones who purport to be value-free and interested only in "pure insight" or "mindfulness," have as a hidden value that one would be better off if thought were still (or at least stiller).

There are many techniques or practices for quieting thought that can provisionally give people a sense of peace by removing them from the field of thought where conflicts and other mentally induced discomforts occur. They can also bring insights as they open more space in between thoughts by interfering with mechanical conditioning patterns. But the often-made assumption that the insights that occur are themselves necessarily value-free and untainted by preferences or other unconscious factors is simply not true. This is why the lengthy practice of any meditation technique almost always ends up affirming the worldview that stands behind the technique.

Repetitive practices can reprogram the way one thinks, but they cannot change the fact that one thinks. This ideal of no-thought operates as a non-conscious meta-program that does serve to detach people from the impact of their thoughts. Instead of stopping people from thinking, devaluing thought and the consequent attempt to detach from it merely hinders thinking clearly. The perspective that regards thought as a hindrance to meditation contains a value that is itself constructed by thought, as are all values. Attempting to disempower thought by creating reactive values against it is really a mechanism of thought itself to create compartments where critical intelligence cannot enter and so disturb other beliefs. The agendas behind the techniques are themselves filters that interfere with insight. Practices with covert agendas create more blind spots, especially if approached uncritically with reverence. Meditation that involves techniques that aim at quieting the mind can bring more awareness and clarity, but often do not because of the worldview and the other agendas at play.

Authoritarian beliefs usually ask us to have "faith" in an ideology, leader, teacher, or tradition. This creates a mental compartment that negates the proper use of thought—which is to test the reasonableness of whatever is being put forth and its relationship to the other positions one holds. When thought creates values that negate its own worth, the controlling dimension of thought does not disappear; it just becomes less conscious. This merely makes one a fragmented, compartmentalized, and thus handicapped thinker, not a non-thinker—for thinking is an inherent part of being human.

The unconscious, which (among other things) is a repository of repressed thought, cannot be disempowered in this manner. On the contrary, it gains power and control whenever conscious thought is devalued. Critical thought, which utilizes comparison, can be alert for discrepancies between the ideals one holds and one's actual actions. Discrepancies of this sort, "behavioral paradoxes," are a sign that there may be non-conscious mechanisms involved in either the formation of the ideals, the causes of the behavior, or both. Moreover, it is not possible to disempower what's underneath conscious thought by a frontal attack that negates it, since the unconscious feeds on denial, which is the very stuff that helps create it. Either/or attitudes, especially when applied to morality, fuel unconsciousness by denying the unwanted (so-called negative) side of the polarity; whereas bringing the hidden to light needs a dialectical integration of both the loving and self-centered aspects of oneself. This explains why so many people who value a spirituality that devalues self-centeredness can be so unconsciously self-absorbed. The denied self-centeredness just displays itself in another form.

So we have serious reservations about both the way meditation has been presented traditionally, and the uses it has been put to. Much of it has fostered conflict-reduction and outmoded authoritarian worldviews rather than awareness. Because these worldviews do not value thought, or to be more accurate, only value the thoughts that affirm their anti-self bias, they are inept at processing the content—emotions, insights, or old memories that can come up. Thus a big problem with meditation lies in the area of meaning, interpretation, and assimilation. It is not possible to integrate any experience without using mental (symbolic) structures and valuing meaning. A useful structure for delving into suppressed areas that surface must contain at least the following: some methodology that can question whether the memory or insight that has arisen is basic or merely another deflection. (This is especially needed for early memories.) Also needed is a way that the interpretative structure itself can evolve through feedback—so that the entire process can be self-correcting.

Meditation techniques rarely aim at expanding one's awareness about the world and our place in it. This is so because meditation negates meaning and interpretation, both of which involve thought. The interpretations that are given come from the worldview it's part of. Meditation is usually presented and done as personal, with personal benefits being the motivator—becoming "more spiritual" is considered an enhancing personal achievement.

Most of the problems and concerns today are social and relational. The kind of meditative frame of mind suggested in this book has neither techniques nor agendas other than seeing what's going on with as much clarity as possible. This necessarily includes looking inward as well as looking outward at the relationships we are a part of and are co-creating with others. In these times of accelerated change, social upheaval, and environmental threats, broadening the spectrum of our awareness becomes an essential ingredient in bringing about the socio-political changes necessary to give human viability a chance. The hope is that more awareness and clarity can bring a movement into conscious social evolution. A refrain running through the original *Passionate Mind* and a theme of this book is "The seeing is the movement." We have all had the experience that when anything is seen with a stark clarity, that seeing has its own momentum with implicit and ongoing repercussions.

True awareness is not simply "being present." It must include as well an awareness of the nature of the filtering process (which comes from the past and includes our genetic heritage) that screens the way the present (the here and now) is experienced. All structures—mental, social, including the structure of being human—organize the way information is integrated. No mere mechanical technique by itself can reveal how information is organized and processed. To grasp organizing principles one needs to view occurrences as they move through time, which always entails thought and specifically memory. What we call the meditative frame of mind involves the clarity to be in touch with "what is," including its possible implications. For us the importance of that state of mind is that it can open a channel to intuition that comes from the source of existence that made us.

10. Evolution

Some historical moments are more critical than others. Transitional periods are such times. We live in a culture and a world that are in transition. What transition actually means is transformation, for as old ways of being crumble, we individually and as a species must forge new meanings for life. We are at a cusp point in our evolution— dangling between the pleasures of adolescence and the urgency of adulthood. Maturation comes when the spectrum of awareness broadens, becoming more inclusive.

In this chapter we focus on the necessity to evolve. The evolutionary mechanisms that previously made us successful are now putting us and other species at risk. In our (the authors') worldview this movement of evolution is not a tragedy or mistake. We do not specifically articulate salient features of our worldview in the body of this chapter, as those have been carefully gone into in the commentaries on evolution and on time. Still, the attentive reader will glean that we do not see the evolutionary process as purposeless—although the purpose is not specific, other than constructing complexities that lead to experiencing itself and from that to self-reflecting intelligence.

For us there is a driving force in the evolutionary process that we call "spirit" that lives in each of us, offering not only hope, but the possibility of we humans becoming conscious participants in the process that made us, and so finding a way to continue our evolutionary journey. This chapter contains our view of what we consider necessary for this to happen. It does not involve trying to change or evolve, nor trying to become something we are not. It does involve an awareness that sees clearly what we are and what works for us and our world, and what doesn't. A major thesis of this book is that real clarity has its own essentially effortless momentum that can move you into what you cannot seek or know beforehand. It is our hope that this book can aid in bringing more awareness to the reader.

Everyone through time and experience constructs some kind of worldview. We operate under the assumption that it's far more likely than not that there exists an underlying reality that different world-views are more or less in touch with. Looking through any worldview is akin to looking through a lens: the more unclouded the lens, the more clearly you see. This book and chapter present a way of looking at oneself and the world that we have found is more in touch with reality than other worldviews we are familiar with, including the purely materialist and the traditionally spiritual. For simplicity's sake, instead of tediously qualifying our views, we'll just state them, fully realizing their fallibility.

We focus on why we humans are where we are, where and why our potential has been blocked, and what opportunities evolution could give us. Although no worldview can be totally encapsulated in words, if you can use what we are presenting as a lens, it opens the poten-tial for seeing more clearly in a living situation. We are not putting this forth as the ultimate lens to look through, but we are saying that it is a clearer and more useful lens than others we've seen. Whether it is for you is your judgment to make.

———————————————————————————————

At first blush it may appear that our inquiry is too self-absorbed, and turning inward could easily be viewed as an escape from external turmoil. Actually, however, the inner and outer to an extent mirror and certainly affect each other. The turmoil of the world is an expression of people's worldviews, beliefs, and inner confusion as people create and recreate social structures and the world. If the world is confused, self-centered, violent, falling apart, it's because we humans have made it so. The hierarchical institutions we created add centralized power to the picture, with its inevitable corruptions. In this final inquiry we look at why broadening and expanding awareness to be more inclusive in these times could have such urgency for individuals and for our species itself.

We live in a time of great turmoil, with enormous problems. There are the problems of ecology involving how we are making the world uninhabitable; and the problems of cities, racial tensions, and the economic blocks to distributing goods in a world where wealth feeds on itself and increasingly polarizes, creating an ever larger gap between haves and have-nots. There are the problems of loneliness and sorrow. So many seemingly insurmountable problems.

We tend to deal with our problems in an isolated way, trying to solve them independently of one another. We create committees, departments, foundations, charities, prisons, yet the problems increase. Many feel helpless, for what can one person do?

The fabric of society is breaking down, and trying to solve these problems from within the old structures that compartmentalize them feeds the confusion. The problems mentioned are symptoms. If only the symptoms are dealt with, the sickness pops out some other place. The real problem is that the old ways no longer work because technology has brought new powers, and with them new challenges. We are conditioned to want and expect immediate gratification, yet we need a much longer view of the repercussions and implications of our actions.

Living is challenge and response, and problems are challenges. What responses are appropriate? What can I do? I'm just a drop in a huge ocean. How can I respond to all this, and even if I do, what difference will it make? Is it possible to be truly responsible, response-able? To help us examine these questions, let us go into the nature and workings of evolution.

Although evolution is always occurring in the present, understanding the process of evolution is more about the past and future—the future because that's what evolution is always moving toward, while the past examined through modern technologies gives us a glimmering of where we and the cosmos came from. Of course for humans, our major interest is where evolution will take us, as it relentlessly moves forward with the arrow of time. The real question for us is how what we do in the ever-moving present moment will affect the manifestations of evolution on Earth.

When we look at a distant star or galaxy, we're seeing how the star looked thousands of years ago because the light has taken that long to travel to us. Cosmologists go back further and further into the past to try to make sense of our present and to predict where the next moment or the next eons will take the universe. Evolution is unfathomable without considering time and the complex instruments that thought created to extend its perception, calculations, and constructive, predictive capacities. Humans have a special role to play in the evolutionary drama on Earth as both the product of it and (ideally) as ongoing participants in it.

In the current scientific view, the main biological evolutionary mechanism involves random mutations in the genes of the reproductive tissue. When changes occur in environmental pressures, the appropriate mutation for functioning in the new environment survives. In popular parlance this is the so-called "survival of the fittest." I call this a "by definition" definition: if a creature survives, it's the fittest—by definition. But what makes the fittest fit? The capacity to run faster, kill better, find an unoccupied ecological niche? The problem with "by definition" definitions is that although they're always true, by definition, they gloss over all the other factors that are or may be at play in the movement of evolution. We will look at this a bit later.

An animal so clever has evolved that it can transform its environment to such a great extent that it (the animal) is no longer subject to the same kind of environmental evolutionary pressures as before. Human pressures have outstripped Earth's capacity to sort things out through the historic evolutionary routes. Species that contribute to the global balance are being lost at an alarming rate. The old non-conscious biological mechanisms of evolutionary change have never—in our species' particular history—faced such enormous impact and cannot tolerate the overall direction we're moving in. Nature's response has made us a species at risk too. Consequently, now we are subject to our own devastating pressures. Either we radically change the way we treat the Earth and each other, or we suffer the alternative—become an evolutionary dead end and go the way of the dinosaur. The true challenge of the times is really quite simple—it's a question of survival, of whether we as a species are going to continue to grow and change, or not.

This, our final inquiry, will not be a condemnation of humanity or of all our unaware excesses. Rather the focus is to look as unsentimentally, matter of factly, and objectively as possible at who we are and how who we are has brought us where we are. Our precarious predicament is not the result of a flaw, failing, or mistake on our part, nor an unfortunate aberration, but rather is related to who we are and how we have evolved so far. We must come to terms with what brought us here: our nature and the social systems that emerged from it that have taken on an out-of-control life of their own.

Our predicament is also related to the way evolution itself works. This factor could be the impetus to move us toward evolving socially as part of our innate drive to survive. As we go further into this, you may find, as I do, that this is a source of hope.

Most of us get our knowledge about evolution from outside authorities and secondhand sources. We read about evolution in school and we are shown external evidence of it in pictures, bones, and fossils. Ordinarily evolution is considered an unconscious biological and geological process following its own laws and routes. And it is true that so far the evolution of life on Earth has been largely in the non-conscious sphere. The old biological evolutionary mechanisms of random mutation of genes selected out by environmental pressure are no longer working for us. Although our genes fostered our survival and even our dominance in earlier environments, they cannot meet the unique ways that our minds through technology have impacted the world and other extraordinary challenges of our making. But evolution itself is not a static unchanging force or operator in the universe (like gravity). It is an operator in the construction of existence that itself evolves. In other words, how change is brought about also evolves in that some of the very mechanisms of change evolve, too. This means that the way evolution moves through us can itself change.

Is a more conscious relationship with evolution possible? Why shouldn't the so far largely non-conscious mechanisms that drive evolution also evolve and be part of a movement from the unconscious to the aware? When life emerged on Earth, and genes and the double helix evolved, the evolutionary mechanisms changed from the purely physical to the non-conscious biological. New rules or "laws" emerged that were not part of the previous evolution of the material cosmos. Through biological evolution a thinking, communicative, self-reflective social animal evolved—with enormous unrealized potential for creativity, connecting, and care—that uses symbols and abstractions to control its environment through technology, while pondering the meaning of it all. This required an unprecedented leap, just like life itself represents a leap of great magnitude that, as with all leaps, can only be "explained" in retrospect. With each leap to a new level of living complexity, new mechanisms and laws for evolution emerge from the complexity itself.

The biological leap to humans is based on non-conscious processes that control us without us having known much about them and their effects until recently. This kept us more on "automatic." Since humans are a leap from what evolution previously manufactured, it would be strange if new evolutionary principles did not emerge with us—and through us. Human awareness is the key to a whole new process of evolution: an evolution within the way evolution operates, with the capacity to break through the mechanical. In the emerging evolutionary shift, a movement from the non-conscious to the conscious, we humans must assume (out of necessity) a more conscious participation in the evolutionary process.

There is no telling reason why the mechanisms of change cannot once again change, this time from being primarily biological to incorporating the interactive conscious participation of thinking minds in a new step toward conscious social evolution—especially if this is what the next stage of human survival requires. If we make another leap into awareness of our genetic conditioning, we will be less determined by it. Then our genes and the necessity of meeting our challenges could work together instead of against us.

The possibility that our genetic, deeply rooted attachment to life will push us to take this crucial and necessary step of making social evolution conscious is a source of hope. I view the expansion of human awareness that would make conscious participation possible as a part of the thrust of evolution itself. Breaking out of one's conditioning is the next step in the evolutionary process. It does not occur through denial or suppression or even effort, but through a radical shift in awareness. I realize that this view of evolution is very different from the way it has mostly been thought of.

So far the old biological evolutionary mechanisms based on the interplay of cooperation and competition, containing both aggression and violence, have manifested without much consciousness. As social animals, humans often use both cooperation and competition to further goals. From an evolutionary perspective and personally too, competition is a honing mechanism that can increase human capabilities. It has pushed human creativity to enlarge our capacity to think, act, and take care of ourselves and others. Human inventiveness uses whatever is current to push against, making a mark that affirms one's uniqueness. This is why prizes are given for accomplishments, and those who win them prize them.

Competition and cooperation are not opposites but are embedded in each other: people, tribes, species, teams, etc., cooperate at one level to compete better at another level. The competition for fame, a place in history, perhaps a Nobel Prize, brought us an awareness of the double helix, among other vital pieces of knowledge. In many aspects of life, from science to corporations, teams compete to better solve problems.

We do use our cooperative abilities toward common goals, but thus far this huge source of potential has been sorely limited by narrow identities, beliefs, and power hierarchies. Consequently, we have more readily used cooperative abilities to further our competitive leverages in relation to other species and each other. Now we need to emphasize cooperation on a worldwide basis to meet common goals that further our survival and that of the intricate web of life we are dependent on.

Unlike other social animals, our addictions to violence and power are unconstrained by instincts. As dimorphic primates, our inbuilt and intertwined social capacities have been, and still are, mostly confined to narrow, highly conditioned gender roles and often-competing ethnic identities. (Dimorphism is a marked difference in size and physical and emotional capacities between genders of the same species.) What is no longer working are the power-driven, gendered, and racist ways we have structured and institutionalized our complex and challenging mix of altruism and egotism, bonding and warring, care and indifference, love and hatred, cooperation and competition, creativity and authoritarianism, heroism and cruelty.

The urgent need to become more aware in order to develop our potential as social animals to care and connect better, and to bring our destructiveness under control, may well be the greatest challenge humanity has ever faced. Simply but not simplistically put, historically "might made right," and as males had more might, they constructed institutions that magnified gender differences to maximize their power, which they believed was their biological right. Because reproduction, the family, and sexual access are at the foundation of the social order, our gender-dimorphic biology has thus far largely determined core aspects of our social systems.

Ordinarily we think of the mind and body as different, yet we're also aware of some of their interconnections. If you drink alcohol or coffee, or take a drug of some sort, it has physical effects on the body. Psychological change, a change in awareness, accompanies the physical changes. We tend to think of this as a one-way causal door, but actually it is not, for if awareness changes, a physiological change necessarily also occurs. Every material change affects the mental and vice versa.

Even our genetic makeup is subject to change since external input and influence can activate or deactivate genes, open or close genetic connections and networks. This is the genetic underpinning of the nature/nurture dialectic. An example of how they are embedded in each other: if a child with gene configurations that can lead to becoming a psychopath is raised with love, the pathology is thwarted; if raised brutally or indifferently an adult psychopath inevitably emerges. Although the thinking mind and the material brain are not identical, they are connected in still unknown ways.

The mind's location is not in the brain, not behind the eyes or between the ears. For me, a metaphor for the body/brain/mind connection is a magnet generating an electromagnetic field. The field is not located in the magnet; but no generator, no field. The "embodied brain" or "thinking body" is the generator creating the field of mind. But unlike the magnet and its electromagnetic field, because the body and consciousness are alive, this makes their mysterious interaction a two-way path of mutual influence. The body with its glands, chemicals, electrical conductivity, and of course the brain generates experiencing and thinking. Seeing a loved one or a horror movie both bring physiological changes. So the phenomenological and the physical (the mind and brain) are interrelated and cross-affecting; they are different modes of a total living energy system. This means that our minds can effect deep physiological and even genetic changes. This interrelationship also implies that a shift in awareness in the mind can affect and change the brain. So differences in the environment, especially during early development, change the very cellular structure itself.

Our extraordinary mind is our great evolutionary advantage—and still today the source of largely untapped potential. What limits our potential are old authoritarian worldviews that fill heads with beliefs that block clear thinking and open-mindedness. Although many people no longer believe in them, the way these worldviews have been institutionalized over millennia is such that they have taken on a momentum of their own: in power hierarchies, unconscious reproduction, and an assortment of childish beliefs that create limited identities, insecurities, wars, overpopulation, greed, polarizing wealth, unsustainable production, to name a few. This goes along with an accumulation mentality that collects things, wealth, power, or "spiritual merits" to justify one's existence. None of this is conducive to freeing the mind to think better or to feel more deeply with more care, which are now needed to survive.

In times of crisis many people have a tendency to turn to religion or a presumed spiritual authority for answers or solace, perhaps following this leader or that who promises some form of salvation through obedience. Many flock to fundamentalist religions offering certainty and absolute values. Would-be "spiritual experts" abound; if you go to them they'll tell you to do this or that, or go back to this sacred text or that—the *Gita,* Bible, *sutras,* Talmud, Koran, Mayan calendar, or whatever because the old masters have all the wisdom. Because of the weight of tradition, giving some credence to a religion opens a risky door that allows some if not all of its beliefs and practices to be given "the benefit of the doubt" (a telling phrase).

Of course, all views that survived the test of time deserve to be examined, as they may contain some valuable wisdom, but this needs to be done with an open yet critical mind. How seriously should we take a virgin birth, a vengeful god, an empty void filling the cosmos, or a unity filling it with illusion? If we rely on tradition for answers we're lost, as all the old structures have gotten us exactly where we are now. The very worldviews and values of these religions, whose authority comes from traditions of the distant past, have constructed the unlivable ideals that are a significant reason why today's world is dysfunctional. No traditional or sacred belief should be exempt from examination. In the marketplace of ideas people have the right to believe as they choose, but people also have the right to challenge any belief that they consider harmful or wrong.

To agree or disagree, or to try to formulate this inquiry into a pleasant or convenient or familiar structure that one can comfortably operate out of, is a distraction from taking in the things that could be pertinent to you. I'm not suggesting that you accept my words without putting them to the test of your own discernment, but that you initially absorb the viewpoint I am offering and then see what meaning might be in it for you. Judgments and criticisms, agreeing or disagreeing, are always possible later. This comes with more clarity if you first get some insight into what I'm saying and why.

Religion provides the most revealing example of how authoritarianism in general works. Because one of religion's basic functions has always been to create beliefs about the unknown (often aligning with people's hopes), religion's susceptibility to being authoritarian has always been great indeed. Whenever an ideology is closed to reason, feedback, or public verification, the potential for abuse and authoritarianism is inherent. Religions make it difficult to examine them by ordaining faith and belief as sacred, while maintaining that no ordinary person can know enough to take issue with these beliefs. A further hindrance to the intelligent examination of religious tradition is the social taboo against doing so. The sacred and taboo are the two faces of any religion with punishable heresy.

The very act of making sacred certain actions, institutions, or ways of being traditionally made them immune from examination and feedback. This continues through social censure and self-censorship related to the almost universal taboo against personally questioning others' religious beliefs. When something was made sacred, this usually meant that it could not stand on its own merit. Traditionally, it was a telling sign that the concept needed protection and shoring up, because of the fear that it could not stand and fall with the truth or examination—thus the socially unacceptable nature of challenging religion. Demanding reverence of the sacred is also an indication that disguised self-interest and power underlie it, with a strong stake in the *status quo.*

Protecting the sacred with taboo petrifies and fossilizes it, creating a museum of beliefs that take up rent-free, eviction-resistant residence in the mind, also fossilizing the mental compartments they live in. This blocks evolution within the people and societies that unshakably revere a particular sacred cow. Obsolete sacred beliefs disconnect people from living reality, which leads to an all-too-prevalent form of non-sanity. They lead to religious wars that battle for people's minds and political power—not only with words but with weapons. The more authoritarian a religion or worldview, the more its sacred aspects get priority over all else—including reality and life itself. "Sacrifice" derives from "sacred"—its two meanings are revealing: offering and loss. Spiritual authorities dictate what must be sacrificed to the sacred. The more precious the better, the epitome being the sacrifice of virgins, one's child, or one's self (ego).

The sacred is a meta-program so powerfully implanted that people will kill others or even themselves to protect and promote it. This is an extreme example of non-sane "ideological uncaringness," where one's ideology and ideals (anti-birth control, for example) take precedence over what's good for people and for the world. What most urgently needs to be reexamined in these fateful and dangerous times are above all the things we hold to be sacred. Indeed, if we want there to be a future at all, we must honor valuing, seeking, and discovering truths more than we honor the relics of the past. Truth is something that each person must find and develop a relationship with. If seeking truth were venerated, there would be no need to revere traditional beliefs, because truth, if honored, will shine through. {The commentary on Time critiques postmodernism's relativistic assault on truth and reason.}

Our mind—like our capacity to love—is a marvelous evolutionary gift whose potential has been retarded. Neither our minds nor our genes are making us "stupid"—we are being made so. We humans are curious, exploratory, intelligent, and creative by nature, especially if taught to think and use our minds well—or at least not inculcated with obsolete worldviews and dogmatic beliefs. Most religions and often societies teach us to mistrust ourselves and are geared at "dumbing us down" to accept huge differentials in power and privilege. The human mind is a relatively untapped resource that, although the source of core problems, is also a core part of the solutions. But sane social circumstances and upbringing are necessary to foster the mind's development and potential.

In looking at oneself, and in looking at the problems we face, what we ordinarily want to do is find ultimate solutions so that all our problems are solved—which often means turning to solutions coming from the past. The past by its nature has a strong pull with its weighty authority and implicit credibility. It's natural for solutions that worked in the past to be given priority. In trying to avoid what caused past failures and apply what brought success, we focus on the old manifestation of a problem instead of the new one.

Although specific past solutions may have value, ultimate solutions and panaceas coming from the past have never worked, nor will they now. Many people who see the need for a transformation or shift in consciousness believe that this would entail moving beyond the so-called negative aspects of being human, like aggression, competition, anger, self-centeredness, egotism, and the like. This frames the ultimate solution as humans needing to become something essentially different from what we are. I see this as an example of a very old hope that we can become nonviolent that has not worked and will not work.

The past has value when assessing the present if it can be a stepping stone to meet the new innovatively, instead of being a vise to squeeze the present into. Our growth and understanding depend on sharing our experience and learning, including accumulating knowledge and whatever wisdom the past has to offer. This is a core part of being the evolving social animal that we are. Knowledge of the past is necessary to understand how and why we find ourselves a species at risk. But the past (our collective memory) cannot deliver a resolution to our evolutionary challenge, for the past as it lives in beliefs, traditions, and identities has brought us to this precarious point. The traditions we are born into have a powerful effect on who we become and how we think and act. Trying to see with objectivity—without the filters of old worldviews, sentimentality, and wishful thinking—which traditions are dysfunctional and obsolete and which ones need to change is the beginning of moving toward adulthood and appropriately reconstructing our societies for the present and future.

The development of the individual as a metaphor is useful. In this analogy, pre-history is humanity's infancy, where the prime need was survival, and lives were totally dependent on belonging to a small band. Discovering agriculture moved humanity into its childhood, a period marked by growth and expansion with ever-larger kingships and authoritarian hierarchies replacing small group interdependence. The world's great ancient civilizations (as far as we can tell) were all based on authoritarian dynasties and worldviews. However sophisticated and esthetically sensitive the elite may be, authoritarianism is still a childish mode of being and thinking. This early authoritarian phase in religion and government is when our current dysfunctional moralities were initiated.

In the age of Western enlightenment, reason took hold, challenging religious and political dogma and hierarchy, moving us into early adolescence—the individuation phase of development that often involves rebelling against authority. Tapping into nature's powers through science and commerce during the resulting industrial revolution accelerated knowledge and moved our adolescence along. Youth is characterized by great self-absorption, experimentation, extreme mood shifts, and feeling and acting as if immortal. Adolescents play with their newly discovered powers without much knowledge or concern for consequences—especially consequences for others. While struggling to individuate, adolescents can be insightful in penetrating the hypocrisy, illusions, and deceits of their elders, but teenagers often construct new idols or fashions to follow and conform to peer pressure. They sometimes develop a misplaced faith in their own point of view and ignore information that does not fit.

Adolescence is also marked by the utilization of power for its own sake, by the expectation of quick rewards for little effort, and minimal concern about repercussions of reckless or self-destructive habits and predilections. In spite of our impressive cleverness and accomplishments as a species, we are still quite adolescent. We have constructed and unleashed extraordinary power that adolescents are not capable of handling. Unfortunately, in many areas humanity is not yet even adolescent—we adopt and aggressively promote childish beliefs, follow authoritarian leaders, and are easily susceptible to manipulation.

The challenge of the times is actually evolutionary and developmental: are we as a species going to move into adulthood, as individuals, groups, and cultures? There is no truly responsible species on the planet today. Yet the planet is crying out for caretakers—for a species that takes care. No other species, no matter what their unique intelligence or care for their environment might be, can deal with human impact. This is not to make humans superior, just far more dangerous. Part of caring about anything is considering repercussions and future consequences. The time for childish beliefs and adolescent carelessness is past if we are to survive. If we are to become adult, this means we must play a more conscious role in our evolution. To do this we must understand and come to terms with the nature of our social and genetic conditioning and how the very things we've been discussing interact with each other. Becoming adult requires seeing the nature of one's conditioning, and consequently not being as controlled by it or manipulated by others.

Maturity is not the mere accumulation of experience. One only grows when one moves, which sometimes means leaving old ways behind. Aspects of maturation may be unappealing or even painful because childhood has permissions and pleasures that one is loath to give up. When one is young and cared for, there's a resistance to move into adulthood, for youth has its beauty and quality of being carefree. You can see this in your own movement out of adolescence. There is a similar resistance to moving into adulthood within humanity—we are undergoing severe growing pains.

Whatever one's beliefs about some kind of afterlife, a key element in becoming an adult is facing one's mortality in this life. Just as the movement from adolescence to adulthood rarely occurs without some struggle, adjusting to the reality of mortality rarely occurs without some discomfort, anxiety, and denial. It can bring a shift in the focus of life, which in turn reorganizes basic habits. Upon seeing aging and dying as part of life, how best to live with care and carefulness can become a concern. One begins to realize that one can and wants to affect not only the length but also the quality of life by one's actions and relationships. Although the emphasis turns more to care and maintenance to get a handle on excesses that the aging body can no longer ignore, there is an unsurprising reluctance to move from carefree (or careless) to care-full. Adulthood is a time when existential issues come to the fore, and acting out of longer-term implications becomes more interesting and vital than insouciant short-term gratifications.

We view humanity as a whole as likewise struggling with the necessity of leaving its adolescence behind, because being a species at risk involves facing mortality. That the species will someday vanish as our sun will someday go *nova* is not the issue. As in infancy, humans are again collectively confronted with the tenuousness of existence. The difference is that now we are the danger we face. Upon facing the possibility of imminent extinction through our out-of-control destructiveness, the real issue becomes whether people can shift their identities and habits to prolong their own and humanity's existence. As with the individual, humanity's confrontation with death and the realization that our survival or demise is in our own hands is part of the developmental process that forces a reexamination of values and priorities.

The very nature of being on an evolutionary cusp is being in uncharted waters. The challenges have never before occurred. There are no authorities about the future because it's all new to everyone. No one can know with certainty what will happen or what you or others should do, so no one can be sure that theirs is the best or right way; no one has definitive answers. Yet we have been trained to give responsibility to authorities and have experts tell us what to do. Although many are eager to tell us, those with the most certainty and seductive confidence are usually minions of the old, of the known, who are the least likely to know (especially if they are protecting their own place within the *status quo*). Certainty, which is all the more appealing in insecure, uncertain times, should be viewed with suspicion.

Authoritarian power, whether political or ideological, has been the major form of social control throughout humanity's childhood and youth. The old paradigms all have some authority—be it a leader, wise man, savior, guru, or prophet—telling the rest of us what life is about and how to lead it. How to replace this old methodology and mythology that have become dysfunctional is a major issue facing humanity. Becoming an adult involves leaving one's parents, gaining or regaining self-trust, and using the mind's potential for creativity and problem-solving.

In a real sense, there is only you and me—all of us—and that may be a frightening thing. We all face the challenges in our individual ways, which cannot be done for us. Each of us has our own particular gifts and concerns to contribute. People can help each other, but giving one's responsibility to someone else is very strange indeed, because responsibility really means response-ability, the ability to respond adequately, which cannot be given away.

A species trying to grow up is like pulling yourself up by your own bootstraps, as there are few grown-ups to point the way. We're entering an unknown territory of our own making. Unlike children with parents to protect and guide them, we are like orphans in the cosmos who have to find our own way. We must be pioneers, explorers, creative problem-solvers, and open-minded truth-seekers.

Ultimately, we can only protect ourselves through protecting each other and the Earth, but our institutions based on power, profit, and a dangerous polarization of wealth and gender are a big part of the total picture and the conundrum we face. Institutions and corporations, though seemingly having a life of their own, are composed of people, and on the top, people with power. If they want themselves, their children, and humanity to thrive they too must take a longer view and exemplify the necessary care.

Since humanity has moved from being isolated to being interconnected around the world, it's a necessary part of the transition into adulthood to be aware that what we do or don't do might have global impact. We can no longer treat the rest of the world as separate from us. The problem is not that an aspect of us is self-centered; it is the childish ways that we are self-centered. Our limited identities based on childish authoritarian beliefs emphasize our differences rather than our similarities, while trumping up artificial superiorities and pandering to the pleasures of feeling superior. This not only limits what we care about and our capacities for altruism, it infiltrates into our predatory nature, magnifying and exacerbating it in cruel and barbaric ways causing torture, sexual slavery, wars, mass rapes as war strategy, and even genocide. Limited identities prevent the world from coming together across cultures to meet common threats. We need a new sense of community that does not create limited identities and ideological boundaries with those outside.

Have you ever wondered where the mechanisms for evolution live inside you—how they display themselves in you? What is the feel of them, the way they express themselves in living, in you? For surely, if there is such a thing as evolution, we all must be products and carriers of it. If there is such a process as evolution, obviously I am the end result of eons of it. Each of us is. Also, quite obviously, evolution must be passed on through us, so the mechanisms of evolution must live somewhere in us. Is it possible to get in touch with these mechanisms from the inside? Not intellectually, but as a living thing. If I observe myself closely, I find that these mechanisms are programmed into me genetically.

Many aspects of who I am, of who we are, have a deep genetic foundation—our ability to talk, to abstract, to empathize, to bond socially, to love, to feel emotions, and to have curiosity about ourselves and the cosmos. As self-reflective tool-makers, we have built devices that extend our senses and thoughts to perceive and understand with a vast reach in ways unimaginable only a century ago. The basis of our abilities to talk, care, love, think, abstract, and be curious are hard-wired into us. They are how we evolved. There is one aspect of our genetic conditioning that needs to be faced and understood more deeply, as it is an important key to understanding where we are. The inner feel of it is aggression. This is an aspect of being human that many people are understandably reluctant to look at because it is related to our predatory nature. Yet if we don't look it squarely in the face, we cannot deal awarely with it and the violence it has propagated—not only in order to mitigate it, but also to tap into its potential and have it work for us instead of against us.

One way that aggression expresses itself is in competition, which can play out on a spectrum from mutually enhancing to violent, with war being an extreme example. Many people tend not to look at aggression or even competition clearly because they don't like to look at themselves in that way, but it's there—the survival of the fittest. We compete for resources, for food, for territory with other species, and with our own species and gender for power, status, sexual partners, entertainment (sports, contests), and for the dominance of beliefs. Overt and covert, conscious and unconscious, subtle and blatant competition is part of daily life.

We can be extraordinarily violent animals, which has helped us be an extraordinarily successful one. We have spread our seed over the whole Earth, and as we do, other species die out. We have casually destroyed entire species around us, and more are dying hourly—ones that could be essential for our survival. Humans are driven by genetic programming, and as successful predators we utilize aggression, violence, dominance, and power over "lesser" species as our birthright.

Our precarious predicament is the unsurprising, even predictable outcome of being a self-reflective but not yet very conscious or aware predatory, dimorphic, social mammal with caring and using, egotism and altruism, violence and love intertwined. We are struggling to become more conscious and aware—and now needing to do so.

Our unprecedented minds have been our evolutionary advantage, giving us dominance on Earth. Thought is comparative, often competitive and aggressive, and it has made our species the successful animal we are. The tiger has its claw, we have thought. I can't beat up the tiger in a fight, but I can invent arrows and guns, which come from thought, and shoot the tiger. This inventiveness along with our ability as social animals to communicate and cooperate allows us to compete better with other animals when we are in groups. Extending our capacity for violence immeasurably through tool-making and cooperation long ago placed us at the top of the animal chain of life. We used this advantage with such extraordinary skill that we became the lords of the planet. No other species has threatened us. On the contrary, we're so "successful" that the ongoing rapid extinction of other species that we have triggered is one of our biggest threats. In fact, we are now our own biggest threat. Having conquered Earth's physical frontiers, our usual external outlets for aggression have diminished, so we're turning it on ourselves and the planet. That's what's happening—we're destroying ourselves.

The ecological destruction of our home planet is a manifestation of our violence that is presently rising to the forefront of everyone's awareness. The momentum of unregulated global capitalism has greatly accelerated this destruction because the bottom line—usually the only line—is profit. The way that acquisitive greed, competition, cooperation, and other genetic programs have been embedded in social structures constitutes a large part of our problems. {This is described in the Pleasure and Power commentary, Chapter 4.} The corporate world, the military, and the arms industry, the race to capture the global computer market, to build the first atom bomb, and war itself are modern versions of internal cooperation furthering aggressive external competition.

Many of us have been conditioned to believe that violence doesn't work and that love can conquer all. There is nearly universal agreement that we have to love more, and all religions preach it. Preaching love, compassion, unity, and the ending of violence by eliminating ego, self-centeredness, attachment, desire, and the like—as all world religions do in their own way—has had thousands of years to prove itself effective and failed. All of these traditions have put forth ideals of unity while creating great division. Ideals of unity only ever create unity among those who share the ideals, and it is sadly this very unity that divides the group from others by creating an "us" and a "them." All communities based on shared belief are only united at the *de facto* price of separating from everyone else—no matter if their ideals espouse unity for all humanity.

Now that our capacity for violence has grown exponentially with technology, and our challenges are ever more global, intertwined, and complex, lofty ideals are even less capable of solving our dilemmas. Religions and societies have long preached nonviolence while engaging in the very violence they condemn. They have separated people everywhere into in- and out-groups by creating often-hostile identities. Religious and ethnic wars, missionaries destroying cultures, torture, inquisitions, crusades, *jihads, fatwas,* and other often-lethal "pressures" to enforce conformity have been routinely unleashed throughout history. The religious injunctions against killing not only have not stopped killing, the willingness to kill rule-breakers reveals that what is really important is not the rule but protecting the authority behind the rule. Infidels and outsiders can all be treated outside the rules in the name of protecting the rules.

As we saw, any closed beliefs can be a catalyst for violence. They underlie and motivate not only one religion being pitted against another, but much of organized violence, racial and ethnic animosities, this country against that, modern men and women mistrusting each other, and in certain medieval-minded cultures men systematically and barbarically abusing women. These polarities and conflicts all stem from outmoded, closed beliefs, including the beliefs that underlie and justify power and privilege. This is a significant part of our history.

One of the not-too-veiled secrets of fighting and war is that violence can be a great pleasure. Look at your own anger—not your judgments about your anger—but your anger itself. What an enormous pleasure and release it is in the moment: the surge of energy, the righteousness, the outrage, and how we cultivate it with blame and justifications.

The simple fact is that although violence did work very well for "success," it no longer does. A species that turns its cleverness and violence on itself as we do is heading for self-destruction.

Please keep in mind that I'm not condemning or saying that aggression or competition is wrong or bad, or suggesting that violence was and is in all instances inappropriate for humanity's evolution and survival. Rather, what I'm doing here is simply looking at aggression and violence and how they (we) work. They were part of the momentum that spread our progeny all over the Earth with great abundance, which has now become a core part of our problems.

Nor am I saying that we can or should try to eliminate all aggression (if we could, which we can't). Aggression is not always violent or even harmful. It's a focused energy. As an evolutionary honing mechanism, the aggressive element in competition moves people to sharpen capabilities, as in athletics and games of mental strategy like chess. But our viability depends on being more conscious of how aggression lives in us and how we use it, in order for it not to work against us. And we must cooperate intelligently to change our institutionalized aggressive tendencies.

In troubled times, hope for a better world is natural and vitally important—but what one hopes for must actually offer real possibilities or else the hope leads one to put energy and attention in the wrong direction. We need hope's energy and positive thrust to meet great challenges, so it is crucial to see where possibilities lie and move toward them. This is where awareness combined with hope and insight is essential. Diana and I call ourselves "possibilists" because we see possibility everywhere that our potential is blocked. So instead of trying to live up to images or inculcated ideals, it is more possible and fruitful to see the nature of the blockages to our evolution and potential leverages to open them up.

People avoid looking at their aggression because it is difficult to look at it without judgment—but judging makes it harder to deal with the issue realistically. For millennia aggression and violence have been judged a human or social flaw by religions, pacifists, and utopian idealists. Their agenda has been to free humanity from it—to no avail. But people do not like to lose or be one down. Aggression has to do with the desire to supersede or defeat an opponent in any win/lose real-life situation or game (chess, soccer, bridge). To see the nature of our aggressive conditioning (genetic as well as social), just to see it, to see it realistically without judging it, is a movement. Aggression can leave in any given moment when you see its workings in yourself and how this impacts you, others, and the world. I cannot eliminate my potential for violence, but I can temper it and move my aggressiveness (which is a form of focused energy) in a positive direction. What can this mean?

These parts of being human long judged to be only negative have a valuable and necessary aspect connected to creativity and the will to make life better. Seeing this clearly brings a shift from trying to eliminate the destructive aspects of our nature to curbing their inappropriate expressions—which it is possible to do. Since aggression is part of who we are, we need to be aware of it, study it very carefully, and channel it into as many viable forms as possible. There is a lot of energy and pleasure in aggression that could be tapped into.

Competition, which contains aggression, can be used in life-furthering ways. Our aggressive genetic heritage could be linked with care and the urgency of common purpose by channeling it into contests with significant rewards for finding sorely needed solutions. Competitions for creatively bettering the world, for clean technologies, and increasing justice and fairness are positive examples of redirecting aggression. Curbing and tempering our potential for violence involves a shift in awareness. Seeing clearly the dangers of the aggression built into us is the beginning of moving to increase the range of its constructive possibilities.

The structures of society that people have contributed to for thousands of years are increasingly revealing their dysfunctionality. But there is no such thing as society apart from the people who create it. The structures that carry us along are actually built and continually regenerated by us. They are a manifestation of what and who we have been, and to an extent of what we still are. It's a two-way feed—we create society and society creates us. If societies are violent, confused, greedy, and dysfunctional, the greater likelihood is that their members will express that in their lives too.

Using force and violence to tear down the old order and install a new one is the way that changes have occurred through the centuries. The new order then becomes the oppressor, with a new elite holding the power, bringing little or no fundamental change. Until the advent of modern democracy to include women and all racial and social groups (a very recent occurrence), it's all been the same thing under a different guise.

Using aggression and violence as a less-than-conscious route to solve problems or advance an agenda—war, arms sales, resource-grabbing, stuffing jails with the disadvantaged, etc.—has severely limited our social capacities for care-taking and retarded our growth and maturity as a species. So our new challenge is to treat each other better, and to infuse our institutions with new values that instill care. This is now a survival necessity, not only a moral imperative, which is what could make it possible at last.

We have the idea that peace or bliss is a life without problems, a life of equanimity and staid equilibrium where nothing affects you. But that is not peace or bliss; it's merely an idea. Peace or bliss is not a cessation of problems but the ability to respond to life and to the problems that come in an unfettered, creative way with the energy that moves through the blockages of our habits and conditioning that clarity can provide.

We began this inquiry by asking why focus on awareness when the threats are so great and urgent. Ordinarily awareness is not at all a marketable item. People mostly don't want it. Civilization certainly hasn't wanted it. Societies that value the continuation of their power structures are afraid of it. Awareness is a wild thing, not a tame beast, and in these times particularly, much of what one sees is clearly neither pleasant nor comforting. Awareness is not respectable, which means it does not respond to the usual button-pushing of sentimentality or conditioned identities. Great pressure is exerted by the forces of the old and the power of tradition to keep people's blinders on.

It seems that awareness only spreads when there is tremendous urgency, with fundamental change being absolutely necessary. And that is what is happening presently. The world is crying out for movement now that the old ways are not working. Awareness is necessary because it is the only way truly to see and confront the unprecedented challenges, and to successfully move into the future. It is only when individuals through awareness of our human nature come to terms with themselves that real change occurs. This includes society coming to terms with how it has incorporated and embodied aspects of our nature within its structures, making it difficult to curtail and regulate our excesses and imbalances. Before looking at how society can change (which can be overwhelming), I need to see if I can.

How can I change? How does it happen? If I try to make it happen out of my old conditioning, this does not bring real change—any core changing I try to do through effort usually creates more conflict. I have an idea that I should be or do something else; I feel the urgency in me and I want to move, yet I cannot see how to go about it. What am I to do? Any time I try to change myself—whether it's through following a technique, a philosophy, psychology, an expert, guru, or whatever I'm involved in—trying to match ideals of what others say is an effort that makes me lose touch with myself. As we saw, the attempted cultivation of love, peace, and nonviolence preached for centuries has clearly failed to contain human violence.

To fix something well, you have to first know how it works and what the nature of the problem is. Curiosity is a handmaiden to awareness. Learning that is not the mere accumulation of knowledge involves asking pertinent questions rather than seeking immutable answers. When you put the right question at the right time, the answer is often contained within it. If you see the problem clearly enough to pin it in a question, you can also often see where possibility lies. Finding where our potential and possibility lie—and how best to leverage them—is the challenge.

The question, once again, is whether people can confront the aspects in themselves they may not like or want to see without getting stuck in self-blame or judgment. To just see oneself directly and with curiosity and hope as part of both the problem and the solution can allow the challenges to be met and dealt with. If the structures are to change and become viable for the pressures and needs of a changing world, we must change so they can. Is it possible for human beings actually to come to terms with the reality of who we are, and in doing so for there to be a newness, a creativity, that is not just a function of the old patterns and conditioning? The transformation I am suggesting, which I think is possible, is not becoming different from what we are—but rather becoming more aware of who we are. We need to understand who we are so that we can be better at it—that is, so we can be who we are more awarely. The important thing is to begin to look at the way one actually works—not only in oneself, but to look at oneself in relationships. This one can do, and it is a good prerequisite for change.

Throughout this inquiry I have been emphasizing the need for care and care-taking, while not extolling the virtues of love. This is not because I doubt the power, wonder, and depth of love. Rather, it is because love has an uncontrollable and non-cognitive aspect to it that makes it difficult to truly love what you have not personally experienced. Care is different, as it can incorporate a net that my mind can throw out based on my knowledge, beliefs, and imagination. I cannot love the dying polar bear that would eat me if it could; but I can and do care about all polar bears that are suffering because of human misuse. I cannot love any or all of the Congolese women who are now being raped, mutilated, and killed whom I never met but know exist. But I can feel empathy and outrage, and care about them and care about stopping this if I could. So as a first step in changing, one can find out what one really cares about, or even would like to care about. The beauty of caring is that your mind has some influence in the direction it takes.

This shift in consciousness is not achieved through asking for it. You don't know what to ask for. One way that change occurs is through "revelation," and by that I don't mean anything mystical, esoteric, or out of the ken of ordinary people or daily life. I mean something quite simple: revelation is seeing—it's seeing with an immediacy that does not occur in time or in thought. It occurs instantly—that instant is a momentary flash of insight, although having an insight sometimes takes a buildup to it that breaks through at some point. Realizations do not occur in time, although it can and usually does take time for them to come. Seeing clearly is revelation in that what it reveals is the living situation, seen from a broader perspective. To see which aspects of our nature are self-destructive and counter to survival, to see all of this clearly is to move. You don't know which way you're going to jump, and where you find yourself is always a surprise. Although a shift in awareness cannot be directly sought, seeing clearly what you in fact do care about can open the door to it. We as a species are facing the challenge of evolution, which has to do with a new principle of personal and social change. With survival once again being the bottom-line consideration for humans, to succeed humanity has to evolve socially. This involves a shift in consciousness, so it is urgent for humans to become more conscious in social spheres.

The more a worldview is in touch with the "reality" within oneself and what's going on "out there," the more it can be a source of revelations in the living moment, in living situations. Awareness is a key to real change and to social evolution. Movement, evolution, and social change can come with awareness of our nature that moves us from unconscious conditioning into the conscious. This can only occur with a real change of awareness within people, within you and me—and in the institutions we create out of our values and worldviews.

It is true that conceptualizing can at times mislead and hinder direct contact with living. Yet the symbols that our memory has stored are partly what allow us to see a tree as a tree. Although a living tree, a human being, or a moment of extraordinary intensity cannot be totally captured by symbols, one still tries to capture and communicate life's ongoing processes with words.

Ideas have changed the world both through changing worldviews (the lens we perceive through) and literally through changing its structures and through materializing the ideas (the computer and Internet being modern examples). Technology has changed the face of the planet and the content of our hopes and fears (what we think about).

Communism is an example of a powerful idea that became a failed experiment, teaching us that the ideal of economic equality and equal distribution of goods cannot be imposed by *fiat* from above through coercion, mental programming, threat, violence, and fear.

A groundbreaking, compelling idea that fits the needs of the times can spread quickly. Democracy, freedom, feminism, and human rights are potent ideas taking root throughout the world as expressions of deep human desires for fairness and justice. Although democracies have not yet managed to prevent many in power from controlling others for their own benefit, democracy is still the form where feedback from different strata can most readily occur. All societies have a tension between individual desires and group cohesion, conformity and the amount of deviance tolerated. Flexibility, a feedback orientation, and societies that permit greater latitude of behavior foster constructive change—a reason why democracies are essential for social evolution.

Making democracy truly democratic is an important step toward social evolution, especially now while social structures are still threatened by authoritarianism from within and without. Leaders can only reflect the awareness and values of the populace that create the climate of opinion they operate in. We need more intelligent, caring people in power, as well as effective regulation that minimizes the corruptions of power. Although politicians can lead and inspire with vision, many are like weathervanes who reflect what they perceive their voters want. It's partly up to the citizenry to help create a favorable and ethical political climate that does not penalize politicians for telling the truth and being principled. The best way to protect and spread democracy is through example, by living up to its ideals.

The shift we have been talking about is a broadening of awareness to be more inclusive, a requisite for making social evolution conscious. The possibility that evolution can move from the unconscious biological to the more conscious social only speaks to the necessity of movement, not what the movement will look like. However, when looking at previous shifts in evolution, where else could the next step be? Change comes in many ways: from person to person, group to group, from the bottom, middle, and top, and all their interactions and permutations. For one person to become aware is a spark of awareness that can spread. Since the inner and the outer to an extent mirror each other, if I change, this affects others and my surroundings in small or not so small ways. Social change starts with individuals and groups and takes on a life of its own. Once it begins it can create its own momentum, eventually becoming part of a planetary movement toward more global consciousness.

Humanity is on an evolutionary crest, a cusp point. Whether we will respond to that challenge or not remains an open question. Different historical epochs have different demands. This epoch is urgently demanding that we deeply change the unworkable ways we do things. Time constraints are putting us under great pressure—the screw is tightening. Evolution works through pressure, for without it there would be no motive to change. When life is relatively secure and pleasures come easily, there isn't much interest in awareness or change. In this day and age it's much more difficult to remain unperturbed in habitual modes. The challenges of the times are great; ignoring them creates extraordinary dangers. Change can be frightening and even at times dangerous. But the world as it is now is more than merely dangerous; it's collapsing around us. So whatever its unknown dangers, change offers hope if we rise to meet this extraordinary moment in our short history on Earth.

Real awareness is a way of seeing oneself and being in the world that lines up with the evolutionary cusp we're on. Our conundrum is that we are not facing an outside enemy but aspects of our nature that no longer work. How do we protect others, the Earth—and ourselves—from ourselves? The answer lies within the nature/nurture dialectic: changing our nature through more aware and caring nurture. Other social animals are largely governed by instincts and biology, including their nurturing. But for human beings, where there is an embedded relationship between nature and nurture, nurture is more important and partly has to be taught and learned. Nurture develops and shapes our nature, even to the extent of influencing which genes fire, creating different neural networks. It's the surest way both to influence our genes and develop our untapped potential. Within this nature/nurture dialectic, our genes, our biological nature, are not the core problem—we are (meaning, our inadequate "nurturing"). Our capacity to care and love is not limited by our genes but by unlivable ideals, the sexual order and its gendered structuring of society, as well as a worldwide lack of societal nurturing and real education.

Our mind's creativity and our capacity to care and connect with each other are great, relatively untapped resources and sources of hope and solutions; but a sane social situation and citizenry are needed to nurture (foster) their development. A sane society conducive to bringing about social evolution and an adult citizenry would include conscious reproduction, actually treating children as our most precious resource, women sharing institutional power, democracy, global identities, pancultural values, and making the process of truth-seeking paramount. This is the only way that our extraordinary mind's untapped potential can be used in the service of care and our deepest will to survive.

This is the seemingly insurmountable wall we face. Can we evolve sufficiently to cross over the wall? Because awareness is a necessary element in the next step, if we believe we can, we might; but if we think it impossible, we won't. Viewing evolution as purposeless and meaningless makes it more difficult to muster hope and positive action.

If "spirit" is the embedded force within existence that is the invisible driver of evolution, spirituality is the connection between self-conscious individuals and the evolutionary momentum they are a part of—this includes how people connect with each other, other species, and the planet that supports us. Spirituality is ignited by the relationship among people (whether we see ourselves as One or not) and how spirit expresses itself within a given epoch, which changes as it too participates in the evolutionary momentum. So spirituality needs to be periodically reframed to mesh with new human challenges, discoveries, and potentials. The challenge facing humanity is to complete the worldview transformation still underway through co-creating a compelling spectrum of values, an adaptable morality that is life-sustaining.

If spirit does drive evolution, then it drives us too as the product of it. Spirituality then is not a personal achievement, nor does it exist in a separate realm. Rather, it is embedded in a relational context that people can participate in, manifesting in the ways people treat each other and their home planet. Unlike traditional spiritual worldviews, this view does not artificially separate spirit from matter, the spiritual from the mundane, nor altruism from self-centeredness. Rather it expresses an evolutionary movement that I believe at this time to be crucial for humanity's survival: bringing spirituality back to Earth. As one delves into the timeless question "Who am I?" the knowledge that comes is not merely about the individual—it includes the understanding of oneself as part of the total fabric of life, and as an active and aware participant in the process of evolution. In the last analysis, these two things are one.

To be aligned with the spirit of the times brings an energy and a sense of possibility that can cut through the accumulation of habits that brought us here. It can be exciting and enlivening, bringing meaning and purpose into life. The next step in the evolutionary process that moves from the unaware biological to the more conscious social is to create and take care of a sane world. It is up to us whether or not there will be a next step.

Question: Worldviews seem so abstract and removed from living. What difference do they make in daily life?

Answer: The mind's responsiveness is limited by the ideas and beliefs with which it views the world. A worldview structures the mind, which affects the way the world is experienced and how one feels in a general way and on a daily basis. Whether viewing the universe as basically benign, malevolent, or randomly neutral (indifferent), these all seem to be abstractions that you might seldom overtly think about, far removed from daily living. These parts of worldviews, however, are the basis of common attitudes (idealism, pessimism, optimism, cynicism, skepticism), which are patterns that color all perceptions by monitoring what comes in.

Believing in the Rapture or that some omniscient intelligence is in control and will set things right can make you feel better. If you believe that the cosmos is totally indifferent to human fate, it's easy to be pessimistic; if your viewpoint is based solely on our history, it's hard *not* to be pessimistic. All these beliefs and attitudes are contained in basic worldviews, and like all worldviews, they only "prove" themselves from within the worldview itself, so proof is always circular and relative—only relevant to those who share the premises within the worldview. All these beliefs about the world have emotional impact and totally influence the way you think, act, perceive, and even who you prefer to relate with, directly affecting the quality of your life.

Question: With so many people in the world, and so many of them just struggling for survival, how can enough people change to meet these huge challenges? It's hard not to feel hopeless.

Answer: Skeptics can claim that evolving socially is a pipe dream, another stick dangling the carrot of unrealistic hope. Around seven billion people in differing stages of cultural development with different and conflicting agendas live on planet Earth, competing for survival, resources, minds, and sometimes the imposition of their values and ways on others. Many of them live so close to the edge of survival that they aren't aware of global problems and issues or even that humanity's survival is at stake. One could reasonably wonder how most or even any of them could have any idea of what we're talking about, let alone care, or have the will or capacity to make needed changes.

Thinking it necessary to influence and change the minds of some seven billion people does seem hopeless. This paralyzes will and action and is not a good frame of mind for facing what we have never faced consciously before—the pressure to make an evolutionary leap into being a more caring social species, and moving through evolution toward greater consciousness. The question is not whether everyone can change, but can a different social climate of awareness and opinion be created, and so be a beacon toward survival?

Change can and is occurring throughout the world in many different ways and at many different levels, from the bottom up to the top down. Anyone who looks past their local surroundings (which technology is making increasingly possible) can see that the world as it is now structured is not working. As those who *do* see this make their move toward possibilities, this ignites others to look more deeply and move too. So one way change occurs is personally—from person to person, whether face to face or through communication technologies like the Internet. This has already led to a worldwide surge of grassroots movements and NGOs initiating changes aimed at sustainability and social justice.

A double-edged aspect of being human is that we are creatures who follow fashion—this is an extension of the primate and the very human proclivity to imitate. On one side this has led us to conformity, authoritarian leaders, obsolete religions and mentalities, and fads that can dilute things to such blithely unaware, vapid, and increasingly destructive superficialities as the shallow and unsustainable hedonism of consumerism.

On a brighter note, people at all levels are reached through what might be called the pace- or fashion- setters. Here following fashion bodes well for us. If some of the world's fashion-setters (a very small percentage of the population) have a shift in awareness, which is already occurring and spreading, through technology's magnification this could have a great effect on large numbers of people. The combination of an awareness shift in the fashion-setters and in the pro-democracy, ecology, social justice grassroots phenomenon throughout the world is creating an ever-increasing, self-propelling momentum with global impact. Ultimately, the energy could be remarkable and spread far and wide.

We not only communicate verbally and cognitively, we also communicate emotionally. When there is fear or joy in a crowd or a sporting event you can feel it, and it's hard to resist being somewhat swept into it. Whereas cognition dates back a few hundred thousand years, rudimentary emotionality goes back one hundred million years. Emotionality is a highly developed mammalian sense organ with sophisticated information-processing capacities of others' emotional states Mammals without language attune and adapt to each other's states and communicate emotionally through the limbic system. Emotions are contagious, able to leap between minds through neural attunement, bringing immediate congruence. Scientists call this synchronistic mutual responsiveness "emotional resonance."

If there is an evolutionary spirit of the times that people can connect with, this could bring about an emotional resonance among people (one school of psychologists calls this a "group unconscious") that can help focus energy where it's most needed. The brain is the seat of emotions, primarily in the limbic system. The brain's wirings can change through environmental impact, like caring nurturing.

This is not merely a simplistic Pollyanna hope; the need for some kind of basic shift is available to most anyone who wants to look. Timely, urgently needed, and eagerly hoped-for breakthroughs, discoveries, and ideas spread like wildfire, as did the American-now-global women's movement. Timely ideas can have an almost immediate and more far-reaching impact through technology. So it ultimately gets down to how much we, people all over the world like you and me, and the powerful, the fashion-setters, want humanity to continue. It depends on whether we can use our genetic desire to survive, while overriding counter-to-survival genetic programming and social manipulation, in order to put our intelligence, emotions, and creativity at the service of passion for life and survival.

Human genes, minds, and emotions have created the world we find ourselves in, and it is they that must create something new that is viable. Can I, can we, change and move? If evolution is itself now moving through us from the biological to emphasizing the social, the good news is that this means we can become conscious participants in the process and take it in our hands to evolve socially. Social evolution is in our power and can move quickly once underway if it meets the challenges of the times.

Question: Since adults are like "cosmic orphans" with no saviors, no last-minute rescuing cavalry, as you say, and few if any role models on how to be more aware, where do we find teachers?

Answer: Life is full of teachers. Obviously I'm teaching. To live is to teach and to learn. We are teachers and learners for each other. A rich source of learning is from those different from you. Different generations, ethnic groups, men and women—they all have much to teach each other. There are countless examples.

A big cultural lack with enormous potential needing to be tapped is cross-generational dialogue. Rapidly changing times cause strange reversals in where the cutting edge lies, and in who knows what, and how they know it and communicate it. Although past guides cannot be relied upon for unprecedented challenges, sharing knowledge among generations is an untapped source of insight, knowledge, and wisdom. Now the generations can and must be teachers and learners for each other if the world is to survive, much less thrive. Cross-generational dialogue is tremendously important—each phase of life and generation has valuable experience, perspectives, and insights to share to help fill each other's gaps. Each generation is conditioned both similarly and differently by their experience and times. Every generation makes different media choices and has different ways of getting and processing information and of using technology to communicate and relate.

Since the young are pioneers more in touch with the new and oriented to the future, they can be far more affected by and adept at using the new technologies—whose varied and still unknown effects are double-edged. Their very nervous systems are connected to technology, which affects everything: their relationships, lifestyle, worldview, and even how and what they think. Their facile, elaborate interconnectivity with others and around the world is changing the very nature of identity and helps them envision new possibilities for global connectivity. The mistakes, failings, and illusions of preceding generations can be more apparent to those who follow, which can make them mistrustful. Those older need to reach out, take and show genuine interest, trust and foster trust, and provide opportunities for intergenerational conversation.

Earlier generations have a different relation to the printed word, books, reading, writing, and communicating, which gives them important sources of information and insights. They are also more in touch with how the past became the present, a needed source of understanding for creating a better future. More life experience can bring more nuanced insights and at times wisdom. Also through having children, and sometimes grandchildren, they can be more cognizant not only of recent history, but of humanity's and their own nature.

Later generations have a remarkable amount of power over the way the young come into themselves and into the world. Each generation has a responsibility to those coming afterward to protect them, especially young girls, from the harms of and fall-out from the out-of-control, unbridled consumerist, and highly sexualized culture. Specifically, sex education, birth control, abortion access, and reliable information about food and drugs are needed to help the youth make informed decisions and to prevent harmful societal habits from being propagated unconsciously. We must protect those younger and their environment, for they are the living thread of humanity moving forward. Our species will only be as good as the next living edge of evolving humans. Valuing humanity necessitates nurturing, educating, and supporting them to the best of our capacity as one of humanity's most important tasks.

COMMENTARY:
Intelligence Without Design

Many years ago, a friend replied to our lengthy laments about the world going down the tubes, "If you're really interested in change, optimism is your best strategy." Intuitively we knew he was right, but how to be optimistic without conjuring up fantasy scenarios geared primarily at making oneself feel better? This is when we began to realize just how much one's worldview frames and influences what one sees and thinks, thereby affecting one's attitude toward life—whether hopeful or hopeless, optimistic or pessimistic, idealistic or cynical. It especially influences how one views a future-oriented topic such as evolution. We came to realize why otherwise intelligent people negate evolution, or put it into religious contexts like monotheism that seem to us to contain contradictory beliefs and rather juvenile myths (at best), and why other people might keep scientific and religious worldviews in separate mental compartments, without trying to make them congruent.

Most people understandably have a hard time believing that existence just appeared out of nowhere. This implies a cold universe indifferent to human concerns, lacking a non-material dimension. So they turn to available worldviews that incorporate purpose and meaning, which are generally religious.

This has resulted in a deep split between a strict materialist worldview and other worldviews that see some intelligence within existence. Many people (on both sides of the split) are not aware of the extent to which this controversy involves significant and complex arguments about the nature of reality. They justify their respective positions by unknowingly simplifying and reducing the issues to a polarity between spirituality and secular materialism, the latter being the foundation of modern science. The media popularizes it more simplistically yet as a split between religion and science.

This conflict is currently playing itself out with much heat in the arena of evolution theory, where raging arguments cut to the foundation of how and why existence exists. At one extreme are the "arguments from design" denying evolution; on the other side are the materialist, evolutionary perspectives. And in the seeming middle are those who say that God designed evolution, which they think explains the jumps and incongruities in the evolutionary process. This "middle ground" is really just a more sophisticated argument from design.

Seeking a resolution to this core divisive conflict, we extend the discourse beyond the simplistic and false polarization of "science versus religion" to the underlying philosophical quandaries. By reframing the debate to address the vital questions of "purpose versus purposelessness" or "meaning versus meaninglessness" within evolution and the cosmos, we are attempting to discern and revision the issues behind the polarizations. The core of the controversy is between "intelligent design" with purpose built in on the one hand, and causation with chance and randomness being the drivers of a purposeless, evolutionary momentum on the other. Purposeless is abhorrent to the intelligent design believers; purpose is anathema to most of traditional science. ("Emergentist" scientists who acknowledge a momentum toward greater complexity likewise deny inbuilt purpose, neither explaining nor addressing the cause or source of emergence.)

The materialist scientists have no truck with what they consider the irrational (unprovable in principle) and anthropomorphic indulgences that the "designers" exhibit. The former focus on the absurdity of a transcendent God—an easy target. The more intelligent

"intelligent designers" rail against science's narrow vision, its refusal to give any real explanation for the extraordinary confluence of statistically improbable events and finely tuned, coordinated configurations of exacting precision down to mathematically unimaginably small sub-atomic levels that allow this universe to be at all. This seems so randomly impossible that it fits some dictionary definitions of "miraculous." All this is related only to the existence of Existence itself. We haven't even begun to take into account the unexplained arrival of experiencing, consciousness, emotions, and human symbol-communicating, abstractive, self-reflecting consciousness.

The design advocates point out that Science cannot prove Design is wrong, just that it does not fit a very narrow scientific paradigm that leaves out most of life's important issues. Materialist scientists in turn say that without using science as a baseline for truth and objectivity, any flight of fancy is possible. It is obvious that these two positions are operating out of worldviews with different conceptions of what "proof" consists of. Scientific worldviews only address what is falsifiable or what they consider provable. Meaning and purpose do not qualify as being within science's realm and are therefore considered off-limits to scientific inquiry or theory (they are too subjective). However, some scientists might need to be reminded that the scientific assumption that no intelligence is involved in the construction of the universe because it does not fit a materialist worldview is likewise not provable by science.

In our view, one root of this heated debate is the fact that both sides are missing something vital that needs to be acknowledged and taken into account. We have found that the crucial missing elements can be given their due by bringing them together in a third worldview that addresses the problem from a different perspective. The way our worldview approaches evolution, like all other speculations about the nature of creation and how things came to be, cannot ultimately be proven in the ordinary sense of proof. This is because what consists of proof is always embedded in a worldview, and thus is always circular. Such relativistic "proof" is of no help because it cannot be a referee in a world of conflicting worldviews. So given that our perspective does not involve proof—just as the other two worldviews cannot—we speak to reasonableness and "most-likelihood." After all, likelihood and reasonableness are all one has to go on when the moorings of science prove insufficient to deal with life's important questions and issues.

What follows is a carefully reasoned argument that sheds light on how our worldview differs from the two polarized ones, and why we think it is far more likely than either of them to be useful in our evolution. This is not merely an intellectual exercise—thinking about this topic has vital ramifications for where humanity is positioned and what is possible for us within evolution. Leaving aside those who deny evolution altogether, let's first agree that evolution of some sort operates within the play of existence. If evolution is not a part of your worldview, this book will probably not be relevant to you, unless you are open to the possibility of it.

Whether one believes in literal scriptures, has faith in a creator God that created evolution, or accepts only a mechanical evolutionary process, each point of view is embedded in a worldview. The worldview we are putting forth features an intelligence without a designer or a specific design. This is both similar to and different from each of the other worldviews. We find that this perspective gives a better explanation of the evolutionary process, including where we find ourselves at this historic and dangerous evolutionary moment. It is also a source of hope, offering a realistic possibility that we are facing an inevitable evolutionary challenge that *can* be met.

Evolution, by the very meaning of the word, implies change. The question is whether or not change has within it any viable foundation to be considered improvement. Improvement is not a value-free notion. This is so no matter what level of evolution one considers. Is greater complexity alone a sufficient reason to consider the more complex an improvement over the less? On the level of cosmic evolution—that is, the way the material of the cosmos seemingly evolves—is having a multitude of galaxies an improvement over the time before galaxies formed? Is a star with planets (as it is more complex) an improvement over planetless ones? On the planetary level, is one with life an improvement over one without? On the biological level, is increasing the range of possible experiencing an evolutionary improvement? And on the social level, does the very evolution of human capacities evolve, and if so does this in any way consist of improvements? Of course, the easy way out is to refuse to link evolutionary change with any vestige of improvement, claiming that values are nothing but a particular human quirk that are simply manufactured by human needs, which is evolution's fancy way of giving humans a survival edge because it allows them (us) the illusions of purpose and meaning that give impetus to social change when necessary.

This question, of course, lies at the crux of how different worldviews incorporate meaning, purpose, and value into their attempts to explain how and why anything exists at all, and why it is that life, experiencing, and consciousness came to be. Some arguments try to persuade that because on a purely physical level the cosmos constructs increasing complexities that both replicate and evolve, life and then consciousness would necessarily likewise evolve given a proper environment to do so. What "necessarily evolve" means is that because of the way evolution works over the long haul, statistically speaking, given the right combination of chemicals in the right environment, life is bound to appear. And then, because consciousness has some significant evolutionary survival advantages, it would also come forth at some point in the evolutionary process. Seeing that life and consciousness have evolved, this is an argument in retrospect that seeks an essentially mechanical explanation free from any hint of intention or purpose—because where would the purpose come from? This would introduce a mystery that science assumes is unwarranted.

An explanation for the occurrence of life and consciousness based on the observable fact that existence does have a momentum toward complexity may be comforting to those who wish to reduce all explanations to strictly materialistic reasons. However, this does not inquire into where this vector toward complexity comes from and why different qualities emerge out of more complex configurations. What is not addressed is why a particular arrangement of chemicals in a particular "soup" does bring forth life; rather it is just observed and stated that it does. The same is true for consciousness in that it does seem to emerge from life at some point, although just why and even where it emerges are murky questions. Are amoebas conscious, or plants, or ants, or snakes, or apes? And then there is the self-reflecting consciousness that humans have, which seems to go with an evolutionarily new linguistic ability. Did this too necessarily emerge simply because language gives social animals enormous facilities in cooperation, which in turn enables humans to out-compete other species?

The question of the evolutionary emergence of something seemingly new out of something old lies at the heart of whether or not something else beside purposeless and totally indifferent mechanisms is going on within the makeup of existence. (This is sometimes referred to as "the ghost in the machine.") In other words, is some kind of intelligence embedded in the very structure of existence itself that moves within the vectors of evolution to construct complexities, and what is more, to bring about emergent qualities including life and consciousness? The arguments in these pages attempt to show that it is more likely than not that there is. It is worth examining emergence again because it is important to not confuse it and other perspectives herein with current conceptions of and controversies around "intelligent design."

Religious thought uses the "argument from design" to affirm that there must be a super-intelligent designer (God) that is the cause of it all. The ultimate justification for this theory essentially rests on a belief that because the cosmos displays such great intelligence in its construction, there must be some super-intelligent constructor. "Intelligent design" is the terminology used to argue that the way that existence is put together is so exact and precise, and human consciousness and biological organs (the eye) so complex, that there had to be a creator intelligence behind it.

God is brought into the picture in different ways: Hard-line fundamentalists use "God's design" to negate the reality of evolution and even the findings of science as to the age of our universe. The extreme fundamentalist position has done away with reasonableness altogether, replacing it with emotional conversions and belief in authoritarian "sacred" texts and pronouncements. It demands absolute faith in ancient words interpreted by living "experts," who punctuate their sentences with phrases like "God says" or "God wants." Their worldview presents an absolute fixed morality with unbending rewards and punishments in the unchangeable realm of an afterlife. No doubt their faith gives them a mooring point of certainty that offers some solace in these fearful, uncertain times. The more fear and insecurity, the more people are seduced by and cling to (presumed) certainty. Although there is no way to penetrate such authoritarian worldviews to prove them wrong, they with the greatest likelihood are wrong because they ignore any reasonable counter-evidence.

Those who take biblical pronouncements less literally—the modernizers who mix faith with reason, science, and democratic values—say that God created evolution as the mechanism for change and has a hand in how it goes. (He could intervene at any time.) This posits a transcendent (separately existing) intelligence (God) as a necessary or better explanation for temporal existence. The more sophisticated form of this position does not deny science; but it too assumes that God the creator is eternal, that he created people with some super-conscious purpose in mind, and he is somehow steering the course. Few monotheists would make God temporal. If God is not eternal, but finite, then where did God come from?

If one wants to hold the eternal God worldview one can, but since modernizers allow a place for science and human reason, it is reasonable to show the problems in this point of view: This boils down to showing that, instead of resolving the mystery of existence, reliance on God as the explanation merely moves it back a step. This living mystery—which modern investigators tend to concede is unknown in many domains, including its origin—then becomes something we are told is caused by an unfathomable, invisible entity, which is an even greater mystery, for where did that entity come from and what is it? Assuming that a separate, conscious, willful, presumed-eternal entity is the cause of and reason for it all only adds an entirely new mystery to the picture, but it makes the new mystery much bigger because it is totally invisible and unreachable (unlike the cosmos), and even more mysterious and opaque than the cosmos itself. Perhaps there will always be some mystery, but many people find it more reassuring to believe in an impenetrable supernatural entity that is the cause of it all, and in charge, with a purpose that is ultimately benign.

But what does this God want—to be worshipped or somehow placated? Is God then the ultimate "ego trip"? Having a personal transcendent God adds another disturbing and irresolvable issue to the confusion: why did God design existence the way it is instead of some other way that results in less misery and cruelty? Why have so much pain and suffering in the mix? Is God a sadist; or are we instead left with "God moves in mysterious ways that we mere mortals cannot fathom"? Having a transcendent super-intelligence as an explanation does not offer a compelling argument for the all-too-often painful nature of existence. Nor does it counter the biggest challenge to monotheism—the existence of "evil." The pat reason given for evil (that it allows humans the freewill needed for God's final judgment) is a paltry excuse. Surely a more benevolent God could have given "good" a bit more edge over "evil." And if God is all-powerful, where did the devil come from?

Though a separate designer is most unlikely, the universe does display regularities and "laws" that fit each other in remarkable ways. To say there seems to be some intelligence of some order in the makeup of things does not imply that a superhuman-like intelligence is the causal factor. The transcendent God position need not imply that God displays the individuated will, intention, and preferences that humans do (on a far grander scale). Many people on both sides of the debate do not seem to realize that there are many ways to look at this—take deism, for example.

The eighteenth-century deist position is similar to the transcendent God position above—with a crucial difference: it says that God created the universe and all the laws of nature (which these days would include evolution) and set them all in motion—and then left everything alone to take care of itself. In fighting monotheism's authoritarianism and dogma, deists got rid of as much of the supernatural as possible, without entirely eliminating God as an explanation for existence. What remained was a detached and indifferent creator God as the first or "prime" mover, much like a clockmaker winding up his clock and setting it in motion. The deist explanation has many of the problems just mentioned, including why a God would do this. However, not needing to pay attention to a God that didn't pay attention to his creation got God "off their backs."

Given all the above problems within transcendence, it is possible to have instead a super-conscious intelligence that emanates from the whole of existence and is immanent within it. This is a form of pantheism where the whole of existence is somehow super-conscious and willful in the design of its own creation. Here God is the whole of creation, with a consciousness that directs how it designs itself. Hegel and de Chardin, among others, said that existence has been designed to move toward a predetermined end (predetermined by either a pantheistic or transcendent super-consciousness). Any worldview that uses some conception of design usually implies that we humans are a predetermined product marching toward a predetermined (designed) end.

These various arguments for intelligent design are presented to clarify a contrast between "intelligent design" (as defined in the past and also in the current religious manifestation) and our perspective. Although the arguments from design are deeply flawed in that they fail to capture the seeming arbitrariness, unfairness, pain, and cruelty that existence displays, nonetheless many people deeply, and we believe rightly, intuit that life and consciousness must mean something more than arbitrary chance. Arguments denying any intelligence or purpose within the makeup of existence have different problems such as: the minute exactitudes necessary in basic particles for this universe to exist at all; why seemingly new qualities emerge through complexity; and how do life, experiencing, and consciousness arrive?

Design in its essence implies meaning, and the different forms of intelligent design are different ways of bringing in premeditated meaning and purpose. They all come from traditional perspectives and placate fear by arguing that something wiser is in control. They can all stand against any onslaught from reason because reason alone cannot penetrate the given beliefs through unassailable proofs to the contrary.

A major difference between the point of view presented here and those in the debate centers on the words "intelligent" and "design." To be intelligent, what is generally assumed is that somewhere there is a conscious awareness with some foresight and hindsight that is cognizant of some of the forces at play that influence perceptions and outcomes. A design is a template for future manifestation. A design for a building constructs parameters about how the actualized building will look. So would a design for cars, humans, and for the structure of existence. Though the finished product could display some novelty outside the design, this involves the builders of the design going beyond the design itself. Still, following or being part of a design places deterministic constraints on the ultimate outcome. The very nature of a design points to a future, to some kind of finished product held in mind. It is very difficult to posit a design for existence without there being some kind of consciousness behind it (or within it).

The differences between this book's view of intelligence and purpose within the makeup of existence and the variants of intelligent design are as follows and not trivial: The intelligence being proposed here does not contain conscious intention about what the conscious parts of itself that come about via an evolutionary process will look like or do. There is therefore no conscious design in regard to outcomes and how existence will manifest. There is only the push to construct unique and novel individuals and species that give existence an endless array of experiencing itself through its creations. The evolutionary stages of buildup and breakdown that create jumps where different qualities emerge, such as life, are part of a momentum toward self-reflection. With the arrival of life and the irreducible miracle of experiencing, evolution moved to its life-and-death dramas that operate in a field of competition/cooperation. Biological evolution displays emergent leaps in the complexity of interaction among the individual constructions. Social interactions increase complexity; and with human beings another leap in complexity and self-reflexivity occurred, with language, abstraction, and curiosity that led to building tools and increasing our power to gain knowledge and comfort, and to create and destroy.

So instead of positing that existence has a specific design or designer manufacturing events, we think it far more likely that existence has an impetus to generate complexities that can and do bring forth emergent and surprising qualities that broaden existence's experience of itself. Novelty as part of an evolutionary vector (not a design because you cannot design novelty) explains better why there is violence within drama, why there is death without which there would be no change, and why we humans have continually pushed against the riddle of existence. It also explains better why each of us (or most of us) somewhere deep down believes that on occasion the choices we make create something new and different than other choices would have brought about. Having a self-conscious entity capable of real choice makes possible, or at least accelerates, the capacity of existence to experience itself more deeply in novel ways. None of this makes it necessarily so.

Yet we humans are what existence has come up with in this particular section of the cosmos. We are what existence constructs. If there is an inbuilt purpose to construct individuals that can experience something of the extraordinary majesty of the cosmos's workings, then for this planet, at this time, humans are at the apex of that capacity. So in a very real way, we humans are examples of the meaning and purpose of existence. It is a fact (archaic notions doubting evolution notwithstanding) that we are what the evolutionary process has brought forth. Whatever meaning or purpose each of us can tease out of our individual lives should take into account our participation in an evolutionary momentum containing severe but necessary challenges to either mature or leave the stage. This is where, in this particular epoch, meaning and purpose lie.

To say that humans are what existence constructs to experience itself does not mean that we have been consciously designed to be the way we are, nor have we been designed for guaranteed success. If this were so, then novelty and real choice would be a charade (it could be argued they are), and people would have no real say in whether they can consciously participate in their own evolutionary momentum. The worldview being presented argues that there is no specific design or conscious designer; that it is more likely that there is a momentum within existence to construct individuals that can consciously experience themselves, and to an extent the world around them. That's why we are here.

There is an argument within complexity theory that, in brief, says that the cosmos creates complexities through "laws." And so in the fullness of time and the endless arrays of possibility, life was bound to happen, and with it experiencing, which eventually led to consciousness and then self-reflexivity. This argument is purely statistical, and also purely retrospective in its assumptions. One of these unprovable assumptions (and an unscientific hope) is that given practically endless possibilities, something like human consciousness was bound to happen. This argument leaves out one major problem, which is that complexity alone has nothing within it that points to consciousness; nor even why out of different levels of complexity different qualities and "laws" emerge at all.

Life seems to emerge from non-life, consciousness from non-consciousness, and human linguistic abstractive abilities are likewise really an extraordinary emergent phenomenon. Humans can build very complex machines that can simulate a great deal of human thought. But it took human thought and will to do this, and as of now, no machine has the capacity of experiencing in the way that living entities do. If we humans are ever able to create self-conscious experiencing life (which is unclear), it is only because we emerged from an evolutionary process that enabled us to do so. Could experiencing and with it consciousness have emerged without there being some vector within the structure of existence for evolution to produce them? Certainly this is possible and arguable, but if consciousness just occurred without any purpose behind it, one would be hard-pressed to say that there is any purpose within life or consciousness. There also would be no reason to think they would ever occur again. For these and other reasons we argue that the emergence of self-conscious, self-reflective life is not arbitrary.

Many people intuitively wonder how the evolutionary exactitudes that led to self-conscious life could be fortuitous or accidental. This has brought many to give different variations of "intelligent design" some credence. Those who argue against "the argument from design" do so by showing that having an external designer explains little and increases the mystery. This book is proposing that there is a different, more likely way of giving purpose and meaning to the evolutionary process and to this particular evolutionary stage than the worldviews of "intelligent design," "meaningless accidental occurrence," or the statistical likelihood advocated by some complexity thinkers. People are facing the need to be more conscious using the gifts and powers we have, so as to continue the evolutionary track of self-reflective expansion. This must involve another leap in evolution into a more conscious involvement in the social sphere. We must care more about how we use ourselves and what is around us.

Insofar as we are conscious, consciousness exists; but more, insofar as we display any intelligence at all, intelligence is a part of existence. So the intelligence that humans on occasion display did not come out of nowhere; rather it is a manifestation of an intelligence that is within the construction of existence. This, of course, cannot be proved or disproved, but what is the alternative? That the regularities the cosmos displays just happen by lucky accident? That human intelligence is a fortuitous (or not) quirk that magically appeared out of nowhere? Even if one were to say that intelligence evolved only because there is survival value in it, it has survival value only because there is intelligence within the makeup of existence. Human intelligence in some fashion mirrors, responds to, and can connect with aspects of existence that it is a part of. If the universe did not behave intelligently in its construction, what good would it be to be intelligent? So, it is most likely that there is some kind of intelligence interwoven in the way existence designs itself. This is one of the pegs that this book hangs its view of evolution upon.

Scientific worldviews that rigidly adhere to a strict methodology of what is "provable" by science assume evolution to be essentially meaningless, in that it has no agendas and operates out of the interface of laws and response to random or unpredictable events. In biological evolution, the bottom line is "the survival of the fittest." This is a circular definition—whatever survives is "fit." Here an uninvolved science considers the extraordinary emergence of different qualities of complexity—including a creature that can use language, have values, self-reflect, love, appreciate beauty, and utilize a capacity to think in abstractions that allow for science—to be merely the outcome of a mix of "laws" with randomness or chance.

"Emergentists" in cosmology do acknowledge that different laws emerge with different levels of complexity. How these emergent aspects appear is not really known, but since emergentists are materialists too, this is just taken as a given, as is electricity, which is not totally understood either. (It is assumed that eventually science will figure it out.) That a universe evolved that could eventually support life is taken for granted, even though if any of the basic particles differed minutely in charge or size, this whole universe would not have formed at all. Science's answer as to why it formed against such astronomical odds is that "It formed as it did, and that's all that can be said—for now."

Science summarily dismisses all questions as "unscientific" that it deems unverifiable and not testable or falsifiable—with the unscientific hope that one day science will answer all the important questions. It is difficult for many (ourselves included, as well as many scientists when they take off their scientific hats) to not think there is some kind of intelligence somewhere in the makeup of existence. What makes it hard is seeing laws on the macro-level displaying an elegant simplicity, while at the quantum level individual particles are indeterminate, but when taken in large numbers, even quantum particles are so statistically predictable that the reliability of microchips in computers can be counted on. Then there are the almost magical occurrences of emergent laws and the extraordinary complexities within life—including the experiencing, communicating, connecting, emotionally resonating, thinking human being. All this makes it extremely difficult for us (and many others) to think it likely that this could have occurred by chance, without an internal momentum in this direction.

Our worldview sees the evolutionary process as having a momentum within it that leads to consciousness and then to self-reflexive intelligence. Although we take exception to the traditional meanings of spirit, we do call this underlying urge or vector "spirit" because it cannot be explained or described by the laws applying to matter. Also, no other word captures what we are trying to express. So we view evolution as having "spirit" embedded in matter, moving it toward form, emergent complexity, life, and eventually self-reflecting experiencing.

We are broad-based evolutionists, meaning we think that everything is evolving, including the mechanisms of evolution itself. First the material of the universe evolved into galaxies, stars, and planets. When life emerged—on this planet at least—the non-conscious mechanism of natural selection with its genetic underpinnings took over. There is no reason to think that the evolution of evolutionary mechanisms has stopped. If our premise is correct, that our survival depends on evolving socially, this is potentially good news. Evolving socially would involve a new evolutionary mechanism based on a shift and broadening of our awareness to enhance ways of relating and connecting, which could happen quickly, not over eons.

Our evolutionary advantage came through our large communicative, emotional brain, which through our vastly enlarged cooperative and tool-making abilities put us on top of the chain. This included eventually separating ourselves off from the rest of the animal kingdom such that we thought of ourselves as different and superior, with the right to use the rest of the world as we pleased. The need to become aware of this and to think differently is what puts humanity on an evolutionary cusp point, and in a sense a spiritual cusp too, that is challenging us to either evolve socially or vanish.

Experiencing, and its extension consciousness, constitutes the great unsolved mystery of life. The neurology that underlies experiencing is so different from consciousness that no one really knows how the connection between them works. Is it a one-way street with matter creating mind (as hard-line materialists, believe)? This makes mind a mere epiphenomenon with no effect on anything that happens. Or can consciousness (mind) in the forms of belief, will, intention, emotions, relationships, awareness, and meditation, change the physiology and the direction that one's life takes—making it a two-way street? This would mean the mind is not reducible to the brain's physiology.

We think the latter is more likely: that the evolutionary process that has produced existence, life, consciousness and experience, emotions, and our brain also produces conscious entities with will, intention, potentials of creativity, and an aesthetic that can appreciate, empathize with, and care for other constructions of existence. This means that nothing is written in stone and that existence is pushing for new ways to experience itself. This piece of a worldview seems to us more likely than a cold indifferent universe in which life fortuitously sprang up, or that came upon life through the statistically remote mix of necessary chemicals and environmental factors.

In addition, a solely material universe does not explain the various forms of experiencing, including will, intention, and the ability to make innovative choices that affect the future. In spite of materialism being largely deterministic in outlook, we suspect that most scientists of all persuasions are secretly convinced that they themselves are not totally determined "robots."

We have not become outright optimists, as we cannot know which way things will go. Instead we call ourselves "possibilists," meaning we believe that humanity has real possibilities and extraordinary untapped social potential. Of this we are certain: If people think and act as if we have a chance of becoming viable, then we might. If we don't, then we surely won't. Whether or not these views resonate with you, one thing is clear and absolute. Either human beings through will and intention have some say in the direction of the course of events, or we don't. This commentary on evolution is predicated on the strong likelihood that we do.

A major premise of this book is that humanity is on an evolutionary cusp. We are a species at risk—a risk of our own making—facing the ultimate challenge, possible extinction. This turning point, which is an unparalleled opportunity for breaking through old ways and seeing what humanity is capable of, comes from the risk. This is the way evolution works. The cosmos and evolution bring change through challenge and response, through forcing its parts to overcome seemingly insurmountable challenges—or not. An evolutionary challenge is by definition seemingly insurmountable. That's what brings necessary change. "Necessity is the mother of invention" is not merely a truism—it's true but not trite. Otherwise we are ruled by the force of habit, pleasure, privilege, and short-sighted, amoral power. The penalty for not rising to the "evolutionary occasion" is always death. So we have no choice but to take it on, and to believe it's possible to succeed.

We face a wall that can seem impossible to break through because doing so involves changing deeply held behaviors, some of them hard-wired. Facing potential extinction is related to a combination of factors in our nature, many of which we have looked at in these discussions, such as a clever brain requiring extended pregnancy and child-rearing; dimorphism causing an oppressive, imbalanced sexual order that has retarded our nurturing and maturing; aggression, male power hierarchies, and so on.

In our favor is the fact that evolution provided us, like most living beings, a deeply implanted drive to survive. (It's a Janus-faced gift for humans, as it also brings the realization of the tragedy of death, which underlies many basic fears.) With people the will to survive is complicated by conflicting priorities between self and other, individual survival versus group survival, and the decision over which group to give one's allegiance to, a narrow "identity" group or the whole species?

Whether or not we evolve into a viable relationship with this planet and each other is to a great extent in our hands. Our challenges are not necessarily a sign that we have made an irredeemable mess of things. On the contrary, this is where a relatively unaware, self-reflecting, clever but dangerously childish and primitively dimorphic predator would be expected eventually to arrive. In hindsight, given our dual nature of love and violence, altruism and egotism, care and carelessly using, it was fairly predictable that we would find ourselves here.

Realizing that, given who we are, where we are is congruent with the nature of evolution can be both comforting and frightening, for though it means we are possibly on track, the stakes and risk could not be higher. Given our nature, we would have to pass this test for evolution to move us from the non-conscious biological to the conscious social. Time constraints are severe; our technological cleverness has pushed our drama to "fast forward," tightening the screws of challenge and response.

Confronting a predictable cusp that forces us to resolve the challenges of our destructiveness can be reassuring. It means that we are not irredeemably flawed, but that we must adapt to continue our journey. The question is whether we will infuse our use with care, becoming care-takers, instead of merely takers and users. Our real challenge is not climate change, overpopulation, poverty, limited resources, and the widening gap between "haves and have-nots," or all the other symptoms of our two-sided nature that has not only gloried in war but is at war with itself. Our "war within" comes from trying to live up to unlivable authoritarian ideals, like selfless love, that breed self-mistrust, conflict, and guilt. This largely unconscious aspect that has retarded our development and awareness is our real challenge. Since we can't eliminate the basic dialectic between self and other, egotism and altruism, the conundrum is how to become more aware of its workings in us.

The core problem is that we are a social animal who has not yet learned how to be viably social in our new world of exploding population, technologies, sophisticated violence, and devastating global ecological threats. Unlike other social animals that are all programmed with a specific social system, we are programmed to have one, but not which one to have. This is our unmet challenge—how to develop a viable system. Current societal stages of development vary widely from medieval patriarchy to modernized, democratic versions of the "sexual order." Nevertheless, globally the oppressively institutionalized dimorphic gender split, authoritarian spirituality, fear-based conditioning, and exploitation have not changed enough in some core structural ways. This history of abuse within a warping sexual order has stunted our relationships, emotional life, thinking, level of maturity, and aware-ness—the very qualities needed to intelligently counterbalance the dual nature of being a predator who both uses and cares.

Humanity has displayed great creativity in most domains, with the exception of relationships. Most of our problems are a function of unworkable relationships between people, groups, religions, regions, and countries, and humanity's relation with the Earth. Because killing, or the threat of it, is and has been the bottom line of power, and given the nature of power and wealth to coalesce and expand, and given that children need lengthy nurturing, humanity has not yet constructed a social system that can sufficiently promote the general well-being of large populations.

We need an evolutionary leap in relationships to match our extraor-dinary recent leaps in science and technology and the resulting jugger-naut taking us we know not where. Developing our relational and social capabilities has to include the global dimension by replacing traditional unlivable, authoritarian ideals with more viable pan-cultural values that can flexibly meet accelerated change. We must learn how to be global social animals at last, through deepening, exploring, and build-ing on the untapped potential in our nature, broadening our awareness, and emotionally maturing—all of which are possible if we care enough about surviving.

That a change of consciousness is needed is widely agreed upon. The question remains as to its nature. The traditional solution has long been to say that a change in consciousness is needed that moves us beyond our competitive, destructive, self-centered nature. This would involve becoming very different from who we are, which has never worked. Like all mechanical reactions, it is shaped and conditioned by the past. Since who we are is partly undefined, or rather defined by the nature/nurture dialectic, and given that nature is much harder to shift, our potential lies on the side of improving care-taking and nurturing. This is the obvious place to start to explore who we are and can be, not to mention that care and nurture can literally change genetic wiring. The necessary shift is to be better at being who we are and can be, instead of trying to become something we are not and cannot be (non-aggressive and non-competitive).

We need emotional connection from infancy throughout life, since our inbuilt potential for relating only develops through being cared for and caring. We must get better at educating and using our amazing brain so we become better thinkers and better believers. To get "better" at aggression and competition means being more aware of their consequences and using them constructively. All these things will affect and temper our aggressive, predatory aspects in ways that trying to negate and eliminate them will not.

If, as we think, a meaning of existence is to construct parts of itself that can uniquely both experience and appreciate, even in a small way, the majesty that is beyond the total conception of any individual, we as a species must move from a self-absorbed adolescence to a care-taking adulthood to continue the adventure. If we begin to align with the "spirit of the times," support can come in unforeseen ways, because we are the outcome of an evolutionary process aimed at experiencing the wonders of itself. Better use of our minds and hearts can allow humanity to continue on our evolutionary journey.

Is evolving socially so that we can better take care of each other and the planet possible? We humans are capable of spectacular things in so many arenas: art, science, technology, athletics. If we were to put the focus and attention into making the planet and ourselves viable we could again be spectacular in totally new ways in relationships. That this challenge seems like an insurmountable wall to cross over is the way evolution works. The good news is that we do not have to evolve biologically; rather we have to evolve socially. Social evolution is in our power and can move quickly once underway if we connect with the spirit of the times.

The Passionate Mind uses "the tree is falling" as an example to illustrate that when one sees with real clarity, the seeing itself moves you. If you see a tree falling toward you, you move. As a species the metaphoric tree is falling on all of us, and our consciousness individually and collectively must see this and move. Evolving socially is not only the morally proper, good, and right thing to do. For the first time in history as we know it, taking care of each other and our home planet—which most of us knew is the right thing to do—is now conjoined with being the nec essary thing to do. Evolution moves through necessity.

Photo by Michael Kranzler

ABOUT THE AUTHORS

Joel Kramer and **Diana Alstad** began their life partnership in 1974. They speak and give seminars on evolution, social issues, yoga, spirituality, values, and relationships. They are coauthors of *The Guru Papers: Masks of Authoritarian Power* (Frog, 1993), which addresses hidden authoritarianism and decodes social and "spiritual" control. Kramer and Alstad have taught at centers such as Esalen and Omega and throughout North America, Europe, and Asia. For more on their shared work, visit joeldiana.com.

Joel Kramer did postgraduate work in philosophy and psychology at the University of Florida, NYU, and Columbia (1959-1963) on the philosophy of science, ethics, epistemology, worldviews, consciousness, and comparative religion. Since he was on the resident faculty at Esalen Institute in Big Sur, California, from 1968 to 1970, he has led seminars on the basic concerns of living and the evolution of awareness. An early innovator of modern American physical and mental yoga, Kramer wrote the seminal *Yoga Journal* article "Yoga as Self-Transformation" (1980) and introduced widely used principles foundational for many of today's leading teachers. Erich Schiffmann's acclaimed 1996 book *Yoga: The Spirit & Practice of Moving into Stillness* (Pocket Books, 1996) features Kramer's approach to physical yoga.

Diana Alstad is an author, lecturer, and seminar leader. A Woodrow Wilson Fellow, Alstad received a PhD from Yale in 1971 and was a professor at Duke University in the humanities. She initiated and taught the first Women's Studies courses at Yale and Duke, co-founded New Haven Women's Liberation in 1968, and was on the board of the Veteran Feminists of America from 1998 to 2004. Her *Yoga Journal* article "Exploring Relationships" (1979) created a foundation for the Yoga of Relationship by extending Kramer's yogic approach to the social arena, a modality they continue to develop and teach. She has been an escort-interpreter and lecturer in French and Italian, and also speaks Spanish.